A History of AMERICAN LITERATURE, 1607–1783

CLASSIC AMERICAN HISTORIANS

Paul M. Angle, GENERAL EDITOR

A History of
AMERICAN LITERATURE

1607-1783

by Moses Coit Tyler

abridged and edited by Archie H. Jones

THE UNIVERSITY OF CHICAGO PRESS   Chicago & London

The selections in this book are taken from Moses Coit Tyler's
A History of American Literature (1878) and *The Literary
History of the American Revolution 1763–1776* (1897), published
by G. P. Putnam's Sons.

Library of Congress Catalog Card Number: 67–20582
THE UNIVERSITY OF CHICAGO PRESS, CHICAGO & LONDON
The University of Toronto Press, Toronto 5, Canada
Abridged edition © 1967 by The University of Chicago
Published 1967. Printed in the United States of America

General Editor's Preface

FEW today read the great American historians. Few can. If one limited himself to those chosen for inclusion in this series —Prescott, Parkman, Bancroft, McMaster, Moses Coit Tyler, Henry Adams, Nicolay and Hay, and Rhodes—he would find himself straining his eyes eight hours a day for at least a year. This, in the modern world, is an impossible requirement.

Yet that the works of these men should remain unknown is deplorable. Something is better than nothing. From that conviction this series was born. But what should that "something" be? A series of condensations? How can one condense the sixteen volumes of Parkman, or the nine volumes of Henry Adams, into one volume without doing inexcusable violence to the whole? On the other hand, representative selections, each of substantial length, can convey a good idea of point of view, breadth of treatment, narrative skill, and style. This was the method chosen.

After this choice was made, the general editor came across a relevant pronouncement which John Hay made during the serialization of *Abraham Lincoln: A History*. "The only question," Hay wrote to Richard Watson Gilder, editor of the *Century*, "is whether you want the Life to run three years or four. If the former, you must take heroic measures. Leaving out a chapter here and there, or retrenching an adjective, will do no good. . . . You must cut great chunks of topics out. . . .

Neither Nicolay nor I can write the work over again for the purpose of saving a half chapter here and there." Nor, we submit, can anyone else.

The books in this series were designed for reading, not research. All documentation, therefore, has been eliminated. Editors of individual volumes have used their discretion in retaining expository footnotes. Such footnotes as they have added are identified by their initials. The typographical style, punctuation, and spelling of the original texts have been followed.

The editor of this volume considers *A History of American Literature during the Colonial Time, 1607–1765*, and *The Literary History of the American Revolution, 1763–1783*, as one book, to which he has given the inclusive title, *A History of American Literature, 1607–1783*,

PAUL M. ANGLE

Introduction

In 1949 no fewer than fifty-five distinguished American scholars collaborated on a literary history of the United States. It was clearly an attempt to produce a definitive work, yet the preface opens, and wisely, with this sentence: "Each generation should produce at least one literary history of the United States, for each generation must define the past in its own terms."[1] This is much more than a justification for writing another history of American literature. It is a fundamental truth about the nature and purpose of history.

The historian, whether he will admit it or not, writes history upon the basis of the present. His history is always to some degree an attempt to use the past to explain the present. Each generation must rewrite history because more data are available, because basic assumptions have changed. A historian writing in 1750 could not have described John Wise as a man whose thought anticipated the Declaration of Independence. The nineteenth-century historian wrote of the history of the United States as a part of God's cosmic plan; the mid-twentieth-century historian is searching for a less supernatural frame of reference.

History is an artist's rendering of the past as he knows it that eventually becomes a part of a larger past that other historians

[1] Robert E. Spiller, Willard Thorp *et al., Literary History of the United States* (New York: Macmillan Co., 1949), p. vii.

incorporate in their histories. Yet, like a great painting, great history is also a work of art which may well reveal for the perceptive reader a glimpse of essential truth. Moses Coit Tyler's literary history is all this; it was written from a point of view no longer completely acceptable, yet it contains insights the loss of which would impoverish us.

In 1903 Emma Lazarus wrote a poem that was inscribed on a tablet in the pedestal of the Statue of Liberty. The last few lines are the most familiar:

> Give me your tired, your poor,
> Your huddled masses yearning to breathe free,
> The wretched refuse of your teeming shores,
> Send these, the homeless, tempest-tossed to me,
> I lift my lamp beside the golden door.

Nearly thirty years earlier Moses Coit Tyler had expressed the same idea when he wrote of a volume published in 1698 that "we catch in this book the tender American note of sympathy with men and women in Europe who have a hard lot there; a cheery voice from this side of the Atlantic sounding out clear above the countless laughter of its billows, and telling all who need a new chance in life that at last they can have it. . . ."

We no longer write this way; perhaps now our shores are "teeming"; perhaps we are too wise to indulge in this sort of optimism; or perhaps we have lost a sense of mission that once made the United States unique among nations. In any case, this passage reveals in Tyler a distinctively nineteenth-century romantic strain.

Tyler's romanticism was primarily the product of the America that made Horatio Alger a favorite author and elected as its President a man who could never decide whether it was more important to be a cowboy, a historian, an "all-around" athlete, or a political leader. And it was only because Tyler was a product of this era that he could describe John Smith as "the wholesomest type of manhood anywhere to be found; body and brain both active, both cultivated; the mind not made fastidious and morbid by too much bookishness, nor coarse and dull by too little. . . ." Words like these came easily to the man who early in his career had written: "Since every part of our nature is the sacred gift of God, he who neglects his body, who calumniates his body, who misuses it, who allows it to grow up puny, frail, sickly, mis-shapen, homely, commits a sin against the Giver of the body."[2] Reading these lines one might assume that the author had, like Theodore Roosevelt, lived a strenuous life, but this would be far from the truth.

Moses Coit Tyler was born on August 2, 1835, in Griswold, Connecticut, the fourth son of parents who were descendants of old New England families. When he was three years old the family moved to Michigan, where young Moses received his early education. In 1852 he enrolled at the University of Michigan, but under pressure from his New England family, he transferred to Yale in September, 1853. After graduating from Yale in 1857, he entered Andover Theological Seminary but stayed only one year.

Despite this abbreviated theological training, he was ordained in August, 1859, and took the pulpit of the Congregational Church in Owego, New York. In October of the same year he was married. Owego was not the most attractive of pastoral plums, and after two years there Tyler moved to Poughkeepsie. Less than two years later, his health broken, he resigned and went to Boston never again to be a pastor.

In Boston he became a devotee of Dr. Dio Lewis' musical gymnastics and eventually went to England to spread the gospel of the new muscular ethics. There he developed into a good lecturer and began to write for magazines. As success came he broadened his scope until in 1865 he hit upon a new lecture topic: "It strikes me as a capital plan to write six or eight elaborate lectures on 'The History of American Literature'...."[3]

By this time his reputation had reached the United States, and he returned to lecture there early in 1867. Andrew D. White, whom Tyler had known at Yale, suggested that Tyler

---

[2] Quoted in Howard Mumford Jones, *The Life of Moses Coit Tyler* (Ann Arbor: University of Michigan Press, 1933), p. 84.

[3] Quoted in Jones, *Moses Coit Tyler,* p. 111.

think of a college teaching career either at the University of Michigan where White had just vacated the chair of history, or at Cornell University where White had just become president. The primitive campus at newly opened Cornell frightened Tyler, but lecturing seemed a risky business, and so after some negotiation, he became professor of rhetoric and English literature at the University of Michigan.

This decision settled Professor Tyler into a career that he continued for the remainder of his life; he died on December 28, 1900. There was one brief interlude (1873–75) as literary editor of *The Christian Union*, during which he learned that he did not want to be an editor or live in New York and that the great Henry Ward Beecher had feet of clay. (Tyler knew both Beecher and Theodore Tilton very well.) Michigan took him back, but in 1881 he made his final move—to Cornell as professor of American history and literature. Tyler found it hard to leave Michigan, but he prayed for guidance, and "my mind became irradiated, and for the first time I seemed to see my way to Cornell made luminous."[4] Tyler best stated the purpose of his life as a professor when he wrote in 1873: "There is something morbid and degrading in the passion with which we have worshipped exotic models in letters and have despised our own. Who shall explain the odd contradiction in our national habits of furiously boasting of American history, and steadily refusing to know anything about it?"[5]

Although he liked teaching, Tyler quickly realized its limitations. There were good days and bad days; one of the latter inspired this entry in his diary:

> Ah me, ah me, what a misery
> In this pedagogue chair, for life to be,
> And listen, and listen eternally,
> While these shallow chicks drone and chatter at me,
> Their talk, talk, talk all stupidity![6]

[4] Jones, *Moses Coit Tyler*, pp. 203–4.

[5] Moses Coit Tyler, *A History of American Literature, 1607–1765* (New York: Collier Books, 1962), p. 11. The foreword to this edition, in which this quotation appears, was written by Perry Miller.

[6] Tyler MSS Diary, May 10, 1881. The Tyler manuscripts are preserved at Cornell University, Ithaca, New York.

The life of a professor is not all teaching and research; there is always academic politics. Tyler's diaries for 1889 and 1890 are full of a struggle for power between the president of Cornell and the faculty senate. At one point Tyler, delighted by a senate triumph, told a member of the board of trustees that the success of the senate would "lead logically to the abolition of the University President. . . ."[7] Tyler's prediction was wrong, and one suspects that he knew it when later he wrote of "a most . . . garrulous Faculty Meeting which I at last quitted when it was in full cry at maggot-hunting."[8]

Professor Tyler undoubtedly left a good number of faculty meetings early, for he somehow found time after becoming a professor to write a number of magazine articles, six books, and to help establish the *American Historical Review*. This listing does not include the four volumes that have established him as a great historian and from which the selections in this book have been taken. *A History of American Literature* was first published in two volumes by G. P. Putnam's Sons in November, 1878. The final two volumes of what is essentially one history were published in 1897 as *The Literary History of the American Revolution*.

Life as a teacher and scholar did not disturb Tyler's deep faith in a personal God; in fact, he continued to preach—often regularly. An entry in his diary made after nearly seven years at Michigan is typical: "Have suspended for a while my . . . labors in American History in order not to divert myself from the mood of writing Sermons."[9] It was not mere rhetoric when Tyler wrote that the three ships that brought the first settlers to Jamestown "were guided by the finger of Him who points out the tracks of the winds and the courses of national destiny. . . ."

For mid-twentieth–century historians this sort of interpretation is naïve and useless, if not pernicious. And we dismiss Tyler's concept of "race" in the same way. At best we would

[7] Tyler MSS Diary, March 31, 1890.
[8] Tyler MSS Diary, October 5, 1894.
[9] Tyler MSS Diary, May 26, 1874.

call the following observation quaint: "Since the year 1640, the New England race has not received any notable addition to its original stock; and today their Anglican blood is as genuine and as unmixed as that of any county in England."[10] But will the modern pursuit of a national character appear less quaint to a historian in 2020 than Tyler's "race" does to us? Probably not.

Although Tyler was both a Christian and proud of his New England heritage, he did not worship at the Puritan shrine. Michael Wigglesworth's poem, *The Day of Doom*, was especially offensive to him. It was a "dreadful example . . . of the distressing illusions once inflicted upon themselves, in the name of religion, by the best of men."[11]

Despite this vehemence, Tyler's attitude toward the Puritans was ambivalent. He could refer to them as among "the best of men" because he was, after all, a member of an old New England family. And disgusted as he was with Wigglesworth's poem, the fact remains that Tyler himself believed in a literal Day of Judgment. In a sermon that he delivered a number of times between 1885 and 1892, Tyler warned his listeners that "there are two events in front of you, and only two, that may be predicted with absolute certainty: one of these is Death, the other is the Judgment after Death."[12]

So it is that Tyler could call Puritan theology "sublime and hideous dogmas."[13] For Tyler belief in God was always "sublime," but like most nineteenth-century American Protestants his theology was little more than a set of simplistic beliefs —in Jesus Christ, in God, in the judgment day—that he did not press to logical and systematic conclusions. Without a systematic theology of his own he could only disagree with certain Puritan conclusions; he could not disagree and at the same

[10] Moses Coit Tyler, *A History of American Literature* (New York: G. P. Putnam's Sons, 1879), I, 94.

[11] *Ibid.*, II, 34.

[12] Tyler MSS Sermon, "The Day of Judgment." Tyler delivered this sermon in eight different churches between November 30, 1885, and November 27, 1892.

[13] Tyler, *American Literature*, II, 24.

time appreciate, even admire, the intellectual structure that supported those conclusions.

Tyler objected to, or did not try to understand, most Puritan theologians, but John Wise was a notable exception. It may be that Tyler approved of Wise because he was reputed to be a great wrestler—perhaps a disciple of an earlier Dr. Dio Lewis. But the more likely explanation is found in Wise's defense of democratic government in both church and state.

In 1710 Wise wrote a book defending the democratic government and independence of each church against a proposal to centralize the government of the New England churches. Seven years later he published a general treatise on church government in which he set down a democratic political theory. Tyler quoted from the work liberally and with obvious pleasure. How could he help admiring a man who said "that the first . . . original of civil power is the people . . ."? If this was not enough to make Tyler happy, consider Wise's definition of religion: "Religion . . . in its transcendent effects, in time the charming peace and joys of conscience, in eternity the joyful retreat and shouts of glory;—is the most incomparable gift of Paladium which ever came from heaven."

John Wise was a muscular, joyously optimistic Christian and a democrat, and so was Moses Coit Tyler. Wise stated the basic assumptions of the Declaration of Independence before it was written; over one hundred years after the adoption of the Declaration, Tyler still believed that it embodied eternal and universal truths, that it was one of the moving forces of history.

As Ralph Gabriel has pointed out, the annual Fourth of July celebration was, during the nineteenth century, a religious event at which the orator delivered a political sermon after hearing a reading of the Declaration of Independence—the national scriptures.[14] Moses Coit Tyler does not mention attending many of these ceremonies, but he certainly believed that the Declaration was virtually the word of God.

[14] Ralph Henry Gabriel, *The Course of American Democratic Thought* (2d ed.; New York: Ronald Press Company, 1956), pp. 98–101.

Assessing the influence of the Declaration, Tyler declared in 1897 that "the influence of this state paper on the political character and the political conduct of the American people has been great beyond all calculation." And the Declaration was not merely an important national document; it was "a stately and a passionate chant of human freedom. . . ." This belief, which was virtually an unconscious assumption in nineteenth-century America, was buttressed for Tyler by his reading of Henry T. Buckle, who argued that the ideas expressed in literature were actual forces operating in history.[15]

Thus, in *The Literary History of the American Revolution*, Tyler chose to write not of generals and armies and battles, but of "persons who, as mere writers . . . still illustrate for us and for all who choose to see, the majestic operation of ideas, the creative and decisive play of spiritual forces, in the development of history, in the rise and fall of nations. . . ."[16]

While our Fourth of July celebrations have been drifting away from the nineteenth-century pattern, American historians have changed their minds several times about the American Revolution. The first break from the nineteenth century was made by the so-called Imperial School of historians. Such men as George Louis Beer and more recently Lawrence H. Gipson have argued that the British were doing their best to develop a viable imperial system, but that the Americans were too selfish and impatient to work out the political and economic problems as reasonable men should have done.[17]

The role of ideas in this context has been described by, among others, Carl Becker and Randolph G. Adams. Both of these men argued that the Americans shifted their constitu-

[15] Tylor was greatly impressed by volume I of Henry Thomas Buckle, *History of Civilization in England* (London, 1858). See Howard Mumford Jones, *The Theory of American Literature* (Ithaca: Cornell University Press, 1948), pp. 103–4.

[16] Moses Coit Tyler, *The Literary History of the American Revolution 1763–1783* (New York: Frederick Ungar Publishing Co., 1963), I, vii.

[17] George L. Beer, *British Colonial Policy, 1754–1765* (New York: Macmillan Company, 1907), *passim*, and Lawrence H. Gipson, *The British Empire before the American Revolution* (New York: A. A. Knopf, 1936–56), IV–IX, *passim*.

tional arguments as the needs arose—from objecting to internal taxation to resisting external taxation, to a refusal of the British right to regulate trade until finally they were denying Parliament all authority over the colonies. In essence, these historians were saying that in the American Revolution ideas were tools, not causal factors.[18]

Another group of historians has insisted that the Revolution was simply a struggle for home rule that was complicated and forced into violence by the internal struggle over who was to rule at home. Arthur Meir Schlesinger, for example, demonstrated that the colonial merchants favored opposition to the British but not revolution; they were forced into radical action by the lower classes and in the years after the war found themselves still opposing the same lower classes.[19] This may explain the friction within the colonies but not the revolt against the British. One explanation of the latter is to put the blame on agitators who used ideas for their own somewhat less than eternal purposes.[20] Perhaps this is true, but a question remains: Why were the ideas attractive?

In answering this question, the present generation of historians is coming back to Tyler's conception of the role of ideas. Helen M. and Edmund S. Morgan contend that the colonial arguments were consistent and that they sweepingly condemned on principle all parliamentary taxation. In another place, Edmund Morgan has "tried to describe the American search for principles of freedom and to see these years as a time of extraordinary unification rather than division."[21]

All of this does not, of course, mean that the twentieth-cen-

[18] Carl L. Becker, *The Declaration of Independence* (New York: Harcourt, Brace, 1922), *passim*, and Randolph G. Adams, *The Political Ideas of the American Revolution* (Durham, N.C.: Trinity College Press, 1922), *passim*.

[19] Arthur M. Schlesinger, *The Colonial Merchants and the American Revolution, 1763–1776* (New York: Columbia University Press, 1918), *passim*.

[20] John C. Miller, *Sam Adams: Pioneer in Propaganda* (Boston: Little, Brown, 1936), *passim*.

[21] Edmund S. Morgan. *The American Revolution: A Review of Changing Interpretations* (New York: Macmillan Company, 1958), p. 15.

tury interpretations are wrong. Far from it. We can never accept the interpretations of Tyler as the final and complete answer. Yet Edmund Morgan is correct when he says that "we must continue to ask, for we still do not fully know, what the Revolution was."[22] It is possible, even probable, that Tyler will in the last analysis contribute significantly to a definition of the American Revolution. Perhaps the Declaration of Independence was and is "a stately and a passionate chant of human freedom."

Because Tyler wrote of the causes and the nature of the American Revolution, his work must be understood in the context of this branch of American historiography; he was, however, primarily a historian of literature and this is in itself a division of historical scholarship.

As in some ways a disciple of the Frenchman Charles-Augustin Sainte-Beuve, Tyler understood literary history as fundamentally biographical. Throughout his four volumes, he sought to " 'place himself at the standpoint of the author,' " while at the same time as a historian he studied "both the producer and the thing produced." In this Tyler was trying to follow " 'a law of relation between living and thinking,' so that 'the conduct of phrase is part of the conduct of life'." Consequently, he did not classify his subject matter into schools but rather into general chronological and regional groups.[23]

But there is more to it than this. Because he believed that literature is "part of the conduct of life" and because he lived in an era that considered history to be past politics, Tyler emphasized "public prose," that is, writing was good or important if it expressed the needs of the society of which it was a product. Literature was for him a form of social "activism." Here is the reason he virtually ignored the beginnings of American fiction and yet another reason why he did not attempt a thorough analysis of Puritan theology.[24]

The socioeconomic theory of literature that has been so im-

---

[22] *Ibid.*, p. 15.
[23] Jones, *The Theory of American Literature*, pp. 103–5.
[24] *Ibid.*, pp. 106–7.

portant in the twentieth century was not a part of Tyler's pattern of thought. Vernon Louis Parrington's preoccupation with the presumed class struggle between the followers (and precursors) of the Jeffersonian and the Hamiltonian traditions was as foreign to Tyler as was Parrington's admission that "I was a good deal of a Marxian."[25]

Men like Parrington find in literary history support for their personal political positions. There is none of this in Tyler's volumes with the exception of his attachment first to John Wise and later to the Declaration of Independence. Parrington made Jefferson and the Jeffersonian tradition the focus of his work.[26] Tyler limited his treatment of Jefferson to his role as chief draftsman of the Declaration. If Tyler had any hero, it was Benjamin Franklin. Although he approved of Franklin's politics, it was Franklin's catholicity as a literary man, as a scientist, as a diplomat that impressed Tyler. Tyler was not in his personal life a political man, and he did not search for the roots of this or that American political movement.

One of the most important modern theories of literary history is that which calls for a history of "literature as literature," not as an expression of the culture in which it is produced. "Literature must not be conceived as being merely a passive reflection or copy of the political, social, or even intellectual development of mankind."[27] Although he did make critical appraisals of the quality of the literature, Tyler was emphatically not writing the history of "literature as literature." As he put it in the first chapter of the Revolution volumes: "The chief purpose of the present work is to call attention to these writings, not so much for their independent artistic value as for their humanistic and historical value, interpreting, as they do, with direct and undisguised speech, the very spirit and life and inward process of the American Revolution. . . ."[28]

[25] *Ibid.*, p. 143.

[26] Vernon Louis Parrington, *Main Currents in American Thought* (New York: Harcourt, Brace, 1927–30), I–III, *passim.*

[27] René Wellek and Austin Warren, *Theory of Literature* (New York: Harcourt, Brace and World, 1956), p. 255.

[28] Tyler, *American Revolution*, p. 28.

Tyler's conception of the purpose of history has not, however, disappeared. Whether it is the literary historian seeking a "constant reinterpretation of American cultural values" or the new breed we call intellectual historians trying "to extricate a unique, indigenous tradition" from American history, the purpose is the same. Modern historians are searching the past for the meaning of the present because the mid–twentieth–century American badly needs a "usable past."[29]

Given a purpose such as this, the historian may distinguish good from bad literature, but he ignores the bad at his peril. Both the good and the bad may well embody the ideas that men live by and for which they are at times willing to die. In part because Tyler did not discard the bad literature his work has an enduring value; it provides for mid-twentieth–century Americans a "usable past."

That the past Tyler offers us rings true is in part the result of his literary style. A contemporary reviewer observed that Tyler's liberal use of adjectives enriched "his pages to a degree that will seem lavish to the stiff stylists who inculcate that two in a sentence make a blot and three constitute a crime."[30] It is indeed difficult to find a better description of Thomas Paine's personal triumph in *Common Sense* than Tyler's "here the vigor of his mind, his shrewdness of insight, his unhesitating confidence, the filmless lucidity of his style, his humor, his asperity, his epigrammatic gift, have victorious play, and give to his pages the most stimulating flavor." And when Tyler remarks that Roger Williams was "never able by the ordinary means of intellectual stagnation to win for himself in his lifetime the bastard glory of doctrinal consistency," the reader can smile and at the same time learn something about both Roger Williams and Moses Coit Tyler.

[29] Jones, *Theory of American Literature*, pp. 119, 185, and John Higham, "The Rise of American Intellectual History," *American Historical Review* LVI (April, 1951): 469.

[30] *Yale Alumni Weekly* (June 22, 1897). This review and many others are preserved in bound scrapbooks at Cornell University, Ithaca, New York.

The combination of a style beautifully adapted to the era in question, the biographical method, a liberal and skillful use of quotations, and a refusal to impose upon the literature an elaborate set of critical or political categories does not produce a neatly organized analysis of a culture pattern; better, it breathes life into the past. For life, which is history as we experience it, is not orderly. It is episodic and only partially explained; it is a chronological string of happenings—glimpsed rather than seen.

To write history such as this a man must possess enormous energy and be profoundly excited about the era of which he writes. He must believe, deeply and personally, that there exists in the men, the events, and the ideas he chronicles eternal truth for all men. All this Moses Coit Tyler had in abundance.

ARCHIE H. JONES

Contents

A History of AMERICAN LITERATURE, 1607–1783

Chicago Historical Society

Virginia: The First Writer

THE three little ships which bore so many hopes, dropping from London down the Thames on the 20th of December, 1606, were vexed by opposing winds and were kept shivering within sight of the English coast for several weeks; then, instead of pursuing the straightforward westerly course to America, they curved southward, meandering foolishly by the Canaries, Dominica, Guadeloupe, and elsewhere, to the great loss of time, food, health, and patience; and did not reach their journey's end until the 26th of April, 1607—a journey's end to which they were at last blown by the providence of a rough storm, after "the mariners had three days passed their reckoning and found no land." No blunder in man's performance could have been more happily condoned by Heaven's pity; for these poor little ships, groping along the coast of America in great geographic darkness, and seeking only "to find out a safe port in the entrance of some navigable river," were guided by the finger of Him who points out the tracks of the winds and the courses of national destiny, into the noblest bay along the whole coast, and upon a land of balm and verdure. They had come to Virginia at the happy moment when nature in that region wears her sweetest smile and sings her loveliest notes. They were amazed, as one of them tells us, at the opulence of life visible all about them; at the oysters "which lay on the ground as thick as stones," many with pearls in them; at the earth "all flowing over with fair flowers of sundry colors and kinds, as though it had been in any garden or orchard in England;" at "the woods full of cedar and cypress trees, with other trees which issue out sweet gums, like balsam." "Heaven and earth," exclaimed another of that delighted company, "never agreed better to frame a place for man's habitation."

Thus began our American civilization; and among those first Englishmen huddled together behind palisadoes in Jamestown in 1607, were some who laid the foundations of American literature. There were about a hundred of them all. As we look over the ancient list of their names and designations, we alight upon some facts which bode little good to an enterprise in which there is no safe room for persons afflicted with constitutional objections to hard work. The earliest formal History of Virginia contains testimony that herein lay the worst peril of the enterprise; that besides one carpenter, two blacksmiths, two sailors, and a few others named "laborers," "all the rest were poor gentlemen, tradesmen, serving-men, libertines, and such like, ten times more fit to spoil a commonwealth than either begin one, or but help to maintain one." But in this heterogeneous party of forcible Feebles, were a few men of some grip and note, such as brave old Bartholomew Gosnold, Edward Maria Wingfield, John Martin, Gabriel Archer, Robert Hunt their saintly chaplain, and George Percy a brother of the Earl of Northumberland. And there was one other man in that little group of adventurers who still has a considerable name in the world. In that year 1607, when he first set foot in Virginia, Captain John Smith was only twenty-seven years old; but even then he had made himself somewhat famous in England as a daring traveller in Southern Europe, in Turkey and the East. He was perhaps the last professional knight-errant that the world saw; a free lance, who could not hear of a fight going on anywhere in the world without hastening to have a hand in it; a sworn champion of the ladies also, all of whom he loved too ardently to be guilty of the invidious offence of marrying any one of them; a restless, vain, ambitious, overbearing, blustering fellow, who made all men either his hot friends or his hot enemies; a man who down to the present hour has his celebrity in the world chiefly on account of alleged exploits among Turks, Tartars, and Indians, of which exploits he alone has furnished the history—never failing to celebrate himself in them all as the one resplendent and invincible hero.

This extremely vivid and resolute man comes before us now for particular study, not because he was the most conspicuous person in the first successful American colony, but because he was the writer of the first book in American literature. It is impossible to doubt that as a storyteller he fell into the traveller's habit of drawing a long bow. In the narration of incidents that had occurred in his own wild life he had an aptitude for being intensely interesting; and it seemed to be his theory that if the original facts were not in themselves quite so interesting as they should have been, so much the worse for the original facts. Yet in spite of this habit, Captain John Smith had many great and magnanimous qualities; and we surely cannot help being drawn to him with affectionate admiration, when we remember his large services in the work of colonizing both Virginia and New England, his sufferings in that cause, and his unquenchable love for it until death. In his later life, after he had been baffled in many of his plans and hopes, he wrote, in London, of the American colonies these words: "By that acquaintance I have with them, I call them my children; for they have been my wife, my hawks, hounds, my cards, my dice, and in total my best content, as indifferent to my heart as my left hand to my right."

Then, too, as students of literature we shall be drawn to Captain John Smith as belonging to that noble type of manhood of which the Elizabethan period produced so many examples—the man of action who was also a man of letters, the man of letters who was also a man of action: the wholesomest type of manhood anywhere to be found; body and brain both active, both cultivated; the mind not made fastidious and morbid by too much bookishness, nor coarse and dull by too little; not a doer who is dumb, not a speech-maker who cannot do; the knowledge that comes of books widened and freshened by the knowledge that comes of experience; the literary sense fortified by common sense; the bashfulness and delicacy of the scholar hovering as a finer presence above the forceful audacity of the man of the world; at once bookman, penman, swordsman, diplomat, courtier, orator. Of this type of manhood, spacious, strong, refined, and sane, were the best men of the Elizabethan time, George Gascoigne, Sir Philip Sidney, Sir Walter Raleigh, and in a modified sense Hakluyt, Bacon, Sackville, Shakespeare, Ben Jonson, and nearly all the rest. To this type of manhood Captain John Smith aspired to belong. "Many of the most eminent warriors," said he, "what their swords did, their pens writ. Though I be never so much their inferior, yet I hold it no great error to follow good examples." In another book, he expanded the thought in a way that shows it to have been a pleasant one to him: "This history . . . might and ought to have been clad in better robes than my rude military hand can cut out in paper ornaments; but because of the most things therein I am no compiler by hearsay but have been a real actor, I take to myself to have a property in them, and therefore have been bold to challenge them to come under the reach of my own rough pen." And that he had achieved his ambition for this spherical form of excellence was the belief of many of his contemporaries, one of whom wrote thus of him and of his book on the history of Virginia and New England:

> Like Caesar now thou writ'st what thou hast done,
> These acts, this book, will live while there's a sun.

Captain John Smith became a somewhat prolific author; but while nearly all of his books have a leading reference to America, only three of them were written during the period of his residence as a colonist in America. Only these three, therefore, can be claimed by us as belonging to the literature of our country.

The first of these books, *A True Relation of Virginia,* is of deep interest to us, not only on account of its graphic style and the strong light it throws upon the very beginning of our national history, but as being unquestionably the earliest book in American literature. It was written during the first thirteen months of the life of the first American colony, and gives a simple and picturesque account of the stirring events which took place there during that time, under his own eye. It was probably carried to London by Captain Nelson of the good ship Phoenix, which sailed from Jamestown on the second of June, 1608; and it was published in London and sold "at the Grey-hound in Paul's Church-Yard," in the latter part of the same year—not far from the very day when the child John Milton was born, and in a house only three streets distant. Perhaps I may be pardoned for indulging what will seem to some a mere literary caprice, by placing these two events side by side in this history, even as they were placed side by side in the happening of actual fact. John Milton was born into life, and the first American book was born into print, in the same year, and in the same part of the year, and almost on the same spot. The child born on that ninth of December, 1608, in Bread Street, a few steps from the book-shop where the earliest of American writings was first placed on sale—the child around whose cradle may have been repeated by his father some of the wild and exciting incidents related in that book—was to grow up into a colossal literary figure not only in that century but in all centuries: he was to be in an eminent degree the exponent of the great ideas of religious and political freedom that were to form the basis of American civilization, which, like himself, was then beginning to live; and the moral peculiarities of his genius, austere earnestness, a devout ethical force, an obstinate habit of judging of life and even of art and letters from the throne of moral laws and of moral tendencies, were to be likewise the most marked spiritual qualities of that remote and unfriended national literature which began its career almost at the very same moment when he began his, and almost on the very same spot.

The title-pages of the seventeenth century are not the least expressive or amusing portions of the books of that century; and if ever an old title-page shall deserve full quotation at our hands, this does so. It is as follows: "A True Relation of such occurrences and accidents of note as hath happened in Virginia since the first planting of that colony, which is now resident in the South part thereof, till the last return from thence. Written by Captain Smith, Coronel of said colony, to a worshipful

friend of his in England. London: Printed for John Tappe, and
are to be sold at the Grey-hound in Paul's Church-Yard, by
W. W. 1608."

Barely hinting at the length and tediousness of the sea-
voyage, the author plunges with epic promptitude into the
midst of the action by describing their arrival in Virginia,
their first ungentle passages with the Indians, their selection of
a place of settlement, their first civil organization, their first
expedition for discovery toward the upper waters of the James
River, the first formidable Indian attack upon their village,
and the first return for England, two months after their arrival,
of the ships that had brought them to Virginia. Upon the departure of these ships, bitter quarrels broke out among the
colonists; "things were neither carried with that discretion nor
any business effected in such good sort as wisdom would; . . .
through which disorder, God being angry with us plagued us
with such famine and sickness that the living were scarce able
to bury the dead. . . . As yet we had no houses to cover us; our
tents were rotten, and our cabins worse than nought. . . . The
president and Captain Martin's sickness compelled me to be
cape-merchant, and yet to spare no pains in making houses for
the company, who, notwithstanding our misery, little ceased
their malace, grudging, and muttering . . . being in such despair
as they would rather starve and rot with idleness than be persuaded to do anything for their own relief without constraint."
But the energetic Captain had an eager passion for making
tours of exploration along the coast and up the rivers; and after
telling how he procured corn from the Indians and thus supplied the instant necessities of the starving colonists, he proceeds to relate the history of a tour of discovery made by him
up the Chickahominy, on which tour happened the famous incident of his falling into captivity among the Indians. The reader
will not fail to notice that in this earliest book of his, written
before Powhatan's daughter, the princess Pocahontas, had
become celebrated in England, and before Captain Smith had
that enticing motive for representing himself as specially fa-

vored by her, he speaks of Powhatan as full of friendliness to him; he expressly states that his own life was in no danger at the hands of that Indian potentate; and of course he has no situation on which to hang the romantic incident of his rescue by Pocahontas from impending death. Having ascended the Chickahominy about sixty miles, he took with him a single Indian guide and pushed into the woods. Within a quarter of an hour he "heard a loud cry and a hallooing of Indians"; and almost immediately he was assaulted by two hundred of them, led by Opechancanough, an under-king to the emperor Powhatan. The valiant Captain, in a contest so unequal, certainly was entitled to a shield; and this he rather ungenerously extemporized by seizing his Indian guide and with his garters binding the Indian's arm to his own hand, thus, as he coolly expresses it, making "my hind" "my barricado." As the Indians still pressed toward him, Captain Smith discharged his pistol, which wounded some of his assailants and taught them all a wholesome respect by the terror of its sound; then, after much parley, he surrendered to them, and was carried off prisoner to a place about six miles distant. There he expected to be at once put to death, but was agreeably surprised by being treated with the utmost kindness. For supper that night they gave him "a quarter of venison and some ten pounds of bread"; and each morning thereafter three women presented him with "three great platters of fine bread," and "more venison than ten men could devour." "Though eight ordinarily guarded me, I wanted not what they could devise to content me; and still our larger acquaintance increased our better affection." After many days spent in travelling hither and yon with his captors, he was at last, by his own request, delivered up to Powhatan, the overlord of all that region. He gives a picturesque description of the barbaric state in which he was received by this potent chieftain, whom he found "proudly lying upon a bedstead a foot high, upon ten or twelve mats," the emperor himself being "richly hung with many chains of great pearls about his neck, and covered with a great covering of raccoon skins. At head sat a woman; at his feet, another; on each side, sitting upon a mat upon the ground were ranged his chief men on each side the fire, ten in rank; and behind them, as many young women, each a great chain of white beads over their shoulders, their heads painted in red; and with such a grave and majestical countenance as drave me into admiration to see such state in a naked salvage. He kindly welcomed me with good words, and great platters of sundry victuals, assuring me his friendship and my liberty within four days." Thus day by day passed in pleasant discourse with his imperial host, who asked him about "the manner of our ships, and sailing the seas, the earth and skies, and of our God," and who feasted him not only with continual "platters of sundry victuals," but with glowing descriptions of his own vast dominions stretching away beyond the rivers and the mountains to the land of the setting sun. "Seeing what pride he had in his great and spacious dominions, . . . I requited his discourse in describing to him the territories of Europe which was subject to our great king, . . . the innumerable multitude of his ships. I gave him to understand the noise of trumpets and terrible manner of fighting were under Captain Newport my father. . . . Thus having with all the kindness he could devise sought to content me, he sent me home with four men, one that usually carried my gown and knapsack after me, two other loaded with bread, and one to accompany me." The author then gives a description of his journey back to Jamestown, where "each man with truest signs of joy" welcomed him; of his second visit to Powhatan; of various encounters with hostile and thievish Indians; and of the arrival from England of Captain Nelson in the Phoenix, April the twentieth, 1608—an event which "did ravish" them "with exceeding joy." Late in the narrative he makes his first reference to Pocahontas, whom he speaks of as "a child of ten years old, which not only for feature, countenance and proportion much exceedeth any of the rest of his people, but for wit and spirit the only nonpareil of his country." After mentioning some further dealings with the Indians, he concludes the book with an account of the preparations for the return to England of Captain Nelson and his ship; and describes those remaining as "being in good health, all our men well contented, free from mutinies, in love one with another, and as we hope in a continual peace with the Indians, where we doubt not but by God's gracious assistance and the adventurers' willing minds and speedy furtherance to so honorable an action in after times, to see our nation to enjoy a country, not only exceeding pleasant for habitation, but also very profitable for commerce in general, no doubt pleasing to Almighty God, honorable to our gracious sovereign, and commodious generally to the whole kingdom."

Thus, with words of happy omen, ends the first book in American literature. It is a book that was written, not in lettered ease, nor in "the still air of delightful studies," but under a rotten tent in the wilderness, perhaps by the flickering blaze of a pine knot, in the midst of tree-stumps and the filth and clamor of a pioneer's camp, and within the fragile palisades which alone shielded the little band of colonists from the ever-hovering peril of an Indian massacre. It was not composed as a literary effort. It was meant to be merely a budget of information for the public at home, and especially for the London stockholders of the Virginia Company. Hastily, apparently without revision, it was wrought vehemently by the rough hand of a soldier and an explorer, in the pauses of a toil that was both fatiguing and dangerous, and while the incidents which he records were fresh and clinging in his memory. Probably he thought little of any rules of literary art as he wrote this book: probably he did not think of writing a book at all. Out of the abundance of his materials, glowing with pride over what he had done in the great enterprise, eager to inspire the home-keeping patrons of the colony with his own resolute cheer, and accustomed for years to portray in pithy English the adventures of which his life was fated to be full, the bluff Captain just stabbed his paper with inken words; he composed not a book but a big letter; he folded it up, and tossed it upon the deck of Captain Nelson's departing ship. But though he may have had no expectation of doing such a thing, he wrote a book that is not unworthy to be the beginning of the new English literature in America. It has faults enough, without doubt. Had it not these, it would have been too good for the place it occupies. The composition was extemporaneous; there appears in it some chronic misunderstanding between the nominatives and their verbs; now and then the words and clauses of a sentence are jumbled together in blinding heaps; but in spite of all its crudities, there is racy English, pure English, the sinewy, picturesque and throbbing diction of the navigators and soldiers of the Elizabethan time. And although the materials of this book are not moulded in nice proportion, the story is well told. The man has an eye and a hand for that thing. He sees the essential facts of a situation, and throws the rest away; and the business moves straight forward.

About three months after the departure for England of the ship which carried to the printing-press the book of which an extended account has just been given, there arrived from England another ship, bringing a new supply of colonists, and bringing likewise a letter of fantastic instructions and of querulous complaints from the London stockholders of the company. It fell to Captain John Smith, as the new president of the colony, to make reply to this document; and he did it in the production which forms the second title in our list of his American writings. This production is brief; but it is a most vigorous, trenchant, and characteristic piece of writing, a transcript of the intense spirit of the man who wrote it, all ablaze with the light it casts into that primal hot-bed of wrangling, indolence, and misery, the village of Jamestown. Let us reproduce some parts of this letter, the sentences of which seem to fly as straight and hard as bullets:—"I received your letter wherein you write that our minds are so set upon faction and idle conceits in dividing the country without your consents; and that we feed you but with if's and and's, hopes, and some few proofs, as if we would keep the mystery of the business to ourselves; and that we must

expressly follow your instructions sent by Captain Newport, the charge of whose voyage amounts to near two thousand pounds,—the which if we cannot defray by the ship's return, we are alike to remain as banished men. To these particulars, I humbly entreat your pardons if I offend you with my rude answer. For our factions, . . . I cannot prevent them. . . . For the idle letters sent to my Lord of Salisbury by the president and his confederates for dividing the country and so forth, what it was I know not; for you saw no hand of mine to it, nor ever dreamt I of any such matter. That we feed you with hopes and so forth, though I be no scholar, I am past a school-boy; and I desire but to know what either you and these here do know, but that I have learned to tell you by the continual hazard of my life. I have not concealed from you anything I know. . . . Expressly to follow your instructions by Captain Newport, though they be performed, I was directly against it; but . . . I was content to be overruled by the major part of the council, I fear to the hazard of us all; which now is generally confessed, when it is too late. . . . For the charge of this voyage of two or three thousand pounds, we have not received the value of an hundred pounds. . . . From your ship we had not provision in victuals worth twenty pounds; and we are more than two hundred to live upon this,—the one half sick, the other little better. For the sailors, I confess they daily make good cheer; but our diet is a little meal and water, and not sufficient of that. Though there be fish in the sea, fowls in the air, and beasts in the woods, their bounds are so large, they so wild, and we so weak and ignorant, we cannot much trouble them. . . . Captain Ratcliffe is now called Sicklemore. . . . I have sent you him home, lest the company should cut his throat. . . . When you send again, I entreat you rather send but thirty carpenters, husbandmen, gardeners, fishermen, blacksmiths, masons, and diggers up of trees' roots, well provided, than a thousand of such as we have; for except we be able both to lodge them and feed them, the most will consume with want of necessaries, before they can be made good for anything. . . . These are the

causes that have kept us in Virginia from laying such a foundation that ere this might have given much better content and
satisfaction; but as yet you must not look for any profitable
returns. So I humbly rest."

Such are the principal portions of Captain John Smith's
letter of explanation to the London proprietors of the company
whose affairs in Virginia he was just then conducting. Certainly
this writing is racy, terse, fearless; a style of sentence carved
out by a sword; the incisive speech of a man of action; Hotspur
rhetoric, jerking with impatience, truculence, and noble wrath.
And it is not without an under-meaning in many ways, that
this production, among the very earliest in American literature,
should communicate to England a foretaste of what proved to
be the incurable American habit of talking back to her. From
the beginning, it was hard for England to see the just limits of
her interference with her own colonial children in America;
and though three thousand miles from them, she could not stay
her motherly tongue from advising and commanding them concerning the details of their life in the wilderness about which
they inevitably knew more than she did. One can easily imagine
what a shock this epistolary retort of Captain John Smith
must have given to the dignified nerves of those kindly and
lordly patrons in London; how its saucy sentences must have
made them gasp and stare. Almost the earliest note, then, of
American literature is a note of unsubmissiveness. Captain
John Smith's letter, in the first decade of the seventeenth century, is a premonitory symptom of the Declaration of Independence.

In the same parcel with this remarkable letter of Captain
Smith's was enclosed by him to the adventurers in London
another document—a proof of his irrepressible activity and of
his versatile talent—a "Map of the Bay and the Rivers, with
an annexed Relation of the countries, and nations that inhabit
them." This document did not get into print until 1612, when
it was published at Oxford, and constitutes the third work in

the list of the author's American writings. It deals with the
climate and topography of Virginia, with its fauna and flora,
and particularly with the characteristics of its earlier inhabitants, the Indians. As a whole the work is uncommonly picturesque and even amusing; for though devoted to climatic
and topographic descriptions, to matters of natural history, and
to the coarse features of savage existence, the genius of the
writer quickens and brightens it all, strewing his pages with
easy and delightful strokes of imagery, quaint humor, shrewdness, and a sort of rough unconscious grace. His introductory
chapter is full of the joy which the first visitors to this country
felt in the sweet air, the rich soil, the waters, the mountains,
in all the large and majestic framework of nature in the new
world: "The temperature of this country doth agree well with
English constitutions. . . . The summer is hot as in Spain; the
winter cold as in France or England. . . . The winds here are
variable; but the like thunder and lightning to purify the air,
I have seldom either seen or heard in Europe. . . . There is but
one entrance by sea into this country, and that is at the mouth
of a very goodly bay, eighteen or twenty miles broad. . . .
Within is a country that may have the prerogative over the
most pleasant places known, for large and pleasant navigable
rivers. . . . Here are mountains, hills, plains, valleys, rivers and
brooks all running most pleasantly into a fair bay, compassed,
but for the mouth, with fruitful and delightsome land. In the
bay and rivers are many isles, both great and small. . . . The
mountains are of diverse natures; for at the head of the bay the
rocks are of a composition like mill-stones, some of marble and
so forth. And many pieces like crystal we found, as thrown
down by water from those mountains. . . . These waters wash
from the rocks such glistering tinctures that the ground in
some places seemeth as gilded; where both the rocks and the
earth are so splendent to behold that better judgments than
ours might have been persuaded they contain more than probabilities. The vesture of the earth in most places doth mani-
festly prove the nature of the soil to be lusty and very rich."

This charming passage, pregnant with adroit hints, must have proved very seductive when it came to be read in England; it must have made many an eye sparkle with the expectation of golden returns from this mysterious new realm of theirs, all bulging and variegated with precious metals and precious stones. And the passage just quoted contains, likewise, not a few of the best traits of the author's descriptive manner, which is vital with the breath of imagination, and tinted with the very hues of nature. One has not to go far along with the sentences elsewhere in this book without finding all the dull and hard details of his subject made delightful by felicities of phrase that seem to spring up as easily as wild flowers in the woods of his own Virginia. He speaks of "an infinite number of small rundels and pleasant springs that disperse themselves for the best service as do the veins of a man's body"; of " a bay wherein falleth three or four pretty brooks and creeks that half intrench the inhabitants of Warraskoyac"; of the river Pamaunkee that "divideth itself into two gallant branches"; of the river Patawomeke "fed . . . with many sweet rivers and springs which fall from the bordering hills." There is often a quaint flavor in his words—that racy and piquant simplicity which so much charms us in the English descriptive prose of the sixteenth century, and the first third of the seventeenth. He speaks of a plum called Putchamins, which when unripe "will draw a man's mouth awry with much torment"; of the Indian men of Virginia who "wear half their beards shaven, the other half long; for barbers they use their women, who with two shells grate away the hair of any fashion they please." Referring to the personal ornaments of the Indians, he mentions that "in each ear commonly they have three great holes, whereat they hang chains, bracelets, or copper. Some of their men wear in those holes a small green and yellow colored snake, near half a yard in length, which crawling and lapping herself about his neck oftentimes familiarly would kiss his lips. Others wear a dead rat tied by the tail." "The men bestow their times in fishing, hunting, wars, and such man-like exercise, scorning

to be seen in any woman-like exercise, which is the cause that the women be very painful, and the men often idle." He says that "for their music they use a thick cane, on which they pipe as on a recorder. . . . But their chief instruments are rattles made of small gourds or pumpions' shells. . . . These mingled with their voices sometimes twenty or thirty together, make such a terrible noise as would rather affright than delight any man." He describes their orators as making speeches of welcome to a public guest, "testifying their love . . . with such vehemency, and so great passions that they sweat till they drop, and are so out of breath that they can scarce speak; so that a man would take them to be exceedingly angry or stark mad." He tells of a certain Indian king who "did believe that our God as much exceeded theirs as our guns did their bows and arrows; and many times did send to me to Jamestown, entreating me to pray to my God for rain, for their gods would not send them any." Remembering those tender-fingered drones calling themselves "gentlemen" who constituted so large and so useless a portion of the first colonists in Virginia, one cannot help relishing the frequent sarcasms with which this impetuous and indomitable man spices his references to them; in one place characterizing them as persons who never "did anything but devour the fruits of other men's labor"; and who, "because they found not English cities, nor such fair houses, nor at their own wishes any of their accustomed dainties, with feather beds and and down pillows, taverns and alehouses in every breathing place, neither such plenty of gold and silver and dissolute liberty as they expected, had little or no care of anything but to pamper their bellies, to fly away with our pinnaces, or procure their means to return for England; for the country was to them a misery, a ruin, a death, a hell."

There are in this book some specimens of portrait-painting that show no slight power. Let us take, for example, his description of the appearance and state of the famous Indian king, Powhatan: "He is of personage a tall well-proportioned man, with a sour look, his head somewhat gray, his beard so thin that

it seemeth none at all, his age near sixty; of a very able and hardy body to endure any labor. About his person ordinarily attendeth a guard of forty or fifty of the tallest men his country doth afford. Every night upon the four quarters of his house are four sentinels, each from other a slight shoot, and at every half hour one from the *corps de garde* doth halloo, shaking his lips with his finger between them; unto whom every sentinel doth answer round from his stand. If any fail, they presently send forth an officer that beateth him extremely." Here, likewise, is some effective description in his account of the Susquehanna Indians, whom he encountered on one of his tours of discovery, and whose huge shapes and strange costumes appear to have impressed him greatly: "But to proceed, sixty of those Susquehannocks came to us with skins, bows, arrows, targets, beads, swords, and tobacco pipes for presents. Such great and well proportioned men are seldom seen; for they seem like giants to the English, yea and to the neighbors, yet seemed of an honest and simple disposition, with much ado restrained from adoring us as gods. Those are the strangest people of all those countries, both in language and attire. For their language, it may well beseem their proportions, sounding from them as a voice in a vault. Their attire is the skins of bears and wolves. . . . One had the head of a wolf hanging in a chain for a jewel, his tobacco pipe three quarters of a yard long . . . sufficient to beat out one's brains; with bows, arrows, and clubs suitable to their greatness. . . . The picture of the greatest of them is signified in the map; the calf of whose leg was three quarters of a yard about, and all the rest of his limbs so answerable to that proportion that he seemed the goodliest man we ever saw."

Near the end of this little book occurs one sentence in which the author has admirably compacted a statement of all the nobler utilities of the young colony of Virginia: "So, then, here is a place, a nurse for soldiers, a practice for mariners, a trade for merchants, a reward for the good; and that which is most of all, a business, most acceptable to God, to bring such poor infidels to the knowledge of God and his holy gospel."

We may be well content to let this strong and beautiful sentence linger on our memories as the last one we shall draw from Captain John Smith's American writings, and as an honorable token of his broad and clear grasp of the meaning of that great national impulse which stirred the heart of England in his time, for the founding of a new English empire in America.

The book which we have just inspected is the third work written by Captain John Smith in America; and as students of American literature, we must here end our study of his writings. He remained in Virginia about twelve months after the time to which the latest of these writings refer, returning to England in the fall of 1609. It is not improbable that he was recalled to England by the displeasure of the London proprietors of the Virginia company. Dropped from their service, he remained in England until 1614, when with two ships he made a voyage of trade and exploration to New England, and came back the same year with a map, drawn by himself, of the country between the Penobscot and Cape Cod. In the year 1615 he sailed again for New England, taking with him a colony for settlement there; but on the voyage out he was captured by a French pirate and carried prisoner to Rochelle, whence he soon escaped and made his way back to England. From that time until his death in 1631 he probably never left England again. His career of daring adventure was over. Though he continued to take the most passionate interest in American colonization, and to agitate and plot and strive for it, he had to appease his restless spirit with the tame joys of authorship. He appears to have been looked upon henceforth as the veteran explorer, and to have been consulted and quoted as an authority in the practical details of colonization. The marvellous tales of his exploits which he told in his books furnished welcome materials for Ben Jonson and other playwrights; so that he himself said, half in pride, half in complaint, "they have acted my fatal tragedies upon the stage and racked my relations at their pleasure." Even then there were not wanting those who suspected the fidelity

of his narratives, and who accused him of adorning his heroic anecdotes with exploits which he had wrought only in imagination. "Envy hath taxed me," he says, "to have writ too much and done too little." Thomas Fuller, in his *Worthies of England,* first published thirty-one years after Captain Smith's death, gives perhaps the cool afterthought of many of the Captain's contemporaries, in these contemptuous and delicately cutting words: "From the Turks in Europe he passed to the pagans in America, where . . . such his peril, preservations, dangers, deliverances, they seem to most men above belief, to some beyond truth. Yet have we two witnesses to attest them, the prose and the pictures, both in his own book; and it soundeth much to the diminution of his deeds, that he alone is the herald to publish and proclaim them." Probably it was this base incredulity of his contemporaries, this hard historical Sadduceeism, that Captain Smith and his immediate champions meant to designate by the words "envy," and "detraction," which meet us in their allusions to the reception then given to his writings. A namesake of the author, one N. Smith, thus bravely steps forward as his defender:

> Sith thou, the man deserving of these ages,
>   Much pain hast ta'en for this our kingdom's good,
> In climes unknown, 'mongst Turkes and salvages,
>   T' enlarge our bounds, though with thy loss of blood,
> Hence damn'd Detraction—stand not in our way!
> Envy itself will not the truth gainsay.

It is quite plain that while the weak spot in Captain Smith's character, his love of telling large stories, was suspected by many of his contemporaries, he nevertheless had among the best of them staunch and admiring friends. Sir Robert Cotton, the Earls of Pembroke, of Lindsay, and of Dover, the Duchess of Lenox, and Lord Hunsdon, were those in the upper spheres of society whom he could publicly name as his patrons and friends. Among the writers of commendatory verses prefixed and affixed to his books, are such eminent persons as Samuel Purchas, George Wither, and John Donne; and nearly all of

these writers, whether now famous or obscure, apply to him terms of homage and endearment. Donne calls him "brave Smith"; Richard James calls him "dear noble Captain"; Ed. Jordan exclaims:

> Good men will yield thee praise; then slight the rest;
> 'Tis best, praise-worthy, to have pleased the best;

while an anonymous writer, after reciting the names of the great explorers, Columbus, Cabot, Frobisher, Humphrey Gilbert, Drake, Gosnold, and others, says:

> Though these be gone and left behind a name,
>   Yet Smith is here to anvil out a piece
> To after ages and eternal fame,
>   That we may have the golden Jason's fleece.
> He, Vulcan-like, did forge a true plantation,
>   And chained their kings to his immortal glory,
> Restoring peace and plenty to the nation,
>   Regaining honor to this worthy story.

After all the abatements which a fair criticism must make from the praise of Captain John Smith either as a doer or as a narrator, his writings still make upon us the impression of a certain personal largeness in him, magnanimity, affluence, sense, and executive force. Over all his personal associates in American adventure he seems to tower, by the natural loftiness and reach of the perception with which he grasped the significance of their vast enterprise, and the means to its success. As a writer his merits are really great—clearness, force, vividness, picturesque and dramatic energy, a diction racy and crisp. He had the faults of an impulsive, irascible, egotistic, and imaginative nature; he sometimes bought human praise at too high a price; but he had great abilities in word and deed; his nature was upon the whole generous and noble; and during the first two decades of the seventeenth century he did more than any other Englishman to make an American nation and an American literature possible.

THE Englishmen who came to North America in the early years of the seventeenth century encountered a wilderness full of danger, excitement, and mystery. It was a New World where all things might be different. What crops would grow? Were the winters cold? The summers hot? Who, or what, were the natives?

Out of this curiosity, tinged upon occasion with awe and even fear, came a number of the earliest American literary efforts. Some were largely the product of fertile imaginations; others achieved the level of natural history.

New England: Its Nature and Its People

A DELIGHTFUL group of writings belonging to our earliest age is made up of those which preserve for us, in the very words of the men themselves, the curiosity, the awe, the bewilderment, the fresh delight, with which the American Fathers came face to face for the first time with the various forms of nature and of life in the new world. We have already seen examples of this class of writings produced by the early men of Virginia; and among the founders of New England there was no lack of the same sensitiveness to the vast, picturesque, and novel aspects of nature which they encountered upon the sea and the land, in their first journeys hither. The evidence of this fact is scattered thick through all their writings, in letters, sermons, histories, poems; while there remain several books, written by them immediately after their arrival here, describing in the first glow of elated feeling the vision that unfolded itself before them, of the new realms of existence, the "vast and empty chaos," upon which they were entering.

The first of these books consists of a journal kept by two renowned passengers upon the Mayflower, William Bradford and Edward Winslow, from the ninth of November, 1620, the day on which they caught their first glimpse of American land, until the return to England of the good ship Fortune, more than thirteen months afterward. Of course, in a book of this kind, made up of extemporized jottings, we ought not to look for careful literary workmanship; and yet, the deliberation and the conscientiousness of the Pilgrim character are stamped upon every line of it. It has the charm of utter sincerity, the effortless grace that we might expect in the language of nobleminded men casting their eyes for the first time, and with unhackneyed enthusiasm, upon the face of a new universe.

"After many difficulties in boisterous storms, at length, by God's providence . . . we espied land. . . . And the appearance of it much comforted us, especially seeing so goodly a land, and wooded to the brink of the sea." Coming round "the spiral bending" of the outermost point of Cape Cod, they found themselves suddenly in "a good harbor and pleasant bay," "wherein a thousand sail of ships may safely ride." Upon land "there was the greatest store of fowl that ever we saw. And every day we saw whales playing hard by us, of which in that place, if we had instruments and means to take them, we might have made a very rich return; which to our great grief we wanted." Some of the pioneers going on shore for the purpose of discovering a place of habitation, they wondered at the density of the forests, and at the scarcity of the inhabitants. "We marched through boughs and bushes, and under hills and valleys, which tore our very armor in pieces, and yet could meet with none" of the inhabitants "nor their houses, nor find any fresh water." At last, "about ten o'clock we came into a deep valley, full of brush, wood-gaile, and long grass, through which we found little paths or tracks; and there we saw deer, and found springs of fresh water, of which we were heartily glad, and sat us down and drunk our first New England water, with as much delight as ever we drunk drink in all our lives." "We went ranging up and down till the sun began to draw low, and then we hastened out of the woods, that we might come to our shallop, which . . .

we espied a great way off, and called them to come unto us. . . .
They were exceedingly glad to see us. . . . So being both
weary and faint, for we had eaten nothing all that day, we fell
to make our rendezvous and get firewood. . . . By that time we
had done, and our shallop come to us, it was within night; and
we fed upon such victuals as we had, and betook us to our rest,
after we had set our watch. About midnight we heard a great
and hideous cry; and our sentinels called 'Arm! Arm!' So we
bestirred ourselves, and shot off a couple of muskets, and the
noise ceased. We concluded that it was a company of wolves
or foxes; for one told us he had heard such a noise in Newfound-
land. About five o'clock in the morning we began to be stirring.
. . . After prayer we prepared ourselves for breakfast and for a
journey; and it being now the twilight in the morning, it was
thought meet to carry the things down to the shallop. . . . As it
fell out, the water not being high enough, they laid the things
down upon the shore and came up to breakfast. Anon, all upon
a sudden, we heard a great and a strange cry, which we knew to
be the same voices, though they varied their notes. One of our
company, being abroad, came running in, and cried, 'They are
men! Indians! Indians!' and withal their arrows came flying
amongst us. Our men ran out with all speed to recover their
arms. . . . In the meantime, Captain Miles Standish, having a
snaphance ready, made a shot, and after him another. After
they two had shot, other two of us were ready; but he wished
us not to shoot till we could take aim, for we knew not what
need we should have. . . . Our care was no less for the shallop.
. . . We called unto them to know how it was with them; and
they answered 'Well! Well!' every one, and 'be of good courage!' . . . The cry of our enemies was dreadful. . . . Their note
was after this manner, '*Woach, woach, ha ha hach woach.*' . . .
There was a lusty man, and no whit less valiant, who was
thought to be their captain, stood behind a tree within half a
musket-shot of us, and there let his arrows fly at us. He was seen
to shoot three arrows, which were all avoided; for he at whom

the first arrow was aimed, saw it, and stooped down, and it flew over him. The rest were avoided also. He stood three shots of a musket. At length, one took, as he said, full aim at him; after which he gave an extraordinary cry, and away they went all. We followed them about a quarter of a mile. . . . Then we shouted all together two several times, and shot off a couple of muskets and so returned. This we did that they might see we were not afraid, nor discouraged. Thus it pleased God to vanquish our enemies and give us deliverance."

On Saturday, the third of March, "the birds sang in the woods most pleasantly. At one of the clock it thundered, which was the first we heard in that country. It was strong and great claps, but short; but after an hour it rained very sadly until midnight."

On Friday, the sixteenth of March, "we determined to conclude of the military orders, which we had begun to consider of before. . . . And whilst we were busied hereabouts, we were interrupted again; for there presented himself a savage, which caused an alarm. He very boldly came all alone, and along the houses, straight to the rendezvous; where we intercepted him, not suffering him to go in. . . . He saluted us in English and bade us 'welcome.' . . . He was a man free in speech, so far as he could express his mind, and of a seemly carriage. We questioned him of many things; he was the first savage we could meet withal. He said he was not of these parts, but of Morattiggon, and one of the sagamores or lords thereof. . . . He discoursed of the whole country, and of every province, and of their sagamores, and their number of men, and strength. The wind beginning to rise a little, we cast a horseman's coat about him; for he was stark naked, only a leather about his waist, with a fringe about a span long or a little more. He had a bow and two arrows. . . . He was a tall, straight man, the hair of his head black, long behind, only short before, none on his face at all. He asked some beer, but we gave him strong water, and biscuit, and butter, and cheese, and pudding, and a piece of mallard; all which he liked well. . . . All the afternoon we spent in communication with him. We would gladly have been rid of him at night, but he was not willing to go this night. . . . We lodged him that night at Stephen Hopkins's house, and watched him."

On the twenty-second of March, the Pilgrims received a visit from the great sagamore, Massasoit. "After salutations, our governor kissing his hand, the king kissed him; and so they sat down. The governor called for some strong water, and drunk to him; and he drunk a great draught, that made him sweat all the while after. . . . All the while he sat by the governor, he trembled for fear. In his person he is a very lusty man, in his best years, an able body, grave of countenance, and spare of speech; in his attire little or nothing differing from the rest of his followers, only in a great chain of white bone beads about his neck. . . . The king had in his bosom, hanging in a string, a great long knife. He marvelled much at our trumpet, and some of his men would sound it as well as they could. Samoset and Squanto, they staid all night with us; and the king and all his men lay all night in the woods, not above half an English mile from us, and all their wives and women with them. That night we kept good watch; but there was no appearance of danger.

"For the temper of the air here," writes Edward Winslow, in a letter appended to the journal from which we have been quoting, "it agreeth well with that in England; and if there be any difference at all, this is somewhat hotter in summer. Some think it to be colder in winter; but I cannot out of experience so say. The air is very clear, and not foggy, as hath been reported. I never in my life remember a more seasonable year than we have here enjoyed; and if we have once but kine, horses, and sheep, I make no question but men might live as contented here as in any part of the world. . . . The country wanteth only industrious men to employ; for it would grieve your hearts if, as I, you had seen so many miles together by goodly rivers uninhabited; and withal, to consider those parts of the world wherein you live to be even greatly burthened with abundance of people."

Thus, with words of happy import, do these earliest Americans close up the story of their first year in their new home; and three years afterward, in 1624, Edward Winslow had a second report to make, which was published in London under the title of *Good News from New England.*

He takes up the narrative at the very point where the previous report had dropped it, and carries it forward in luminous and spirited style down to September, 1623. It is a story of the griefs and perils and escapes of the young settlement, of their various encounters, in amity and in enmity, with mean red men and meaner white ones; of the interior administration of the little commonwealth, and of its steady advancement through all obstructions into solid security; above all else, it is a description of the country, with reference to its desirableness as the seat of a new English community. Winslow was a brave man, most expert in dealing with the Indians, and was several times sent upon embassies to them; and his book abounds in vivid and amusing descriptions of these savages, and of the manner of their lives. In one place, for example, he gives this account of their mode of preserving the memory of historical events: "Instead of records and chronicles, they take this course. Where any remarkable act is done, in memory of it, either in the place or by some pathway near adjoining, they make a round hole in the ground, about a foot deep, and as much over; which when others passing by behold, they inquire the cause and occasion of the same, which being once known, they are careful to acquaint all men, as occasion serveth, therewith; and lest such holes should be filled or grown up by any accident, as men pass by, they will oft renew the same; by which means many things of great antiquity are fresh in memory. So that as a man travelleth, if he can understand his guide, his journey will be the less tedious, by reason of the many historical discourses [which] will be related unto him." Perhaps nothing in all the book is more graphic or entertaining than his description of a journey which in the company of "one Master John Hamden, a gentleman of London, who then wintered with us," he made for the medical relief of Massasoit.

The conclusion of the work is a racy and vigorous admonition addressed to Englishmen who might meditate emigration to America, and warning them against the danger of entering upon that grim business without sufficient consideration of its inevitable tasks and pains: "I write not these things to dissuade any that shall seriously, upon due examination, set themselves to further the glory of God and the honor of our country, in so worthy an enterprise, but rather to discourage such as with too great lightness undertake such courses; who peradventure strain themselves and their friends for their passage thither, and are no sooner there, than seeing their foolish imagination made void, are at their wit's end, and would give ten times so much for their return, if they could procure it; and out of such discontented passions and humors, spare not to lay that imputation upon the country, and others, which themselves deserve. As, for example, I have heard some complain of others for their large reports of New England, and yet, because they must drink water and want many delicates they here enjoyed, could presently return with their mouths full of clamors. And can any be so simple as to conceive that the fountains should stream forth wine or beer, or the woods and rivers be like butchers' shops or fishmongers' stalls, where they might have things taken to their hands? If thou canst not live without such things, and hast no means to procure the one, and will not take pains for the other, nor hast ability to employ others for thee, rest where thou art; for, as a proud heart, a dainty tooth, a beggar's purse, and an idle hand, be here intolerable, so that person that hath these qualities there, is much more abominable. If, therefore, God hath given thee a heart to undertake such courses, upon such grounds as bear thee out in all difficulties, namely, his glory as a principal, and all other outward good things but as accessories, . . . then thou wilt with true comfort and thankfulness receive the least of his mercies; whereas on the contrary, men deprive themselves of much happiness, being senseless of greater blessings, and through prejudice smother up the love and bounty of God; whose name be ever glorified in us, and by us, now and evermore.   Amen."

Among the Argonauts of the first decade of New England colonization there was perhaps no braver or more exquisite spirit than Francis Higginson, a graduate of St. John's College, Cambridge, who, entering the ministry of the Church of England, soon became noted for his eloquence, and who, turning away from very brilliant prospects of promotion, became a resolute non-conformist, and finally accepted the office of religious teacher to the little pioneer community of Salem, in Massachusetts. It was in April, 1629, that this saintly and gifted man, with his wife and eight little children, sailed away from England, on the Talbot, "a good and strong ship," carrying "above a hundred planters, six goats, five great pieces of ordnance, with meal, oatmeal, pease, and all manner of munition and provision for the plantation for a twelvemonth."

Of this journey over the Atlantic, then a thing of great novelty and risk, Francis Higginson kept a journal, which he promptly sent back to England, and which was circulated in manuscript under the title of "A True Relation of the last Voyage to New England, declaring all circumstances, with the manner of the passage we had by sea, and what manner of country and inhabitants we found when we came to land, and what is the present state and condition of the English people that are there already; faithfully recorded, according to the very truth, for the satisfaction of very many of my loving friends, who have earnestly requested to be truly certified in these things." Arriving at Salem on the twenty-ninth of June, the author passed the next three months in getting established in his new home, and in making himself acquainted with the youthful-seeming world he had come to live in. The results of his observations were compressed into a little book, entitled

New England's Plantation, giving a "description of the commodities and discommodities of that country." This work was instantly printed in London; and so eager was the thirst of the English people for information concerning their recent settlements in New England, that three editions of the book were called for within a single year. In little more than thirteen months from his arrival in America, however, Francis Higginson died, in the prime of his life, and on the threshold of a great career.

Upon the title-page of his first book there is the hint of an apology to any "curious critic" who may look into it "for exactness of phrases"; and yet, unlabored as is the composition of both his books, we find in them a delicate felicity of expression, and a quiet, imaginative picturesqueness. Thus, for Wednesday, May thirteenth, he writes: "The wind still holding easterly, we came as far as the Land's End, in the utmost part of Cornwall, and so left our dear native soil of England behind us; and sailing about ten leagues further, we passed the isles of Scilly, and launched the same day a great way into the main ocean. And now my wife and other passengers began to feel the tossing waves of the western sea."

Again, under the date of May twenty-seventh, he gives this forcible description of a storm: "About noon there arose a south wind which increased more and more, so that it seemed to us that are landmen, a sore and terrible storm, for the wind blew mightily, the rain fell vehemently, the sea roared, and the waves tossed us horribly; besides, it was fearful dark, and the mariner's mate was afraid, and noise on the other side, with their running here and there, loud crying one to another to pull at this and that rope. The waves poured themselves over the ship, that the two boats were filled with water. . . . But this lasted not many hours, after which it became a calmish day." What pathos and simple beauty are in these words, which were written for Wednesday, the twenty-fourth of June: "This day we had all a clear and comfortable sight of America."

Two days afterwards the author wrote the following sentences, so vivid and real in their descriptiveness, that they enable us to enjoy the very luxury of drawing near to America and of beholding it with the eyes of the Fathers themselves: "Friday a foggy morning, but after clear, and wind calm. We saw many schools of mackerel, infinite multitudes on every side of our ship. The sea was abundantly stored with rockweed and yellow flowers, like gillyflowers. By noon we were within three leagues of Cape Ann; and as we sailed along the coasts, we saw every hill and dale and every island full of gay woods and high trees. The nearer we came to the shore, the more flowers in abundance, sometimes scattered abroad, sometimes joined in sheets nine or ten yards long, which we supposed to be brought from the low meadows by the tide. Now, what with fine woods and green trees by land, and these yellow flowers painting the sea, made us all desirous to see our new paradise of New England, whence we saw such fore-running signals of fertility afar off." On Monday, the twenty-ninth of June, "as we passed along, it was wonderful to behold so many islands, replenished with thick wood and high trees, and many fair, green, pastures. ... We rested that night with glad and thankful hearts that God had put an end to our long and tedious journey through the greatest sea in the world. . . . Our passage was both pleasurable and profitable. For we received instruction and delight in beholding the wonders of the Lord in the deep waters, and sometimes seeing the sea round us appearing with a terrible countenance, and, as it were, full of high hills and deep valleys; and sometimes it appeared as a most plain and even meadow. And, ever and anon, we saw divers kinds of fishes sporting in the great waters, great grampuses and huge whales, going by companies, and puffing up water-streams. Those that love their own chimney-corner, and dare not go beyond their own town's end, shall never have the honor to see these wonderful works of Almighty God."

In describing New England with reference to its fitness as the seat of an English commonwealth, the author arranges his facts, rather quaintly, under the topics of "the four elements—

earth, water, air, and fire." All his pages are full of sunshine, and the fragrance of flowers, and the gladness of nature in New England during the balmy season in which he came to it. Indeed, he was accused by some who came afterward, of having given too attractive a picture of the country; but for this he was hardly to blame. When he wrote, he had seen only the season of roses: no wonder that his descriptions were rosy. After a voyage of six weeks upon the ocean, any land seems good, much more a delicious, flowery summer-land; and Francis Higginson wrote in the first flush of excitement at being on shore, in a bounteous realm, in an exhilarating new life. It seems to him a paradise regained. All things are delightful. He even exults in the domestic felicity of having "already a quart of milk for a penny," and in having candles of "the wood of the pine tree cloven in two little slices something thin, which . . . burn as clear as a torch." Concerning the climate of the country, he declared that "a sup of New England's air is better than a whole draught of Old England's ale." He was not long in making a study of the Indians, whom in one passage he describes with great zest, even weaving into his account a stroke of gentle raillery at a certain English fashion then prevalent, and very distasteful to the Puritans. The Indians "are a tall and strong-limbed people. Their colors are tawny. . . . Their hair is generally black, and cut before, like our gentlewomen, and one lock longer than the rest, much like our gentlemen, which fashion, I think, came from hence into England." But best of all, "we have here plenty of preaching, and diligent catechising, with strict and careful exercise. . . . And thus we doubt not but God will be with us; and if God be with us, who can be against us?"

A very sprightly and masterful specimen of descriptive literature, embodying the results of precise observation directed toward the topography, climate, and productions of the country, is *New England's Prospect*, published in London in 1634, and written by William Wood, whose residence in Amer-

ica is supposed to have begun five years before that date. It will
not be easy for us to give a more felicitous account of the book
than it gives of itself, when, upon its old title-page, it assures
us that it is indeed "a true, lively, and experimental description" of the region that it treats of. The author had attained the
fine art of packing his pages full of the most exact delineation of
facts, without pressing the life and juice out of them; and, besides the extraordinary raciness and vivacity of his manner, he
has an elegance of touch by no means common in the prose of
his contemporaries. His style, indeed, is that of a man of
genuine literary culture, and has the tone and flavor of the best
Elizabethan prose-writers; almost none of the crabbedness of
the sermon-makers and pamphleteers of his own day. There
are dainty strokes of beauty in his sentences; a forceful imaginative vigor; gayety, and good-hearted sarcasm; all going to
make up a book of genial descriptions of nature such as Izaak
Walton must have delighted in, if perchance his placid eye ever
fell upon it. The book is broken into two parts, the first being a
description of the country, the second an account of its Indian
inhabitants. Under the first division, we have in twelve chapters a sketch of the geographical features of New England; of
the seasons; of the climate, "with the suitableness of it to English bodies for health and sickness"; of the soil; "of the herbs,
fruits, woods, waters, and minerals"; "of the beasts that live on
the land," or in the water, or both; finally, of the colonies already established there, and of the best preparations to be made
by those who intended to remove into the new world. The
second division of the work contains twenty chapters, all relating to the Indian tribes of New England; their places of abode;
their apparel, ornaments, paintings; their food; their personal
characteristics, such as friendship, fortitude, intellectual condition; their politics; their worship; their wars, diversions,
domestic customs, and means of livelihood.

Thus the book has a wide range of topics and a multitude of
details; but it moves easily through them all, with an alert and
thorough treatment, not once blundering out of the straight

path or lapsing into dulness. In the preface, the author has a
spirited passage avowing that in all his statements he had been
careful of the truth, and wittily defending the reputation of
travellers against the calumnies of those home-keeping souls
who denounce as false whatever is beyond the petty sweep of
their own horizons. "I would be loath to broach any thing which
may puzzle thy belief, and so justly draw upon myself that unjust aspersion commonly laid on travellers; of whom many say,
'They may lie by authority, because none can control them;'
which proverb had surely his original from the sleepy belief of
many a home-bred dormouse, who comprehends not either the
rarity or possibility of those things he sees not; to whom the
most classic relations seem riddles and paradoxes; of whom it
may be said, as once of Diogenes, that because he circled himself in the circumstance of a tub, he therefore contemned the
port and palace of Alexander, which he knew not. So there is
many a tub-brained cynic, who because anything stranger than
ordinary is too large for the strait hoops of his apprehension, he
peremptorily concludes that it is a lie. But I decline this sort of
thick-witted readers, and dedicate the mite of my endeavors to
my more credulous, ingenious, and less censorious countrymen,
for whose sake I undertook this work. . . . Thus, thou mayest,
in two or three hours' travel over a few leaves, see and know
that which cost him that writ it, years, and travel over sea and
land, before he knew it."

It is a discovery soon made by us, as we turn over the pages
of this writer, that in a book in which description needs to be
the principal thing, his style is most happily descriptive. He
seems to have the very gift of picture-making, describing objects so well that, as the Arabs say, the ear is converted into the
eye. For example, having to tell us of Massachusetts Bay, he
lets us look at it for ourselves. It "is both safe, spacious, and
deep, free from such cockling seas as run upon the coast of
Ireland, and in the channels of England. . . . The mariners . . .
may behold the two capes embracing their welcome ships in
their arms, which thrust themselves out into the sea in form of

a half-moon, the surrounding shore being high, and showing many white cliffs in a most pleasant prospect. . . . This harbor is made by a great company of islands, whose high cliffs shoulder out the boisterous seas."

Another literary trait of the author, which he shares with many of the writers of his period, is that of sprinkling verses along the landscape of his prose; and his verses have this singularity, that they are often of considerable poetic merit. In giving a description of the forest trees of New England, he compresses a multitude of particulars into these terse lines, in which the literary aptness and even imaginative force of his epithets are as striking as is their scientific precision:

> Trees both in hills and plains in plenty be;
> The long-lived Oak, the mournful Cypress-tree;
> Sky-towering Pines, and Chestnuts coated rough,
> The lasting Cedar, with the Walnut tough;
> The rosin-dropping Fir, for masts in use;
> The boatmen seek for oars, light, neat-grown Spruce;
> The brittle Ash, the ever-trembling Asps,
> The broad-spread Elm, whose concave harbors wasps;
> The water-spongy Alder, good for naught;
> Small Eldern, by the Indian fletchers sought;
> The knotty Maple, pallid Birch, Hawthorns;
> The horn-bound tree, that to be cloven scorns,
> Which from the tender vine oft takes his spouse,
> Who twines embracing arms about his boughs.
> Within this Indian orchard fruits be some:
> The ruddy Cherry, and the jetty Plum,
> Snake-murthering Hazel, with sweet Saxifrage,
> Whose spurs, in beer, allays hot fever's rage.
> The dyer's Sumach, with more trees there be,
> That are both good to use, and rare to see.

In his chapters on animals are many paragraphs illustrating an amusing quaintness and quiet mirthfulness of tone, as well as the author's power of condensed and graphic description in verse: "Having related unto you the pleasant situation of the country, the healthfulness of the climate, the nature of the soil, with his vegetatives and other commodities, it will not be amiss to inform you of such irrational creatures as are daily bred and continually nourished in this country, which do much conduce to the well being of the inhabitants, affording not only meat for the belly, but clothing for the back. The beasts be as followeth:

> The kingly Lion, and the strong-armed Bear,
> The large-limbed Mooses, with the tripping Deer;
> Quill-darting Porcupines and Raccoons be
> Castled in the hollow of an aged tree;
> The skipping Squirrel, Rabbit, purblind Hare,
> Immurëd in the selfsame castle are;
> Lest red-eyed Ferrets, wily Foxes should
> Them undermine, if rampired but with mould;
> The grim-faced Ounce, and ravenous, howling Wolf
> Whose meagre paunch sucks like a swallowing gulf;
> Black-glistering Otters, and rich-coated Beaver,
> The civet-scented Musquash smelling ever.

"Concerning lions I will not say that I ever saw any myself; but some affirm that they have seen a lion at Cape Ann, which is not above six leagues from Boston; some likewise being lost in woods have heard such terrible roarings as have made them much aghast; which must either be devils or lions; there being no other creatures which use to roar saving bears, which have not such a terrible kind of roaring. Besides, Plymouth men have traded for lions' skins in former times." "The Porcupine is a small thing not much unlike a Hedgehog; something bigger, who stands upon his guard, and proclaims a 'Noli me tangere' to man and beast that shall approach too near him, darting his quills into their legs and hides." "The beasts of offence be Skunks, Ferrets, Foxes, whose impudence sometimes drives them to the good-wives' hen roost to fill their paunch." "The Oldwives be a fowl that never leave tattling day or night; something bigger than a duck."

Altogether the most remarkable literary quality of this writer is shown in his delineation of objects in natural history: he has in these an extraordinary union of comprehensiveness, minute accuracy, brevity, and pictorial vividness. Thus, in his account of wolves and hummingbirds are passages that indicate in the author an uncommon power of close and definite observation, together with an easy command of the words that are at once nicely, concisely, and poetically descriptive. Wolves "be made much like a mongrel, being big-boned, lank-paunched, deep-breasted, having a thick neck and head, prick ears, and long snout, with dangerous teeth, long staring hair, and a great bush-tail. It is thought of many that our English mastiffs might be too hard for them; but it is no such matter, for they care no more for an ordinary mastiff, than an ordinary mastiff cares for a cur; many good dogs have been spoiled with them. Once a fair greyhound hearing them at their howlings, run out to chide them, who was torn to pieces before he could be rescued. One of them makes no more bones to run away with a pig than a dog to run away with a marrow bone. . . . Late at night and early in the morning they set up their howlings, and call their companies together at night to hunt, at morning to sleep; in a word they be the greatest inconveniency the country hath, both for matter of damage to private men in particular, and the whole country in general." "The Humbird is one of the wonders of the country, being no bigger than a hornet, yet hath all the dimensions of a bird, as bill and wings, with quills, spider like legs, small claws. For color she is as glorious as the rainbow; as she flies she makes a little humming noise like a humblebee: wherefore she is called the Humbird."

"Having done with these," he says, "let me lead you from the land to the sea, to view what commodities may come from thence;" and in the course of this description, he mentions with his usual excellence of apt epithets:

> The king of waters, the sea-shouldering Whale;
> The snuffing Grampus, with the oily Seal;
> The storm-presaging Porpus; Herring-Hog;
> Line-shearing Shark, the Catfish, and Sea-Dog;
>
> .   .   .   .
>
> The stately Bass, old Neptune's fleeting post
> That tides it out and in from sea to coast.

It was not the author's plan to deal at any length with the history and social development of the colonies established in New England; yet he does not altogether pass them over, nor does he forget the needs of those in the mother-land who might be considering the project of coming to America. He speaks sarcastically of the ignorant questions often asked in England concerning the new land, as, "whether the sun shines there or no;" and of the "groundless calumniations" of those who had come to the country with fantastic and impossible notions of what was to be found there, and had of course abandoned it in disgust: "I have myself heard some say that they heard it was a rich land, a brave country; but when they came there they could see nothing but a few canvas booths and old houses, supposing at the first to have found walled towns, fortifications and cornfields, as if towns could have built themselves, or cornfields have grown of themselves without the husbandry of man. These men, missing of their expectations, returned home and railed against the country." The second part of the book is devoted to the Indians, and is written, as the author says, "in a more light and facetious style, . . . because their carriage and behavior hath afforded more matter of mirth and laughter, than gravity and wisdom; and therefore I have inserted many passages of mirth concerning them, to spice the rest of my more serious discourse and to make it more pleasant." But the author's merry eye, never failing to catch a glimpse of whatever is amusing, is likewise alert for whatever is instructive; and the really fine and wise sketch which he has given of the various savage tribes of New England, is not likely to be scorned by us, even though he may have committed the crime of paving the highway of knowledge with entertainment. His study of the Indians seems to have embraced not only their habits in this world, but their notions about the world to come; and in his chapter on "their deaths, burials, and mourning," we find these nimble and affluent sentences, which, besides giving us considerable amusing information, reproduce for us the very manner of the best Elizabethan prose: "Although the Indians be of lusty and healthful

bodies, not experimentally knowing the catalogue of those
health-wasting diseases which are incident to other countries,
. . . but spin out the thread of their days to a fair length, num-
bering three score, four score, some a hundred years, before the
world's universal summoner cite them to the craving grave;
but the date of their life expired, and death's arrestment seizing
upon them, all hope of recovery being past, then to behold and
hear their throbbing sobs and deep-fetched sighs, their grief-
wrung hands, and tear-bedewed cheeks, their doleful cries,
would draw tears from adamantine eyes, that be but spectators
of their mournful obsequies. The glut of their grief being passed,
they commit the corpse of their deceased friends to the ground,
over whose grave is for a long time spent many a briny tear,
deep groan and Irish-like howlings. . . . These are the mourners
without hope; yet do they hold the immortality of the never-
dying soul, that it shall pass to the South-West Elysium, concerning which their Indian faith jumps much with the Turkish
Alcoran, holding it to be a kind of paradise, wherein they shall
everlastingly abide, solacing themselves in odoriferous gardens,
fruitful cornfields, green meadows, bathing their tawny hides in
the cool streams of pleasant rivers, and shelter themselves from
heat and cold in the sumptuous palaces framed by the skill of
Nature's curious contrivement; concluding that neither care
nor pain shall molest them, but that Nature's bounty will administer all things with a voluntary contribution from the overflowing storehouse of their Elysian hospital."

So vigilant an observer as was this author, would not be
likely to let slip any trait that might illustrate the grotesque
and droll effects wrought by the contact of English culture with
the mental childhood of the Indians. Nothing in this kind has
ever ministered more to the white man's mirth than the impression made upon the savages by our improvements in the arts,
which of course seemed to them to be things enormous, superhuman, and dreadful: "These Indians being strangers to arts
and sciences, and being unacquainted with the inventions that
are common to a civilized people, are ravished with admiration

at the first view of any such sight. They took the first ship they saw for a walking island, the mast to be a tree, the sail white clouds, and the discharging of ordnance for lightning and thunder, which did much trouble them; but this thunder being over, and this moving island steadied with an anchor, they manned out their canoes to go and pick strawberries there; but being saluted by the way with a broadside, they cried out 'what much hoggery,' 'so big walk,' and 'so big speak,' and 'by and by kill,' which caused them to turn back, not daring to approach till they were sent for. They do much extol and wonder at the English for their strange inventions, especially for a windmill, which in their esteem was little less than the world's wonder, for the strangeness of his whisking motion and the sharp teeth biting the corn (as they term it) into such small pieces. They were loath at the first to come near to his long arms, or to abide in so tottering a tabernacle, though now they dare go anywhere so far as they have an English guide."

His chapter on the Aberginians, a tribe of savages renowned for their stalwart and superb physical proportions, furnishes us with another instance of his remarkable gift of concentrated, exact, and vivid description. They are "between five or six foot high, straight-bodied, strongly composed, smooth-skinned, merry-countenanced, of complexion something more swarthy than Spaniards, black-haired, high-foreheaded, black-eyed, out-nosed, broadshouldered, brawny-armed, long- and slender-handed, out-breasted, small-waisted, lank-bellied, well-thighed, flat-kneed, handsome-grown legs, and small feet. In a word, take them when the blood brisks in their veins, when the flesh is on their backs, and marrow in their bones, when they frolic in their antique deportments and Indian postures, and they are more amiable to behold (though only in Adam's livery) than many a compounded fantastic in the newest fashion." "But a sagamore with a humbird in his ear for a pendant, a black hawk on his occiput for his plume, mowhackees for his gold chain, good store of wampompaege begirting his loins, his bow in his hand, his quiver at his back, with six naked Indian spatter-lashes at his heels for his guard, thinks himself little inferior to the great Cham; he will not stick to say, he is all one with King Charles. He thinks he can blow down castles with his breath, and conquer kingdoms with his conceit."

A writer of more pronounced scientific intentions, though of far less literary skill, was John Josselyn, who, belonging to an ancient and aristocratic family in England, had the distinction of being able to subscribe his name with the proud affix, "Gentleman." His father, Sir Thomas Josselyn, of Kent, was an associate of Sir Ferdinando Gorges in schemes of American colonization; his brother was that Henry Josselyn, who, from about the year 1634 onward for forty years, was a leading landholder and magistrate in the province of Maine, and who, in life-long contests with white men and Indians, displayed an unslumbering activity of courage and of hate,—a characteristic exactly touched by Whittier in a single vivid line of Mogg Megone—

Grey Jocelyn's eye is never sleeping.

John Josselyn, the author, was twice an inhabitant of this country. He came first in 1638, remaining only fifteen months; he came again in 1663, and remained eight years: in both cases passing the most of his time on his brother's plantation at Scarborough. In connection with his first arrival in Boston, he mentions a fact that gives us a pleasant glimpse of the intellectual exchanges already begun between the men of books in America and the men of books in England: he states that he first paid his respects to "Mr. Winthrop, the governor," and that he next called upon the great pulpit-orator, John Cotton, to whom he "delivered from Mr. Francis Quarles, the poet, the translation of the 16th, 25th, 51st, 88th, 113th, and 137th Psalms, into English metre, for his approbation." Though his family in England appear to have been attached to the Puritan party, he himself certainly had little sympathy with the Puritans of New England, concerning whom he in one place frees his mind, with a refreshing copiousness of frank words. Their leading men, he tells us, "are damnable rich, . . . inexplicably covetous and proud: they receive your gifts but as an homage or tribute due to their transcendency. . . . The chiefest objects of discipline, true religion, and morality, they want; some are of a linsey-woolsey disposition, . . . all like Ethiopians, white in the teeth only; full of ludification, and injurious dealing, and cruelty."

There is no evidence that he engaged in any kind of business in America. He was probably a bachelor; and finding a comfortable home on his brother's estate, he had leisure to indulge his love of reading and particularly his fondness for researches in natural history. He made it his ambition, as he informs us, "to discover the natural, physical, and chirurgical rarities of this new-found world." He appears to have wandered at his will in the forests and on the mountains of Maine, to have dropped his hook in many waters, and to have explored the islands along the coast, everywhere soliciting nature to deliver up to him her mysteries. Some of these mysteries, indeed, did not consent to be delivered up passively to the prying stranger, even for the advancement of science among mankind; as was made apparent, for example, in his somewhat too zealous investigation of that uneasy Americanism, a hornet's nest: "In the afternoon I walked into the woods . . . , and happening into a fine broad walk, . . . I wandered till I chanced to spy a fruit, as I thought, like a pine-apple planted with scales. It was as big as the crown of a woman's hat. I made bold to step unto it, with an intent to have gathered it. No sooner had I touched it, but hundreds of wasps were about me. At last I cleared myself from them, . . . but by the time I was come into the house, . . . they hardly knew me but by my garments." This grim practical joke of the wasps at the expense of the learned naturalist, which must have long supplied food for bucolic mirth among the woodmen of New England, is deftly used by Longfellow in his "Tragedy of John Endicott," when he makes the troubled inn-keeper of Boston, Samuel Cole, exclaim:

> "I feel like Master Josselyn when he found
> The hornet's nest, and thought it some strange fruit,
> Until the seeds came out, and then he dropped it."

It is as a naturalist, and as the writer of two books embodying the results of his observations in that capacity, that John Josselyn has a place in our literary annals. He appears indeed to have been a man of some general learning. He quotes Pliny, Lucan, Isidore, and Paracelsus; all his Biblical citations are from the Vulgate; he brings in a proverb in the Italian; and among the writers of his own country, he has references to Drayton, Ben Jonson, Sir John Davies, Sylvester, George Sandys, Captain John Smith, and to Charles the First; to the last of whom, as the supposed author of "Eikon Basilike," he alludes in the sympathetic cant of the Restoration, as "the royal martyr." John Josselyn's first book, entitled *New England's Rarities Discovered in Birds, Beasts, Fishes, Serpents, and Plants of that Country*, was published in London in 1672; his second book, considerably larger than the first, and entitled *An Account of Two Voyages to New England*, was published in the same place in 1674.

Although his main purpose in these books was to give an account of American productions in natural history, he did not altogether leave out descriptions of the country in general. Thus he speaks of "a ridge of mountains . . . known by the name of the White Mountains, upon which lieth snow all the year, and is a landmark twenty miles off at sea." One of the highest of these mountains is "called the Sugar Loaf, . . . a rude heap of massy stones piled one upon another. . . . From this rocky hill you may see the whole country round about: it is far above the lower clouds, and from hence we beheld a vapor, like a great pillar, drawn up by the sunbeams out of a great lake or pond into the air, where it was formed into a cloud. The country beyond these hills northward is daunting terrible, being full of rocky hills . . . and clothed with infinite thick woods."

In dealing with objects in natural history, the most valuable part of his work is in botany. Of course that science was then in a crude condition, and it may be that even in that condition Josselyn had not perfectly mastered it. According to the decision of Professor Edward Tuckerman, Josselyn is "little more than a herbalist; but it is enough that he gets beyond that entirely unscientific character. He certainly botanized, and made botanical use of Gerard and his other authorities. The credit belongs to him of indicating several genera as new which were so, and peculiar to the American Flora. . . . There are important parts of his account of our plants, in which we know with certainty what he intended to tell us; and farther, that this was worth the telling."

Beyond the realm of botany, his contributions to natural history are less esteemed. Indeed, even within that realm, he was capable of making the announcement that, in America, barley "commonly degenerates into oats," and that "summer-wheat many times changeth into rye"; while in the domain of the other sciences, he indulges in many assertions that exhibit the uncritical habits of even scientific observers in the seventeenth century. He informs us, with all gravity, that in their assemblies the Indians commonly carry on their discussions "in perfect hexameter verse," doing this "extempore." He assures us that there is in New England a species of frog, "which chirp in the spring like sparrows, and croak like toads in autumn"; some of which "when they sit upon their breech are a foot high"; while "up in the country" they are "as big as a child of a year old." He tells of swallows which, loving to dwell in chimneys, construct their nests so as to hang down "by a claw-like string a yard long." These swallows, he adds, "commonly have four or five young ones, and when they go away, which is much about the time that swallows use to depart, they never fail to throw down one of their young birds into the room by way of gratitude. I have more than once observed that, against the ruin of the family, these birds will suddenly forsake the house and come no more." He gives a brilliant description of the Pilhannaw, "a monstrous great bird . . . four times as big as a goshawk, white-mailed, having two or three purple feathers in her head as long as geese's feathers; . . . her head is as big as a child's of a year old; a very princely bird. When she soars abroad, all sort of feathered creatures hide themselves; yet she never preys upon any of them, but upon fawns and jackals. She aeries in the woods upon the high hills of Ossapy." These sentences upon the Pilhannaw are indeed delightful, the last one in particular being very sweet, with a certain far-off, appealing melody; and the artistic merit of the whole picture is perhaps enhanced by the consideration, that it seems to have been on his part an exploit of pure imagination, supplemented by some guess-work and hear-say—this princely bird of Josselyn's being probably nothing but "a confused conception made up from several accounts of large birds" seen in different parts of America.

It may not surprise us to ascertain that this author, whose scientific methods had in them so little severity, should have stopped occasionally to reproach his "skeptic readers" for "muttering out of their scuttle-mouths" expressions of derisive unbelief in his statements. As a student of nature, his own capacity for receiving at the hands of other narrators prodigious gift-horses which he was too polite to look very sharply in the mouth, implied in him at least this compensating merit—a tolerant and catholic mood. And is it not possible, after all, that in our search for knowledge, swiftness to reject may be as great an impediment to progress as swiftness to accept? If extreme credulity swallows down a good deal of error, may it not be that extreme incredulity spurns away a good deal of truth? At any rate, our gentle author seems to have had some such notion; for in his life-time he walked quite freely about this earth, keeping his eyes and ears open for the discovery of such matters as he had not known before, and believing, as he tells us, "that there are many stranger things in the world than are to be seen between London and Stanes."

Jоhn Wіnthrop, *preaching in the spring of 1630 to the Puritans bound for New England aboard the* Arabella, *clearly stated their purpose when he declared: "Wee shall be as a Citty upon a Hill, the eies of all people are uppon us; soe that if wee shall deale falsely with our god in this worke wee have undertaken and soe cause him to withdrawe his present help from us, wee shall be made a story and a by-word through the world."*

The chief New England colonies actually became God-centered communities. For about a generation, the sermon and the theological treatise dominated their literature as thoroughly as men like John Cotton and John Winthrop dominated the social and political systems.

New England: Theology and Religion

Aмоng the earliest official records of Massachusetts, there is a memorandum of articles needed there and to be procured from England. The list includes beans, pease, vine-planters, potatoes, hop-roots, pewter-bottles, brass-ladles, spoons, and ministers. It is but just to add that in the original document the article here mentioned last, stands first; even as in the seventeenth century, in New England, that article would certainly have stood first in any conceivable list of necessaries, for this world or the world to come. An old historian, in describing the establishment of the colony of Plymouth, gives the true sequence in the two stages of the process when he says, they "planted a church of Christ there and set up civil government." In the year 1640, a company of excellent people resolved to found a new town in Massachusetts, the town of Woburn; but before getting the town incorporated, they took pains to build a meeting-house and a parsonage, to choose a minister, and to fix the arrangements for his support. New England was a country, as a noted writer of the early time expresses it, "whose interests were most remarkably and generally enwrapped in its ecclesiastical circumstances"; it followed that for any town within its borders the presence or absence of a "laborious and illuminating ministry" meant the presence or absence of external prosperity. Indeed, the same writer stated the case with delightful commercial frankness when he remarked: "The gospel has evidently been the making of our towns." During the first sixty years, New England was a theocracy, and the ministers were in reality the chief officers of state. It was not a departure from their sphere for them to deal with politics; for everything pertaining to the state was included in the sphere of the church. On occasion of an exciting popular election, in 1637, Mr. John Wilson, one of the pastors of Boston, climbed upon the bough of a tree, and from that high pulpit, with great authority, harangued the crowd upon their political duties. The greatest political functionaries, recognizing the ministers as in some sense their superior officers, "asked their advice upon the most important occasions," and sometimes even appealed to them for the settlement of personal differences that had arisen among themselves. In 1632, the deputy-governor, Thomas Dudley, having a grievance against the governor, John Winthrop, made complaint to two ministers, John Wilson and Thomas Welde; whereupon a council of five ministers was convened to call before them the governor and the lieutenant governor, and to hear what they had to say for themselves; having heard it, the ministers "went apart for one hour," and then returned with their decision, to which the governor meekly submitted. To speak ill of ministers was a species of sedition. In 1636, a citizen of Boston was required to pay a fine of forty pounds and to make a public apology, for saying that all the ministers but three preached a covenant of works.

The objects of so much public deference were not unaware of their authority: they seldom abused it; they never forgot it. If ever men, for real worth and greatness, deserved such preëminence, they did; they had wisdom, great learning, great force of will, devout consecration, philanthropy, purity of life. For once in the history of the world, the sovereign places were filled by the sovereign men. They bore themselves with the air of leadership: they had the port of philosophers, noblemen, and kings. The writings of our earliest times are full of reference to the majesty of their looks, the awe inspired by their presence, the grandeur and power of their words.

Men like these, with such an ascendency as this over the public, could not come before the public too often, or stay there too long; and on two days in every seven, they presented themselves in solemn state to the people, and challenged undivided attention. Their pulpits were erected far aloft, and as remote as possible from the congregation, typifying the awful distance and the elevation of the sacred office which there exercised its mightiest function. Below, among the pews, the people were arranged, not in families, but according to rank and age and sex; the old men in one place, the old dames in another; young men and maidens prudently seated far apart; the boys having the luxury of the pulpit stairs and the gallery. Failure to attend church was not a thing to be tolerated, except in cases of utter necessity. People who stayed away were hunted up by the tithing-men: for one needless absence they were to be fined; for such absence persisted in four weeks, they were to be set in the stocks or lodged in a wooden cage. Within the meeting-house, the entire congregation, but especially the boys, were vigilantly guarded by the town constables, each one being armed with a rod, at one end of which was a hare's foot, and at the other end a hare's tail. This weapon they wielded with justice tempered by gallantry: if a woman fell asleep, it was enough to tingle her face gently with the bushy end of the rod; but if the sleeper were a boy, he was vigorously thumped awake by the hard end of it.

In the presence of God and of his appointed ministers, it was not for man to be impatient; and the modern frailty that clamors for short prayers and short sermons had not invaded their sanctuaries or even their thoughts. When they came to church, they settled themselves down to a regular religious siege, which was expected to last from three to five hours. Upon the pulpit stood an hour-glass; and as the sacred service of prayer and psalm and sermon moved ruthlessly forward, it was the duty of the sexton to go up hour by hour and turn the glass over. The prayers were of course extemporaneous; and in that solemn act, the gift of long continuance was successfully culti· vated: the preacher, rising into raptures of devotion and storm-ing heaven with volleys of petitionary syllogism, could hardly be required to take much note of the hour-glass. "Mr. Torrey stood up and prayed near two hours," writes a Harvard student in the seventeenth century; "but the time obliged him to close, to our regret; and we could have gladly heard him an hour longer." Their sermons were of similar longitude, and were ob-viously exhaustive—except of the desire of the people to hear more. John Winthrop mentions a discourse preached at Cam-bridge by Thomas Hooker when he was ill: the minister at first proceeded in his discourse for fifteen minutes, then stopped and rested half an hour, then resumed and preached for two hours. Well might Nathaniel Ward, in his whimsical satire, make this propensity of himself and his brethren the theme of a confession which was at least half in earnest: "We have a strong weakness in New England that when we are speaking we know not how to conclude. We make many ends before we make an end. . . . We cannot help it, though we can; which is the arch infirmity in all morality. We are so near the west pole that our longitudes are as long as any wise man would wish, and somewhat longer. I scarce know any adage more grateful than 'Grata brevitas'."

In his theme, in his audience, in the appointments of each sacred occasion, the preacher had everything to stimulate him to put into his sermons his utmost intellectual force. The entire community were present, constituting a congregation hardly to be equalled now for its high average of critical intelligence: trained to acute and rugged thinking by their habit of grap-pling day by day with the most difficult problems in theology; fond of subtile metaphysical distinctions; fond of system, min-uteness, and completeness of treatment; not bringing to church any moods of listlessness or flippancy; not expecting to find there mental diversion, or mental repose; but going there with their minds aroused for strenuous and robust work, and demanding from the preacher solid thought, not gushes of sentiment, not torrents of eloquent sound. Then, too, there was time enough for the preacher to move upon his subject carefully, and to turn himself about in it, and to develop the resources of it amply, to his mind's content, hour by hour, in perfect assurance that his congregation would not desert him either by going out or by going to sleep. Moreover, if a single discourse, even on the vast scale of a Puritan pulpit-performance, were not enough to enable him to give full statement to his topic, he was at liberty, according to a favorite usage in those days, to resume and continue the topic week by week, and month by month, in orderly sequence; thus, after the manner of a professor of theology, traversing with minute care and triumphant completeness the several great realms of his science. If the methods of the preacher resembled those of a theological professor, it may be added that his congregation likewise had the appearance of an assemblage of theological students; since it was customary for nearly every one to bring his note-book to church, and to write in it diligently as much of the sermon as he could take down. They had no newspapers, no theatres, no miscellaneous lectures, no entertainments of secular music or of secular oratory, none of the genial distractions of our modern life: the place of all these was filled by the sermon. The sermon was without a competitor in the eye or mind of the community. It was the central and commanding incident in their lives; the one stately spectacle for all men and all women year after year; the grandest matter of anticipation or of memory; the theme for hot disputes on which all New England would take sides, and which would seem sometimes to shake the world to its centre. Thus were the preachers held to a high standard of intellectual work. Hardly anything was lacking that could incite a strong man to do his best continually, to the end of his days; and into the function of preaching, the supreme function at that time in popular homage and influence, the strongest men were drawn.

Their pastorships were usually for life; and no man could long satisfy such listeners, or fail soon to talk himself empty in their presence, who did not toil mightily in reading and in thinking, pouring ideas into his mind even faster than he poured them out of it.

Without doubt, the sermons produced in New England during the colonial times, and especially during the seventeenth century, are the most authentic and characteristic revelations of the mind of New England for all that wonderful epoch. They are commonly spoken of mirthfully by an age that lacks the faith of that period, its earnestness, its grip, its mental robustness; a grinning and a flabby age, an age hating effort, and requiring to be amused. The theological and religious writings of early New England may not now be readable; but they are certainly not despicable. They represent an enormous amount of subtile, sustained, and sturdy brain-power. They are, of course, grave, dry, abstruse, dreadful; to our debilitated attentions they are hard to follow; in style they are often uncouth and ponderous; they are technical in the extreme; they are devoted to a theology that yet lingers in the memory of mankind only through certain shells of words long since emptied of their original meaning. Nevertheless, these writings are monuments of vast learning, and of a stupendous intellectual energy both in the men who produced them and in the men who listened to them. Of course they can never be recalled to any vital human interest. They have long since done their work in moving the minds of men. Few of them can be cited as literature. In the mass, they can only be labelled by the antiquarians and laid away upon shelves to be looked at occasionally as curiosities of verbal expression, and as relics of an intellectual condition gone forever. They were conceived by noble minds; they are themselves noble. They are superior to our jests. We may deride them, if we will; but they are not derided.

Of all the great preachers who came to New England in our first age, there were three who, according to the universal opinion of their contemporaries, towered above all others—Thomas

Hooker, Thomas Shepard, John Cotton. These three could be compared with one another; but with them could be compared no one else. They stood apart, above rivalry, above envy. In personal traits they differed; they were alike in bold and energetic thinking, in massiveness of erudition, in a certain over-powering personal persuasiveness, in the gift of fascinating and resistless pulpit oratory.

Thomas Hooker, though not the eldest, died the first, namely in 1647, aged sixty-one. He had then been in America fourteen years. Before coming to America he had achieved in England a brilliant, influential, troubled career. He was a graduate of Emmanuel College, Cambridge; taking holy orders, he was for some years a preacher in London; in 1626, being forty years old, he became religious lecturer and assistant minister in Chelmsford; and there, if not before, he planted himself conspicuously upon grounds of non-conformity to several doctrines and usages of the established church. In no long time, of course, Bishop Laud was upon his track, storming with ecclesiastical fury. Hooker was cast out of the pulpit. At once he set up a grammar-school near Chelmsford, whence, however, once more the echoes of his eloquent and brave talk even in private, reached the ears of the bishop. Hooker had to flee for his life. Of course he fled to Holland; and there for two or three years he preached to English congregations at Delft and at Rotterdam. Already many of his friends had gone across the Atlantic to the great Puritan colony of Massachusetts Bay; and in 1633 he himself went thither, in the same ship with his illustrious compeer, John Cotton. For three years after his arrival in New England, he preached to the church in Cambridge; and in 1636 he led his entire flock, about a hundred families, westward through the wilderness to the lovely valley of the Connecticut, where they built the town of Hartford—a town which then seemed to the people of Boston to be so close to the western verge of the world that, as they used to say, the last great conflict with antichrist would certainly take place there. Of this colony, Hooker was priest and king; and here, during the last eleven years of his life, he did perhaps his best work, studying hard, preaching hard, shaping for all time the character of the community which he founded, and pouring forth in swift succession through the press of London, those glowing and powerful religious treatises of his which at once became classics in Puritan literature. Soon after his death, a noble young minister, John Higginson, revering his genius, went through the toil of copying two hundred of Hooker's sermons, and sent them to England for publication. There, under various titles, about one half of them were printed. In 1830, one hundred and eighty-three years after Hooker's death, the old parsonage at Hartford was torn down, and in it were found large quantities of manuscripts, supposed to have been his. What they were, we know not. They may have contained letters, diaries, and other invaluable personal and historical memoranda; but there happened to be no one then in the city which Hooker founded, to give shelter to these venerable treasures, and to save them from the doom of being thrown into the Connecticut River.

In the living presence of Hooker there appears to have been some singular personal force, an air both of saintliness and kingliness, that lofty and invincible moral genius which the Hebrew prophets had, and with which they captivated or smote down human resistance. Even during his life-time and shortly afterward, there gathered about him the halo of spiritual mystery, a sort of supernatural prestige, anecdotes of weird achievement that in a darker age would have blossomed into frank and vivid legends of miraculous power. In his youth there was noticed in him "a grandeur of mind" that marked him out for something uncommon. As he came on into manhood, his person and bearing partook of peculiar majesty; the imperial dignity of his office made him imperial. "He was a person," they said, "who when he was doing his Master's work, would put a king into his pocket." People, seeing how fiery was his temper, marvelled at his perfect command of it: he governed it as a man governs a mastiff with a chain; "he could let out his dog," they said, "and pull in his dog as he pleased." As he ruled himself, so he ruled other men, easily; they felt his right to command them. In his school near Chelmsford, a word or a look from him was all the discipline that was needed. His real throne was the pulpit. There he swayed men with a power that was more than regal. His face had authority and utterance in it; his voice was rich, of great compass and flexibility; every motion of him spoke. The impressiveness of his preaching began in his vivacity; he flashed life into any subject, no matter how dead before. He so grappled the minds of his hearers that they could not get away from him. While he preached at Chelmsford, an ungodly person once said to his companions: "Come, let us go hear what that bawling Hooker will say to us." The mocker went; but he was no longer a mocker. Hooker had that to say to him which subdued him: he became a penitent and devout man, and followed his conqueror to America. Once Hooker was to preach in the great church at Leicester. A leading burgess of the town, hating the preacher and thinking to suppress him, hired fiddlers to stand near the church door and fiddle while Hooker should preach; but somehow Hooker's preaching was mightier and more musical than the fiddlers' fiddling. The burgess, astonished at such power, then went near to the door to hear for himself what sort of talking that was which kept people from noticing his fiddlers; soon even he was clutched by the magnetism of the orator, sucked in through the door in spite of himself, smitten down by stroke after stroke of eloquent truth, and converted. Hooker's personality had in it something which made it easy for his disciples to think, that the Almighty would require even the forces of nature to pay considerable deference to so wonderful a man. On his flight toward the sea-side, as he was escaping to Holland, an attendant, knowing that an officer was in full chase not far behind, said anxiously: "Sir, what if the wind should not be fair when you come to the vessel?" "Brother, let us leave that with Him who keeps the wind in the hollow of his hand." And they noticed that, though the wind was against them before Hooker reached the vessel, as soon as he got aboard "it immediately came about fair and fresh," and swept the ship out to sea just in time to leave his pursuer panting and baffled upon the shore. Hooker, like many another strong man, seems to have had a Caesarean faith in himself and his fortunes. On the voyage to Holland the vessel struck by night upon the sands. A panic ran through the ship. Hooker, though unknown to them, by sheer force of personal greatness, restored them to quiet: he just told them not to be frightened; that they should surely be preserved. They had to believe the man who could say that. Multitudes of his contemporaries supposed him to have the gift of prophecy. He himself assumed to have it. Long before the civil war in England he said openly in a sermon: "It has been told me from God, that God will destroy England, and lay it waste, and that the people shall be put unto the sword, and the temples burnt, and many houses laid in ashes." When this man prayed, they noticed that there was some very strange power in it. "His prayer," says Cotton Mather, "was usually like Jacob's ladder, wherein the nearer he came to an end, the nearer he drew towards heaven." Such praying as his, they were sure, God would take particular notice of. Once during a war between the weak Mohegans, who were our friends, and the strong Narragansetts, who were our enemies, this holy man prayed strenuously against the Narragansetts. "And the effect of it was," says the historian, "that the Narragansetts received a wonderful overthrow from the Mohegans."

Every Monday was set apart by him as a day for private consultation upon cases of conscience. It was simply an involuntary Protestant confessional, born of the great need people had to tell their secrets to this particular man; and all sorts of perturbed beings came, and laid their spiritual maladies before him, and were comforted.

It is not to be supposed that, at the close of a life into which so many marvellous things had entered, death would come unheralded by supernatural tokens. On the last Sunday of his life, when he preached and administered the Lord's Supper, "some of his most observant hearers" perceived "an astonishing sort of a cloud" in the room, and among themselves "a most unaccountable heaviness and sleepiness . . . not unlike the drowsiness of the disciples when our Lord was going to die." In a few days the mystery was explained. After a short illness, "at last he closed his own eyes with his own hands, and gently stroking his own forehead, with a smile in his countenance, he gave a little groan, and so expired his soul into the arms of his fellow-servants, the holy angels."

From all the communities of New England a wail of grief went up at the tidings of his death: this was the first one of their mighty leaders that had fallen in the wilderness. One writer mourned him in a Latin elegy, two lines of which have this sense in English:

> The thought will come when o'er him thus we moan,
> That in his grave New England finds her own.

One of his clerical brethren, Peter Bulkley, contenting himself with English verse, thus celebrated Hooker's traits as a preacher:

> To mind he gave light of intelligence,
> And searched the corners of the conscience.
> To sinners stout, which no law could bring under,
> To them, he was a son of dreadful thunder,
> When all strong oaks of Bashan used to quake,
> And fear did Libanus his cedars shake.
> The stoutest hearts he fillëd full of fears;
> He clave the rocks, they melted into tears;
> Yet to sad souls, with sense of sin cast down,
> He was a son of consolation.

His great contemporary, John Cotton, saluted him with tender congratulation:

> Now, blessed Hooker, thou art set on high,
> Above the thankless world and cloudy sky;
> Do thou of all thy labor reap the crown,
> Whilst we here reap the seed which thou hast sown.

Finally, the process of Protestant canonization was completed some time afterward, when one writer gave expression to the general belief, by calling him "Saint Hooker."

The published writings of Thomas Hooker number twenty-three titles. Many of them are large treatises; all of them are on matters of theology, church-polity, or religious life. A noted English preacher of that age said, that to praise the writings of Hooker would be "to lay paint upon burnished marble, or add light unto the sun." This of course is the rapture of contemporaneous enthusiasm; and yet even for us there remains in Hooker's words a genuine vitality, the charm of clearness, earnestness, reality, strength. Remembering what the man was, who once stood behind these words, we cannot much wonder at the effects produced by them. He has many of the traits common to the Puritan writers of his time: minute and multitudinous divisions and subdivisions; the anatomy of his discourse exposed on the outside of it; a formal announcement of doctrine, proofs, sequences, applications; showers of quotation from Scripture. He has also some exceptional literary advantages: a copious and racy vocabulary; an aptitude for strong verbal combinations; dramatic spirit; the gift of translating arguments into pictures; cumulative energy, oratorical verve. This orator is dead: his words after all are not dead.

What he wrote is literature meant for the ear, not the eye; having the rhythm and cadence of a good speech. It is constructed for swift practical effect on the minds, passions, resolutions of men. Its lines of thought are straight, rugged, bold; its movement is like the unhesitating tramp of an advancing army; it quite omits the graces of reserve, the dallying and tenderness of literary implication. We are apt to startle at the blunt integrity of his speech. His theology has a fierce and menacing side to it, the mention of which he takes no pains to conceal from ears polite. He uses frankly all the stern and haggard words of his sect. He awards punishment to sinners in good, round, English curses, that are plain and fructifying. He assures them of damnation right heartily. His pages gleam and blaze with the flashes of threatened hellfire. His ink has even yet a smell of theological sulphur in it.

It was one part of his duty, as he thought, to "fasten the nail of terror deep into their hearts"; and in rhetoric well-seasoned for the use of "proud sinners" he greatly excels: "Do you think to out-brave the Almighty? . . . Dost thou think to go to heaven thus bolt-upright? The Lord cannot endure thee here, and will he suffer thee to dwell with himself forever in heaven? What, thou to heaven upon these terms? Nay, . . . how did the Lord deal with Lucifer and all those glorious spirits? He sent them all down to hell for their pride." "The Lord comes out in battle array against a proud person, and singles him out from all the rest, and . . . saith, 'Let that drunkard and that swearer alone a while, but let me destroy that proud heart forever. You shall submit in spite of your teeth, when the great God of heaven and earth shall come to execute vengeance.' " "There must be subjection or else confusion. Will you out-brave the Almighty to his face, and will you dare damnation? . . . As proud as you, have been crushed and humbled. Where are all those Nimrods, and Pharaohs, and all those mighty monarchs of the world? The Lord hath thrown them flat upon their backs, and they are in hell this day."

He gives sinners to understand, also, that the hell-torments which await them are none of those metaphorical and altogether tolerable hell-torments that are now usually signified by that term: "Judge the torments of hell by some little beginning of it, and the dregs of the Lord's vengeance by some little sips of it; and judge how unable thou art to bear the whole, by thy inability to bear a little of it. . . . When God lays the flashes of hell-fire upon thy soul, thou canst not endure it. . . . When the Lord hath let in a little horror of heart into the soul of a poor sinful creature, how he is transported with an insupportable burden . . . roaring and yelling as if he were in hell already. . . . If the drops be so heavy, what will the whole sea of God's vengeance be?"

The doctrine of the total depravity of man lay in his mind under a light of absolute certainty; and in commending this doctrine to his congregations, he did not dim it by any glozing or euphemistic words: "Thou art dead in trespasses and sins.

What is that? A man is wholly possessed with a body of corruption, and the spawn of all abomination hath overspread the whole man. . . . All noisome lusts abound in the soul, and take possession of it, and rule in it, and are fed there. . . . No carrion in a ditch smells more loathsomely in the nostrils of man, than a natural man's works do in the nostrils of the Almighty." "Alas, the devil hath power over you. As it is with a dead sheep, all the carrion crows in the country come to prey upon it, and all base vermin breed and creep there; so it is with every poor, natural, carnal creature under heaven—a company of devils, like so many carrion crows, prey upon the heart . . . and all base lusts crawl, and feed, and are maintained in such a wretched heart."

His speech is vigorous in denunciation of religious formalism. He tells them that the outward duties are important, but that these without Christ cannot save any one. Forms are but the bucket; Christ is the well: "If you say your bucket shall help you, you may starve for thirst if you let it not down into the well for water; so, though you brag of your praying, and hearing, and fasting, and of your alms, and building of hospitals, and your good deeds, if none of these bring you to Christ, you shall die for thirst." "I do not dishonor these ordinances, but I curse all carnal confidence in them. . . . Hell is full of hearers, and dissemblers, and carnal wretches that never had hearts to seek unto Christ in these duties, and to see the value of a Saviour in them."

As outward forms of piety cannot save the sinner, neither can ministers of the gospel, potent as they are, save him: "Dost thou think that a few faint prayers, and lazy wishes, and a little horror of heart, can pluck a dead man from the grave of his sins, and a damned soul from the pit of hell, and change the nature of a devil to be a saint? No, it is not possible. . . . We are as able to make worlds, and to pull hell in pieces, as to pull a poor soul from the paw of the devil." "Should you pray till you can speak no more; and should you sigh to the breaking of your loins; should every word be a sigh, and every sigh a tear, and every tear a drop of blood, you would never be able to recover that grace which you lost in Adam."

As he passes thus from realm to realm in the vast empire of Christian persuasion, he reaches at times those which appeal to nobler passions than terror or shame; and when he will, he can make a most gallant spiritual charge, and carry for his Master the batteries of self-respect, magnanimity, honor: "Christ must needs take this unkindly that you should give the devil the flower of your age, and give to Christ but the decrepit and infirm parts of your lives; that the devil should suck out the marrow of your youth, and only give God the dry bones, a palsy head, a dim eye, a weak body."

He depicts dramatically, and with a soothing tenderness, the struggle of the soul to find its way to Christ and to be saved: "When a poor travelling man comes to the ferry, he cries to the other side, 'Have over! have over!' His meaning is he would go to the other side by a boat. . . . So Christ is in heaven; but we are here on earth . . . on the other side of the river. The ordinances of God are but as so many boats to carry us and to land us at heaven where our hopes are, and our hearts should be. . . . 'Have over! have over!' saith the soul. The soul desires to be landed at the stairs of mercy, and saith, 'Oh, bring me to speak with my Saviour.' "

He tells them that if they have found Christ and have received his gifts, then are they rich with treasures outshining all the world's riches: "Though a man should beg his bread from door to door, if he can beg Christ and have it, and beg grace and have it, he is the richest man upon earth."

He points out the true method of success in the Christian life, warning them, for example, against idleness, and against impatience: "Whilst the stream keeps running, it keeps clear; but let it stand still, it breeds frogs and toads and all manner of filth. So while you keep going, you keep clear; but do but once flag in your diligence, and stand still, and oh! what a puddle of filth and sin thy heart will be." "We must wait God's leisure, and stay his time for the bestowing of his favors. Beggars must not be choosers."

He seeks to draw them to the higher spiritual life by the imagery of love and utmost tenderness: "Let us be led by all means into a nearer union with the Lord Christ. As a wife deals with the letters of her husband that is in a far country, she finds many sweet inklings of his love, and she will read these letters often and daily, . . . because she would be with her husband a little, and have a little parley with him in his pen, though not in his presence; so these ordinances are but the Lord's love-letters, and we are the ambassadors of Christ, and . . . we bring marvellous good news that Christ can save all poor broken-hearted sinners in the world."

He assures them that in the grace of utter resignation they touch the very essence of felicity and victory: "Be content to want what God will deny, and to wait God's good pleasure, and to be at his disposing. . . . Whatsoever can or shall befall you by the devil and his instruments, and if every spire of grass were a devil, be humbled, and then be above all the devils in hell, and all temptations, and oppositions." "God hath but two thrones; and the humble heart is one." "An humble soul, a poor soul, a very beggar at the gate of mercy, the Lord will not only know him, . . . but he will give him such a gracious look as shall make his heart dance in his breast. Thou poor humbled soul, the Lord will give thee a glimpse of his favor, when thou art tried in thy trouble; and when thou lookest up to heaven, the Lord will look down upon thee." "Men, brethren, and fathers, if there be any soul here that is content in truth and sincerity to be humbled, and to be at God's disposing, . . . do not you make too much haste to go to heaven; the Lord Jesus Christ will come down from heaven and dwell in your hearts." "In thy distempers be humbled and yet comforted: Christ hath overcome the power of them. They may plague thee: they shall not prevail against thee. . . . The power of Christ's prayer will outlive thy life, and the life of thy sins, and set heaven's gates open before thee." "It is with the soul in this case as it is with a mariner; though his hand be upon the oar, yet he ever looks homeward to the haven where he would be."

New England has perhaps never quite appreciated its great obligations to Archbishop Laud. It was his overmastering hate of non-conformity, it was the vigilance and vigor and consecrated cruelty with which he scoured his own diocese and afterward all England, and hunted down and hunted out the ministers who were committing the unpardonable sin of dissent, that conferred upon the principal colonies of New England their ablest and noblest men. Indeed, without Laud, these principal colonies would perhaps never have had an existence. His dreadful name is linked to our early story by sickening memories of terror and brutal insult and grief, of darkened fire-sides, of foul prisons opened to receive saints instead of felons, of delicate women and little children set adrift in the world without shelter or protector; of good men—scholars, apostles —fleeing for their lives, under masks, under false names, skulking in the guise of criminals, from the land they were born in.

The short and easy way with dissenters that Laud adopted, is happily shown in his treatment of Thomas Shepard. In the year 1630, this gifted and consecrated man, then twenty-five years old, a graduate of Emmanuel College, Cambridge, and admitted to holy orders by the bishop of Petersborough, was preaching in the little town of Earles-Colne, in Essex. The odor of his Puritanical piety had reached the nostrils of Laud, then bishop of London. On the sixteenth of December, of the year just named, at about eight o'clock in the morning, the poor parson, in obedience to a citation presented himself before the face of the bishop in his palace in the great city. Of the vivacious conversation that then ensued, the parson himself has left us a narrative. "As soon as I came, . . . falling into a fit of rage he asked me what degree I had taken in the university. I answered him, I was a Master of Arts. He asked, of what col-

lege? I answered, of Emmanuel. He asked, how long I had lived
in his diocese. I answered, three years and upwards. He asked,
who maintained me all this while, charging me to deal plainly
with him; adding withal that he had been more cheated and
equivocated with by some of my malignant faction than ever
was man by Jesuit. At the speaking of which words he looked as
though blood would have gushed out of his face, and did shake
as if he had been haunted with an ague fit, to my apprehension,
by reason of his extreme malice and secret venom. I desired him
to excuse me. He fell then to threaten me, and withal to bitter
railing, . . . saying, 'You prating coxcomb, do you think all the
learning is in your brain?' He pronounced his sentence thus:
'I charge you that you neither preach, read, marry, bury, or
exercise any ministerial function, in any part of my diocese;
for if you do, and I hear of it, I'll be upon your back, and follow you wherever you go, in any part of the kingdom, and so
everlastingly disenable you.' . . . I prayed him to suffer me to
catechise in the Sabbath days in the afternoon. He replied,
'Spare your breath. I'll have no such fellows prate in my
diocese. Get you gone; and now make your complaints to whom
you will.' So away I went." Very naturally the young parson
was at first somewhat dazed by the Laudean hurricane that
had swept over him; and two days afterward, he met half a
dozen of his clerical brethren who "consulted together," as he
tells us, "whether it was best to let such a swine to root up
God's plants in Essex, and not to give him some check."

Unfortunately, in the present case, the mighty hunters were
all on the side of the swine; and the check which the parsons
had hoped to give to him was abundantly bestowed upon themselves. They were routed and scattered, this way and that. For
four years Thomas Shepard was a wanderer in England, eager
to preach the gospel and having a wonderful aptitude that way,
but unable to find anywhere in England a spot that was not
interdicted to him by Laud's unslumbering hostility. Accordingly, in 1635, resolving to put the ocean between himself and
his enemy, he came to New England; and early in the following

year, he took charge of the church in Cambridge, and there remained until his death in 1649.

Even during his life-time his fame as a pulpit-orator and a writer rose high in both Englands; and it rose still higher after his death. In person he had some disadvantages. He lacked the bodily vigor, the massive proportions, the stateliness, of his two compeers, Thomas Hooker and John Cotton. His contemporaries describe him to us as a poor, weak, pale-complexioned man, whose physical powers were feeble but spent to the full. He was a cloistered student and an invalid, recoiling from the crisp breath of a New England winter; during which season, as he tells us, there was a near relation between him and the fireside. But his fragile body was possessed by a spirit of uncommon beauty, devoutness, and power. He had a subtile and commanding intellect; he was a profound thinker; his style was in the main clear, terse, abounding in energy, with frequent flashes of eloquence; and the charm of his diction was enhanced by the manner of his speech, which was almost matchless for its sweet and lofty grace, its pathos, its thrilling intensity, its ringing fulness and force. His successor in office spoke of "the lively voice of this soul-melting preacher." John Higginson described him as one who was both "a Timothy in his family" and a "Chrysostom in the pulpit." His writings, which have been honored by a modern edition, have had among theologians of his school a permanent reputation. He has been much read by his own profession. He may be described as the preacher's preacher. His brethren have paid to him the flattering tribute of lavishly borrowing both his ideas and his words. From a single one of Thomas Shepard's books, Jonathan Edwards, it is said, drew nearly a hundred citations for his celebrated *Treatise concerning Religious Affections.*

The theology of Thomas Shepard, of course, derived its characteristic features not from him, but from his age and his sect: it was harsh, dark, inexorable; most sincere in its exaggerations of the sinfulness of man and the wrathfulness of God;

placing on the throne of the universe a stark divine justice, upon which scarcely fell one glimmer of divine pity; copious in maledictions; having a marvellous alacrity in making its consignments of souls to the devil.

The doctrine, for example, that "in Adam's fall we sinned all," is expounded by this preacher with a courage and a candor that never flinched before considerations either of humanity or of common-sense: "We are all in Adam, as a whole country in a parliament man; the whole country doth what he doth." To some, the felicity of this comparison may be damaged by the fact that, while the country chooses its parliament man to stand for it, "We made no particular choice of Adam to stand for us"; but the reply is, that the choice was made not by us but on our behalf, ages before we were born, by a Being infinitely better and wiser than we are. This first step being made secure, every subsequent step is logical and easy. Each man, having thus fallen into sin thousands of ages before he was born, finds, on arriving to take possession of the existence thus blighted for him in advance, that his fall is an exceedingly complete one— dragging down with itself every faculty and atom of his nature. Nowhere else, perhaps, is the dogma of total depravity presented to us in braver, or more sprightly limning: "Every natural man and woman is born full of all sin, as full as a toad is of poison, as full as ever his skin can hold; mind, will, eyes, mouth, every limb of his body, and every piece of his soul, is full of sin; their hearts are bundles of sin." "Thy mind is a nest of all the foul opinions, heresies, that ever were vented by any man; thy heart is a foul sink of all atheism, sodomy, blasphemy, murder, whoredom, adultery, witchcraft, buggery; so that if thou hast any good thing in thee, it is but as a drop of rosewater in a bowl of poison. . . . It is true thou feelest not all these things stirring in thee at one time . . . ; but they are in thee, like a nest of snakes in an old hedge."

Certainly this is a dire condition of affairs; and it is entailed upon every man at his birth, in consequence of the personal misconduct of an individual, named Adam, who lived some sixty centuries ago; who was the moral representative of every man, but who was chosen as representative by no man. And what is to be done about it? Is there any escape? If the man be one of the elect, yes; if he be not one of the elect, no. In the latter case, "God shall set himself like a consuming infinite fire against thee, and tread thee under his feet, who hast by sin trod him and his glory under foot all thy life. . . . I tell thee all the wisdom of God shall then be set against thee to devise torments for thee. . . . The torment which wisdom shall devise, the almighty power of God shall inflict upon thee; so as there was never such power seen in making the world, as in holding a poor creature under this wrath, that holds up the soul in being with one hand, and beats it with the other; ever burning like fire against a creature, and yet that creature never burnt up. Think not this cruelty: it is justice. What cares God for a vile wretch, whom nothing can make good while it lives? If we have been long in hewing a block, and we can make no meet vessel of it, put it to no good use for ourselves, we cast it into the fire. God heweth thee by sermons, sickness, losses and crosses, sudden death, mercies and miseries, yet nothing makes thee better. What should God do with thee, but cast thee hence? O consider of this wrath before you feel it. . . . Thou canst not endure the torments of a little kitchen-fire, on the tip of thy finger, not one half hour together. How wilt thou bear the fury of this infinite, endless, consuming fire, in body and soul, throughout all eternity?" "Death cometh hissing . . . like a fiery dragon with the sting of vengeance in the mouth of it. . . . Then shall God surrender up thy forsaken soul into the hands of devils, who, being thy jailers, must keep thee, till the great day of account; so that as thy friends are scrambling for thy goods, and worms for thy body, so devils shall scramble for thy soul. . . . Thy forlorn soul shall lie moaning for the time past, now it is too late to recall again; groaning under the intolerable torments of the wrath of God present, and amazed at the eternity of misery and sorrow that is to come; waiting for that fearful hour, when the last

trump shall blow, and body and soul meet to bear that wrath,—
that fire that shall never go out."

Not far from the year 1612, the ancient church of Saint
Mary, in Cambridge, was filled one day by a great concourse
of persons—under-graduates, fellows, professors—who had
been attracted thither by the brilliant reputation of a member
of their own university, a fellow of Emmanuel College, John
Cotton by name, then only about twenty-seven years old. This
person had been in the university ever since he was a lad of
thirteen; he had continually distinguished himself as a scholar;
he had risen to be catechist, head-lecturer, and dean in the college to which he belonged. He was proficient in the logic and
philosophy then taught in the schools; was a critical master of
Greek; could converse fluently either in Latin or in Hebrew.
Beyond all other things, he had genius for oratory, particularly
the oratory of the pulpit. It was his extraordinary fame in that
direction which had drawn together the great crowd to hear him
on the occasion to which reference has been made. Several
times before, he had preached in the presence of the whole university, always carrying off their applause; for he had never
failed to give them the sort of sermons that were then in fashion
—learned, ornate, pompous, bristling with epigrams, stuffed
with conceits, all set off dramatically by posture, gesture, and
voice. Meantime, however, his religious character had been
deepening into Puritanism. He had come to view his own
preaching as frivolous, Sadducean, pagan. In preparing once
more to preach to this congregation of worldly and witty folk,
he had resolved to give them a sermon intended to exhibit Jesus
Christ, rather than John Cotton. This he did. His hearers were
astonished, disgusted. Not a murmur of applause greeted the
several stages of his discourse as formerly. They pulled their
shovel-caps down over their faces, folded their arms, and sat it
out sullenly—amazed that the promising John Cotton had
turned lunatic or Puritan.

Evidently there was stuff in this man; and he it was who,

twenty years later, came over to New England, and acquired there a marvellous ascendency, personal and professional—an ascendency more sovereign, probably, than any other American clergyman has ever reached. The interval of twenty years that fell between that brave university-sermon, and his great career in New England, was by no means a blank. In fact it was a period for him very rich and intense in incident. He left the university to take charge of the great church of St. Botolph's, at Boston, in Lincolnshire, and there he remained till his removal to Boston, in New England. Year by year, while he lived in the elder Boston, he grew in knowledge about the Bible, and in the science of God and man as seen through the dun goggles of John Calvin; his singular faculty as a preacher greatened every way, in force and splendor; his fame filled all the kingdom; and though he was far from being a good churchman, the powerful prelate, Lord Keeper Williams, told King James that Cotton was a good man and a good preacher, and got from the king a promise that Cotton should not be disturbed; finally, under the reign of Charles, the preacher drew upon himself the fatal eye of Bishop Laud. It was in 1633 that Laud became primate of England, which meant, among other things, that nowhere within the rim of that imperial island was there to be peace or safety any longer for John Cotton. Some of his friends in high station tried to use persuasive words with the archbishop on his behalf; but the archbishop brushed aside their words with an insupportable scorn. The earl of Dorset sent a message to Cotton, that if he had only been guilty of drunkenness, or adultery, or any such minor ministerial offense, his pardon could have been had; but since his crime was Puritanism, he must flee for his life. So, for his life he fled, first hiding himself here and there about London, dodging his pursuers; and finally slipping out of England, after innumerable perils, like a hunted felon; landing in Boston in September, 1633.

His arrival filled the colony with exceeding joy. It was a thing they had been praying for. Even the name of Boston had been given to their chief town as a compliment and an enticement to him.

> The lantern of St. Botolph's ceased to burn,
> When from the portals of that church he came
> To be a burning and a shining light,
> Here in the wilderness.

At once, the most conspicuous pulpit was given to him; and from that hour till his death nineteen years afterward, he wielded with strong and brilliant mastership the fierce theocracy of New England. Laymen and clergymen alike recognized his supremacy, and rejoiced in it. He was the unmitred pope of a pope-hating commonwealth. "I hold myself not worthy," said an eminent minister of Massachusetts, "to wipe his slippers." Roger Williams wrote, evidently with a subdued smile, that some people in Massachusetts used to say that "they could hardly believe that God would suffer Mr. Cotton to err." The contemporary historian, William Hubbard, states that whatever John Cotton "delivered in the pulpit was soon put into an order of court . . . or set up as a practice in the church." Another clergyman of that day, trying to utter his homage for John Cotton, found the resources of prose inadequate:

> A man of might at heavenly eloquence,
> To fix the ear and charm the conscience;
> As if Apollos were revived in him,
> Or he had learned of a seraphim.
>
> .   .   .   .
>
> Rocks rent before him, blind received their sight,
> Souls levelled to the dunghill stood upright.

When in 1651, he, the mightiest man in New England, wrote to Cromwell, the mightiest man in old England, the latter promptly "took this liberty from business to salute" John Cotton, as his "dear friend," to confess to him his own sense of unworthiness, and to inform him of the progress of events then big with the fulfilment of prophecies, adding, "We need your prayers in this as much as ever," and closing with this cordial subscription, "Your affectionate friend to serve you."

It was, of course, rather strange that the Almighty should permit such a man to die; but when at last death did come to him, the services of his interment, we are told, made "the most grievous and solemn funeral that was ever known perhaps upon the American strand." Nay, it was commonly believed at the time, that even the heavens as well as the earth took note of the dreadful event, and that Providence set aflame in the sky an indubitable signal of it. "About the time of his sickness," says the historian, Nathaniel Morton, "there appeared in the heavens over New England a comet, giving a dim light; and so waxed dimmer and dimmer, until it became quite extinct and went out; which time of its being extinct was soon after the time of the period of his life: it being a very signal testimony that God had then removed a bright star, a burning and a shining light out of the heaven of his church here, unto celestial glory above."

Although John Cotton was a prolific author, his place in our early literary history bears no proportion to his place in our early religious and political history. As a student, he was of the heroic pattern of the seventeenth century. A sand-glass which would run four hours stood near him when he studied, and being turned over three times, measured his day's work. This he called "a scholar's day." Esteeming John Calvin to be greater than all the fathers and all the school-men, he was accustomed to read in him last of all every evening: "I love to sweeten my mouth with a piece of Calvin before I go to sleep." His grandson, Cotton Mather, who upon such a theme never lapsed into an understatement, tells us that John Cotton "was indeed a most universal scholar, and a living system of the liberal arts, and a walking library."

Upon better testimony we know that he certainly had large reading, a retentive memory, great intellectual poise, agility, and self-command, all his accomplishments and accumulations at ready call; while the character and range of his work as a writer, during the nineteen years of his American life, may be seen by a glance over the mere titles of his principal publica-

tions: *The Bloody Tenet washed and made white in the Blood
of the Lamb; A Brief Exposition upon Ecclesiastes; A Brief Exposition upon Canticles; The Covenant of Grace; An Exposition upon the Thirteenth Chapter of the Revelation; The
Grounds and Ends of the Baptism of the Children of the Faithful; Of the Holiness of Church Members; The Keys of the
Kingdom of Heaven; A Modest and Clear Answer to Mr. Ball's
Discourse of Set Forms of Prayer; The New Covenant; A Practical Commentary upon the First Epistle of John; Spiritual
Milk for Babes; A Treatise of the Covenant of Grace as it is
dispensed to the Elect Seed; The Way of the Congregational
Churches Cleared; The Way of Life; A Treatise concerning
Predestination.*

Let us open, now, any of these old books of John Cotton. At
once, the immensity of his contemporaneous influence becomes
a riddle to us. In the writings of his great associates, Hooker,
Shepard, Peter Bulkley, William Hooke, and Charles Chauncey, at least some threads of immortal light, some lingering
movements of a once glorious energy, some half-blurred foot-
prints of a departed genius, may still be traced by us, after
these two centuries; marks of literary superiority; quotable
passages. The same can hardly be said of the writings of John
Cotton. These are indeed clear and cogent in reasoning; the
language is well enough; but that is all. There are almost no
remarkable merits in thought or style. One wanders through
these vast tracts and jungles of Puritanic discourse—exposition, exhortation, logic-chopping, theological hair-splitting—
and is unrewarded by a single passage of eminent force or
beauty, uncheered even by the felicity of a new epithet in the
objurgation of sinners, or a new tint in the landscape-painting
of hell.

Evidently the vast intellectual and moral force of John
Cotton was a thing that could not be handed over to the printing-press or transmitted to posterity: it had to communicate
itself in the living presence of the man himself. The traditions
of that living presence are certainly notable. He was of medium

size; his hair, brown in early years, with advancing time grew white as snow; and "in his countenance there was an inexpressible sort of majesty, which commanded reverence from all that approached him." Thus the inn-keeper at Derby, having once John Cotton for a guest, very naturally wished him gone from the house; since he "was not able to swear while that man was under his roof." His voice was not powerful, but clear, mellow, sympathetic. One contemporary says that "Mr. Cotton had such an insinuating and melting way in his preaching that he would usually carry his very adversary captive after the triumphant chariot of his rhetoric." But the chariot of his rhetoric ceased to be triumphant when the master himself ceased to drive it.

Such were the three foremost personages among the theological and religious writers of New England, in our first literary period. In the throng of their professional associates—scholars, thinkers, devotees—were not a few others who did famous work in the one form of writing that then suited best the intellectual appetite of the people, and that still preserves best the very form and pressure of that unique time.

One of these men was Peter Bulkley, born in 1583, sometime fellow of St. John's College, Cambridge, a man of considerable estate and social position. For twenty-two years he was rector of Woodhill, Bedfordshire; but at last the hand of the terrible archbishop being laid heavily upon him, he came to Cambridge, Massachusetts, in 1635. The next year "he carried a good number of planters with him up further into the woods," where they established the town of Concord, and where he abode as pastor until his death in 1659. He was a sufferer from bodily pains; his will was exacting, his temper quick, his tongue sharp; yet in heart and hand he was benignant and bountiful; noted even among Puritans for the superlative stiffness of his Puritanism, his austere looks, his prim dress, his incredible brevity of hair. He was a great scholar too; having, as Cotton Mather saith, "a competently good stroke at Latin poetry," even down to old age blossoming oft into fragrant Latin epigrams. A large place in Puritan literature was held by him in his life-time and long afterward, on account of his book, *The Gospel Covenant, or the Covenant of Grace Opened*, made up of a series of systematic sermons preached at Concord, first published in London in 1646; one of those massive, exhaustive, ponderous treatises into which the Puritan theologians put their enormous Biblical learning, their acumen, their industry, the fervor, pathos, and consecration of their lives. It deals with a topic which at that time stirred the minds of all men in New England, which made and unmade reputations, which shook the whole commonwealth. The style, though angular, sharp-edged, carved into formal divisions, and stiff with the embroidery of Scriptural texts, is upon the whole direct and strong. The book has a peculiar interest for us still, on account of its occasional episodes of reference to the mighty things then taking place in England. Near the close of it, is this impressive appeal to the people of New England: "And for ourselves here, the people of New England, we should in a special manner labor to shine forth in holiness above other people. We have that plenty . . . of ordinances and means of grace, as few people enjoy the like. We are as a city set upon a hill, in the open view of all the earth; the eyes of the world are upon us because we profess ourselves to be a people in covenant with God. . . . Let us study so to walk that this may be our excellency and dignity among the nations of the world. . . . There is no people but will strive to excel in something. What can we excel in, if not in holiness? If we look to number, we are the fewest; if to strength, we are the weakest; if to wealth and riches, we are the poorest of all the people of God through the whole world. We cannot excel, nor so much as equal, other people in these things; and if we come short in grace and holiness too, we are the most despicable people under heaven. . . . Be we an holy people, so shall we be honorable before God, and precious in the eyes of his saints."

The whole work carries momentum with it. It gives the impression of an athletic, patient, and orderly intellect. Every advance along the page is made with the tread of logical victory. No unsubdued enemies are left in the rear. It is a monumental book. It stands for the intellectual robustness of New England in the first age. It is an honor to that community of pioneers, drudging in the woods of Concord, that these profound and elaborate discourses could have been produced, and endured, among them.

Another man deserving at least a glance from posterity is John Norton. He came to New England in 1635, being then twenty-nine years of age, a Cambridge scholar, sometime domestic chaplain to Sir William Masham. Soon after his arrival in America he was settled at Ipswich; in 1653 he went to Boston as John Cotton's successor; ten years later he went with Simon Bradstreet to England on an embassy of conciliation to Charles the Second; soon returning he died in 1663. He was remarkable for his early and brilliant attainments as a scholar, the thoroughness of his knowledge of Puritan theology, the multitude of his writings, and his frank advocacy of persecution for all who dared to live in New England without holding orthodox opinions. Longfellow, in his "Tragedy of John Endicott," permits Norton to describe himself as

> A terror to the impenitent, and Death
> On the pale horse of the Apocalypse
> To all the accursèd race of heretics.

Whosoever peeps into John Norton's writings will note their excessively technical character, the frequency and the hardness of their divisions, their dry and jagged diction. The most readable of his books is *The Life and Death of that deservedly famous man of God, Mr. John Cotton,* published in London in 1658. Though promising to be a biography, it has the didactic and hortatory tone of a sermon; the thread of the narrative is strung thick with beads of moralizing; its statements are embellished with citations, from a wide range of history and literature; it abounds in the antitheses that were then in demand.

A thoroughly wholesome personage was William Hooke, a

cousin of Oliver Cromwell and brother-in-law of Cromwell's
general, Edward Whalley. He was born in 1601; was educated
at Trinity College, Oxford; was for many years vicar of Ax-
mouth, Devonshire; was emigrant to America for conscience'
sake about the year 1636; was minister of Taunton, Massachusetts, from 1637 to 1644 or 1645; then, for about twelve
years was teacher of the church in New Haven; having great
inducements to return to England he went thither in 1656, and
became chaplain to the Protector, master of the Savoy, and man
of influence generally; in 1677, he died and was laid to rest in
Bunhill Fields. His life in America made him a true American;
and he never ceased to be one, even after his restoration to
England, keeping always his interest warm in American affairs,
and his "old brotherly affection" for the young communities
there, of which he had been for twenty years a strong and honored member. Not many of his writings ever got into print.
Those of them that were printed are sermons, and are of singular interest to us now for their literary merit, and for a certain
flavor of American thought and emotion that still lurks in them.
Altogether the best is his sermon preached at Taunton, on the
twenty-third of July, 1640, "on a day of public humiliation . . .
in behalf of our native country in time of feared dangers." As
observers of public affairs in England at that time, the people
of America had, in their very distance in space, something of
the advantage that is given to posterity by distance in time.
They were a contemporaneous posterity; they had the knowledge possessed by those who were upon the spot, and the per-
spective enjoyed by those who were afar off. In that great year,
1640, the men and women of New England saw, perhaps more
clearly than did their brethren in the old home, the meaning
and the drift of events in England, then rushing forward into
tears and blood. This sermon of William Hooke's is a striking
instance of their foresight. Its title, "New England's Tears for
Old England's Fears," worthily indicates the touching and
passionate love for the motherland which the whole sermon
breathes. "Old England, dear England still, . . . left indeed by

us in our persons, but never yet forsaken in our affections."
"There is no land that claims our name but England; . . . there
is no nation that calls us countrymen but the English. Brethren did we not there draw in our first breath? Did not the sun
first shine there upon our heads? Did not that land first bear
us, even that pleasant island, . . . that garden of the Lord, that
paradise?" But before the eyes of the preacher, as he spoke,
seemed to be unrolled an appalling vision of the scenes that
were to be enacted in the old land they had left—the chaos,
havoc, and misery of its oncoming civil war. One picture drawn
by him of the horrors of a battlefield, had a realism and an intensity of coloring not easily to be matched in any prose. "Oh,
the shrill, ear-piercing clangs of the trumpets, noise of drums,
the animating voice of horse-captains and commanders, learned
and learning to destroy! . . . Here ride some dead men swagging
in their deep saddles; there fall others alive upon their dead
horses; death sends a message to those from the mouth of the
muskets; these it talks with face to face, and stabs them in the
fifth rib. In yonder file there is a man who hath his arm struck
off from his shoulder; another by him hath lost his leg; here
stands a soldier with half a face; there fights another upon his
stumps, and at once both kills and is killed; not far off lies a
company wallowing in their sweat and gore; such a man whilst
he chargeth his musket is discharged of his life, and falls upon
his dead fellow. Every battle of the warrior is with confused
noise and garments rolled in blood. Death reigns in the field,
and is sure to have the day, which side soever falls. In the mean-
while—O formidable!—the infernal fiends follow the camp to
catch after the souls of rude nefarious soldiers . . . who fight
themselves fearlessly into the mouth of hell, for revenge, for
booty, or a little revenue. . . . A day of battle is a day of harvest
for the devil."

At least one more of these great New England preachers must
be named here, Charles Chauncey, whose early and conspicuous influence upon American letters was such as to suggest to

Cotton Mather the freak of calling him our Cadmus: a great man in many ways, in originality, learning, brain-force, physical endurance, zest for work, enthusiasm, eloquence; a man of impetuous and stormy nature, apt to assert himself strongly and to expect immediate assent, lacking somewhat in tact, capable of lapses from heroism and of penitential agonies in consequence thereof. He was a boy of thirteen at Westminster School at the very time of Guy Fawkes's failure to blow up the adjacent parliament-house, and thereby lost his one opportunity of going to heaven or elsewhere in extremely aristocratic company. At Trinity College, Cambridge, Chauncey took his degrees; he became professor of Greek at his Alma Mater; and in 1627 he became vicar of Ware, where, with his views, he had not long to wait before getting into trouble. He sadly objected to the *Book of Sports*; for in that book the clergy were forbidden to preach on Sunday afternoons, and their parishioners were encouraged to employ that happy time in dancing, archery, vaulting, may-games, and other recreations. Chauncey tried to evade the prohibition by filling the Sunday afternoons with a catechetical exercise for old and young; but this arrangement the bishop stamped on, telling him "that catechising was as bad as preaching." In 1635, he got into a new difficulty. He was cited before the High Commission Court for the crime of objecting to a rail around the communion table, and to the act of kneeling in the communion service. For this he was thrown into prison, sentenced to pay heavy costs, and suspended from the ministry till he should recant. At last in open court he did recant, making confession "that kneeling at the receiving of the holy communion is a lawful and commendable gesture, and that a rail set up in the chancel of any church . . . is a decent and convenient ornament." Of this inglorious act Chauncey was soon ashamed; and to the end of his days he lacerated himself for it, even saying in his will that he kept ever before him his "many sinful compliances with . . . vile human inventions, and will-worship, and hell-bred superstitions, and patcheries stitched into the service of the Lord which the English mass-book . . . and the Ordination of Priests . . . are fully fraught withal."

Of course such a man could not then stay in England, except in jail; and he escaped to America, reaching Plymouth in 1638. There he stayed as minister three years. In 1641, he was invited to Scituate, and continued there thirteen years, preaching, teaching, practising medicine, studying many books, and encountering many griefs. Especially did he suffer from the rebuffs of opponents and of extreme poverty. So wretched was the support allowed him that he had to write to a friend, "deest quidem panis." At last, in 1654, Laud being quiet in his grave, and all things in England having a pleasant look for men like Chauncey, he resolved to go back thither; but on his way to the ship in Boston harbor, he was overtaken by an offer of the presidency of Harvard College in place of the noble-minded Henry Dunster, who had been driven from the office on account of his frank avowal of the Baptist heresy. Chauncey, who also had some taint of the same heresy, promised not to avow it, and was inducted into the great office. It proved to be the right place for him; and he filled it with illustrious success, not without sorrows, until his death in 1672 at the age of eighty. He was a great educating force in those years and long afterward. Neither labor nor age could quell his energy. He rose at four o'clock winter and summer; he outdid all his students in devotion to books; "wittily he moderated their disputations and other exercises"; at College prayers he caused a chapter of the Hebrew Bible to be read in the morning, and of the Greek Testament in the evening, and upon these he always gave an extemporaneous comment in Latin; to all the students he was father, inspirer, guide; and he greatly helped to fill the land with scholars, gentlemen, and Christians. His old age was of the glorious, gritty kind. His friends begged him not to work so hard; but he gave the proud answer, "Oportet imperatorem stantem mori." One day, in winter, the fellows of the College were leading him toward the chapel where he was to preach;

and hoping to dissuade him from the labor, they said, "Sir, you will certainly die in the pulpit." But this, so far from intimidating the grand old man, gave him a new delight; and pressing on more eagerly through the snow-drifts, he exclaimed, "How glad I should be if what you say might prove true!"

His published writings are not many, and all are sermons excepting one—a controversial pamphlet, "Anti-synodalia Scripta Americana," 1662. His most important work is a volume of twenty-six sermons, published in London, in 1659, and entitled, *The Plain Doctrine of the Justification of a Sinner in the Sight of God.* On the title-page we are told that the doctrine is "explained . . . in a plain . . . and familiar way for the capacity and understanding of the weak and ignorant"; yet the leading title of the book is in Hebrew, the dedication is in Latin, and the discussion well sprinkled with quotations from Hebrew, Latin, and Greek, and with such technical terms as synecdoche, equipollent, and the like. In spite of this, the ideas are indeed as clear as crystal, and are generally stated in English that is vigorous and keen. Though the formality of stiff topical divisions cramps the movement of his style, and denies him room for swing and flight, the author's mind breaks out often with genuine brightness and power. There are strokes of condensed force, flashes of imagination and passionate light, felicities of epithet and comparison, vivifying words, memorable sayings: "God . . . stabs the wicked as an enemy with his sword, but lances the godly as a surgeon does his patient with the lancet." "As the moon is nearest to the sun when the least light doth outwardly appear; so is God nearest to the godly when they have the least outward light of comfort." "Let all . . . careless wretches know that if justification be a state of blessedness, then their state is a state of cursedness." "We are singing and chanting to the sound of the viol, while God sounds an alarum by the trumpet of war. We are dancing in jollity, while God is marching in battalia. We are drinking in the wine and strong drink, while God is letting out our blood." "If death arrests you, how will you scramble for bail? How will you wish you had pleased God? . . . Oh, leave not that to the last gasp that should be done first. Thou mayest be great and rich and honorable, and yet not fit to live nor to die; but he that is justified is fit for both." "It was unknown torment that our Saviour underwent. He encountered both the Father's wrath . . . and entered the lists with Satan and all the powers of darkness. . . . All the devils in hell were up in arms, and issued out of their gates; principalities and powers are all let loose against the Redeemer of the world." "Then let us pursue our sins with all possible detestations. . . . Let us stab them to the heart, till they bleed their last, that drew the blood of Christ."

The works of President Chauncey that were published, formed but a small portion of those that he wrote. His manuscripts descended to his eldest son, thence to his grandson, who dying left them in possession of his widow. This lady subsequently married again; and her new husband, a godly man, to wit, a deacon and pie-maker of Northampton, straightway proceeded to utilize the learned labors of the deceased president of Harvard, by putting those manuscripts at the bottom of his pies in the oven; and thus the eloquent and valuable writings of Charles Chauncey were gradually used up, their numerous Hebrew and Greek quotations, and their peppery Calvinism, doubtless adding an unwonted relish and indigestibility to the pies under which they were laid.

By *1700 the character of the New England colonies had begun to change. What had been the Puritan's "Citty upon a Hill" was becoming instead the nucleus of a new nation with its own economic and political system, a distinctive political theory, and the germs of a secular literary tradition. Although the Puritan decline had been gradual, the publication in 1717 of John Wise's* Vindication of the Government of the New England Churches *signaled both the beginning of the end of religious domination and the start of the theoretical argument that culminated in the* Declaration of Independence.

New England: Topics of Popular Discussion

IN the history of literature in New England during the colonial time, one fact stands out above all others—the intellectual leadership of the clergy, and that, too, among a laity neither ignorant nor weak. This leadership was in every sense honorable, both for the leaders and the led. It was not due alone to the high authority of the clerical office in New England; it was due still more to the personal greatness of the men who filled that office, and who themselves made the office great. They were intellectual leaders because they deserved to be; for, living among a well-educated and high-spirited people, they knew more, were wiser, were abler, than all other persons in the community. Of such a leadership, it was an honor even to be among the followers. And in our record of the literary achievements of New England in the colonial time, the clergy fill by far the largest space, because, in all departments of writing, they did by far the largest amount of work.

After the first half century of New England life, another fact comes into notice—the advance of the laity in literary activity. By that time, many strong and good men, who had been educated there in all the learning of the age, either not entering the clerical profession or not remaining in it, began to organize and to develop the other learned professions—the legal, medical, and tuitionary—and, appealing to the public through various forms of literature, to divide more and more with the clergy the leadership of men's minds. Moreover, in the last decade of the seventeenth century, an attempt was made to establish a newspaper in New England. The attempt failed. In the first decade of the eighteenth century, another attempt was made, and did not fail; and long before the end of our colonial epoch, a new profession had come into existence, having a power to act on the minds of men more mightily than any other—the profession of journalism.

Thus, as public discussion grew in the number of those who were participators in it, so also did it increase in the variety of its methods, and in the range of its themes. Henceforward we may trace the intellectual life of New England, not merely in sermons, in formal theological treatises, in grave narratives of civil and military experience, in sombre and painful religious poetry, but likewise in compact literary essays, in pamphlets sprightly or brutal or stupid, in satires, in almanacs, in popular songs, in editorial articles. Public discussion became secularized. At last, even this world began to receive some attention, and to be written about. Witchcraft, state-craft, the small-pox, the behavior of the royal governors, the words and deeds of preachers, quarrels of churches, quarrels of towns and of colonies, agriculture, the currency, repudiation, manufactures, the training of soldiers, the founding of colleges, Whitefield, religious mania, dress, drunkenness, wars with the Indians, wars with the French, earthquakes, comets, the new wonders of science, the impiety of averting lightning by the "electrical points," the truth of Christianity, the damnation of infants, the right to think, the conquest of Canada, the consolidation of the English colonies in America, the grand future of the American continent, the virtues of the English kings, the love and loyalty of America for England—these were some of the subjects that, year by year, along with our second colonial period, possessed the thoughts of men and women in New England, and found some sort of utterance in literature.

In 1691, a thrifty old merchant of Boston, Joshua Scottow, who had grown up with the colony almost from the beginning, published a little book of senile lamentations over the degeneracy of the age. It was called *Old Men's Tears for their own Declensions*. Encouraged by this stroke at authorship, he gave to the press, three years afterwards, *A Narrative of the Planting of the Massachusetts Colony*, beginning with 1628, and particularly accenting the fact of "the Lord's signal presence the first thirty years." Both books have some historical and psychological value, but as literature are worthless. His method of expression is spasmodic, ecstatic, full of apocalyptic symbols, cant, forced allusions, and the croakings of decrepitude. In the dedication of his second book to Simon Bradstreet, he had the good sense to anticipate that his writings might be pronounced "the delirious dotage of his puerile and superannuated brains."

The paroxysms of terror and of frenzy into which, during the last decade of the seventeenth century, multitudes of people in New England were thrown by the witchcraft excitement, gave birth to numerous publications, chiefly hortatory, minatory, and inflammatory; and to one publication that was at least rational, *More Wonders of the Invisible World*, published in London in 1700, and written by a merchant of Boston, Robert Calef, then forty-eight years of age. Though the book is quite destitute of literary expertness; is without symmetry in substance or felicity in form; is indeed, a hodge-pudding of facts, hints, queries, and conjectures; it is not destitute of expertness of other kinds—particularly that kind of expertness which, in a time of general enravishment, may enable one cool head to be an antidote to a multitude of hot ones. It is a reservoir of weird psychological phenomena, first frankly described in the credulous speech of the brotherhood and sisterhood of victims, then chilled and taken to pieces by a process of Sadducean counter-

evidence and cross-examination. It is, also, a monument of the
moral courage and the intellectual poise of its author; of his
firm, placid tenacity in demanding some real evidence as the
price of his belief; of his obstinate incredulity to the end; all
this in contrast with the intolerant eagerness of his contemporaries to rush headlong into folly; their hectic mental spasms;
and their appetency—at once voracious and ferocious—for
marvels, born in malice or in madness, and ending in infamy
and in death. For the chief clerical leaders in the witchcraft
excitement, especially the two Mathers, this book, both by its
scepticism and by its personal irreverence, was most exaspera-
ting. The younger of these two divines wreaked his rage upon
the book by calling it "a firebrand thrown by a madman"; and
the elder of them, at that time president of Harvard College,
tried to extinguish the book by having it publicly burned in
the college-yard. But its peculiar power could not be stifled
in a hangman's smudge; and one may truly say of it, that it
went far to unmadden a whole population of devout and learned
lunatics.

There is one form of writing—the diary—that costs little to
produce; that is usually valued at little by its producers; but
that often gathers incalculable worth with time, outlives many
laborious and ambitious literary monuments, and becomes a
storehouse of treasures for historians, poets, and painters. It
cannot be said that our ancestors failed to write diaries. Unluckily, however, the diaries that they wrote in great abundance, were generally records of events which took place only
inside of them; psychological diaries, more or less mystical and
unhealthy; chronicles of tender, scrupulous, introverted natures, misled into gratuitous self-torture; narratives of their
own spiritual moods fluctuating hour by hour, of the visita-
tions of Satan, of dullness or of ecstasy in prayer, of doubts or
hopes respecting their share in the divine decrees; itineraries
of daily religious progress, aggravated by overwork, indiges-
tion, and a gospel of gloom.

There has come down to us, however, from our second literary period, one specimen of the diary, which, though crude enough in texture, is refreshingly carnal, external, and healthy. It is *The Journal* kept by Mistress Sarah Kemble Knight, a dame of Boston—buxom, blithe, and debonair—who in October, 1704, being then thirty-eight years of age, a wife and a mother, travelled on horseback from Boston through Rhode Island and southern Connecticut to New Haven, a journey of five days; thence, in December, to New York, a journey of two days; returning home by the same route, and reaching Boston in March, 1705. In the pauses of her journey each day, she carefully jotted down her adventures and her own comments upon them, doing this with no little sprightliness and graphic power. The roads were rough, often uncertain; the crossings of the rivers were perilous; the inns were abominable; the manners of the people churlish, their speech a jargon of disgusting slang. Her *Journal,* published for the first time in 1825, is an amusing little book, and has special value as a realistic picture of rural manners in New York and New England in the first decade of the eighteenth century. She had no companions upon her expedition, except as she hired them or fell in with them by the way; and she bore the annoyances of the journey with a sort of mocking and recalcitrant resignation, which was only saved from going to pieces altogether by help of an eye quick to see the ludicrous aspects of disagreeable things—particularly as soon as they were past. Her note-book, indeed, was a sovereign safety-valve to her, forming a harmless conduit through which she could pour her hourly vexations, in playful little puffs of prose and verse. Thus, having to cross a certain river, and not daring to do so by fording it on horseback, she went over it in a wretched canoe—a far less safe ferry-boat than her horse would have been. "The canoe was very small and shallow, so that when we were in," it "seemed ready to take in water, which greatly terrified me, and caused me to be very circumspect, sitting with my hands fast on each side, my eyes steady, not daring so much as to lodge my tongue a hair's breadth more on one side of my mouth than t'other, nor so much as think on Lot's wife; for a wry thought would have overset our wherry." On another day, she relates, the road was furnished even worse than usual "with accommodations for travellers, so that we were forced to ride twenty-two miles by the post's account, but nearer thirty by mine, before we could bait so much as our horses, which I exceedingly complained of. But the post encouraged me by saying we should be well accommodated anon at Mr. Devil's, a few miles further; but I questioned whether we ought to go to the Devil to be helped out of affliction. However, like the rest of the deluded souls that post to the infernal den, we made all possible speed to this Devil's habitation; where, alighting in full assurance of good accommodations, we were going in; but meeting his two daughters, (as I supposed, twins—they so nearly resembled each other, both in features and habit, and looked as old as the Devil himself, and quite as ugly,) we desired entertainment, but could hardly get a word out of them, till with our importunity . . . they called the old sophister; who was as sparing of his words as his daughters had been. . . . He differed only in this from the old fellow in t'other country—he let us depart. However, I thought it proper to warn poor travellers to endeavor to avoid falling into circumstances like ours, which at our next stage I sat down and did, as followeth:

> May all that dread the cruel Fiend of Night
> Keep on, and not at this curst mansion light.
> 'Tis hell; 'tis hell; and Devils here do dwell;
> Here dwells the Devil—surely this is hell.
> Nothing but wants—a drop to cool your tongue
> Can't be procured these cruel fiends among.
> Plenty of horrid grins, and looks severe,
> Hunger and thirst; but pity's banished here.
> The right hand keep, if hell on earth you fear!

A strong, gentle, and great man was Samuel Sewall, great by almost every measure of greatness—moral courage, honor, benevolence, learning, eloquence, intellectual force, and breadth and brightness. Both his father and his grandfather were among the pioneers of New England colonization; although his father, who founded the town of Newbury, Massachusetts, seems to have passed and repassed between England and America without bringing hither his wife and children, until 1661, when the boy, Samuel, was nine years old. This boy, destined to great usefulness and distinction in the new world, thus came to it in time to have that personal shaping for his life here, only to be got from early and direct contact with it. He had the usual education of a New England gentleman in those days. He was graduated at Harvard College. He tried his hand for a time at preaching—a vocation for which he was well qualified, but from which he was diverted into a prosperous and benign secular career. He became a member of the board of assistants, then of the council, judge of the supreme court, and finally its chief-justice, holding the latter office until 1728, two years after which date he died. He was a man built, every way, after a large pattern. By his great wealth, his great offices, his learning, his strong sense, his wit, his warm human sympathy, his fearlessness, his magnanimity, he was a visible potentate among men in those days.

> Stately and slow, with thoughtful air,
> His black cap hiding his whitened hair,
> Walks the Judge of the great Assize,
> Samuel Sewall, the good and wise.
> His face with lines of firmness wrought,
> He wears the look of a man unbought,
> Who swears to his hurt and changes not;
> Yet touched and softened nevertheless
> With the grace of Christian gentleness;
> The face that a child would climb to kiss;
> True and tender and brave and just,
> That man might honor and woman trust.*

He had the courage to rebuke the faults of other people; he had the still greater courage to confess his own. Having, in 1692, fallen into the witchcraft snare, and having from the

---

* J. G. Whittier, "Prophecy of Samuel Sewall."

bench joined in the sentence of condemnation upon the witches, five years later—when more light had broken into his mind—he made in church a public confession of his error and of his sorrow. The Indians of Massachusetts had then no wiser or more generous friend than he; and he was, perhaps, the first of Americans to see and renounce and denounce the crime of negro slavery as then practiced in New England. In 1700, he spoke out plainly on this subject, publishing a tract named "The Selling of Joseph"; an acute, compact, powerful statement of the case against American slavery, leaving, indeed, almost nothing new to be said a century and a half afterwards, when the sad thing came up for final adjustment. In this pamphlet one sees traces both of his theological and his legal studies; it is a lawyer's brief, fortified by Scriptural texts, and illuminated by lofty ethical intuitions. Within those three pages he has left some strong and great words—immortal and immutable aphorisms of equity: "Liberty is in real value next unto life; none ought to part with it themselves or deprive others of it, but upon most mature consideration." "All men, as they are the sons of Adam, are co-heirs, and have equal right unto liberty, and all other outward comforts of life." "Originally and naturally there is no such thing as slavery." "There is no proportion between twenty pieces of silver and liberty."

All his lifetime he made the Biblical prophecies his favorite study—a study out of which all manner of marvels, not always edifying, may be educed upon occasion; and the special marvel drawn from them by this sagacious Puritan judge was their palpable predictions of America as the final "rendezvous for Gog and Magog," and as the true seat of the New Jerusalem. In his *Phaenomena Quaedam Apocalyptica; . . . or . . . a Description of the New Heaven as it makes to those who stand upon the New Earth,* a book first published in 1697, he unfolds this theory, going over the applicable prophesies clause by clause. Toward the end of his book, he replies to the objections that might be urged against his doctrine—one of them being that in America the human race inevitably deteriorates, becomes barren, dies off early. The accusation he repels with an affluence of facts illustrating the productiveness and longevity of the human family here; and having done so, he rises into this rhythmical and triumphant passage, which in its quaint melody of learned phrase, and in a gentle humor that lurks and loses itself in the stiff folds of his own solemnity, has a suggestion of the quality of Sir Thomas Browne: "As long as Plum Island shall faithfully keep the commanded post, notwithstanding all the hectoring words and hard blows of the proud and boisterous ocean; as long as any salmon or sturgeon shall swim in the streams of Merrimac, or any perch or pickerel in Crane Pond; as long as the sea-fowl shall know the time of their coming, and not neglect seasonably to visit the places of their acquaintance; as long as any cattle shall be fed with the grass growing in the meadows, which do humbly bow down themselves before Turkey-Hill; as long as any sheep shall walk upon Old-Town Hills, and shall from thence pleasantly look down upon the River Parker, and the fruitful marshes lying beneath; as long as any free and harmless doves shall find a white oak or other tree within the township, to perch, or feed, or build a careless nest upon, and shall voluntarily present themselves to perform the office of gleaners after barley-harvest; as long as Nature shall not grow old and dote, but shall constantly remember to give the rows of Indian corn their education by pairs; so long shall Christians be born there, and being first made meet, shall from thence be translated to be made partakers of the inheritance of the saints in light."

It gives still another charm to the memory of this practical and hard-headed mystic of New England, this wide-souled and speculative

Puritan,
Who the halting step of his age outran,

to discover, that, in a matter of very serious concern, he had the chivalry to come forward as the champion of woman. He tells us that once, while "waiting upon a dear child in her last sickness," he took up a book to read. It was a book called *The British Apollo*. Presently, his eye fell upon a startling question, worded thus: "Is there now, or will there be at the resurrection, any females in heaven; since there seems to be no need of them there?" Very likely he then closed the book; and there, by the death-bed of his daughter, over whose resurrection this question threw its cold shadow, his mind set to work upon the problem thus presented; and afterwards he fully resolved it, in an essay bearing this delectable title: "Talitha Cumi; or, An Invitation to Women to look after their Inheritance in the Heavenly Mansions." He begins by quoting the question that he had met with; then he proceeds to say: "This malapert question had not patience to stay for an answer, as appears by the conclusion of it—'since there seems to be no need of them there.' 'Tis most certain there will be no needless, impertinent persons or things in heaven. Heaven is a roomy, a most magnificent palace, furnished with the most rich and splendid entertainments; and the noblest guests are invited to partake of them. But why should there seem to be no need of women in heaven? . . . To speak the truth, God has no need of any creature. His name is exalted far above all blessing and praise. But by the same argument there will be no angels nor men in heaven, because there is no need of them there." He then discusses, with judge-like care and fulness, all the arguments, on both sides, that may be drawn from reason, Scripture, and the ancient and modern theologians, reaching at last this assertion: "There are three women that shall rise again,—Eve, the mother of all living; Sarah, the mother of the faithful; and Mary, the mother of our Lord. And if these three rise again, without doubt all will." In the course of the discussion he meets the objection that, upon a certain branch of his subject, "the ancients are divided in their opinions." His answer to this objection comes edged by a flash of wit: "If we should wait till all the ancients are agreed in their opinions, neither men nor women would ever get to heaven."

When Chaucer visited the house of the goddess Fame, he observed that the outer gate

so well y-corven was,
That never suche another nas;
And yit it was be aventure
Ywrought, as often as be cure.

It is an illustration of the caprice which everywhere prevails in the domain of this goddess, that the one American who, upon the whole, was the most powerful and brilliant prose-writer produced in this country during the colonial time, and who in his day enjoyed a sovereign reputation in New England, should have passed since then into utter obscurity; while several of his contemporaries, particularly Increase and Cotton Mather, who were far inferior to him in genius, have names that are still resounding in our memories. This writer was John Wise, born at Roxbury, probably in 1652; graduated at Harvard College in 1673; and, from 1680 until his death in 1725, minister of the Second Church of Ipswich. He had almost every quality that gives distinction among men. He was of towering height, of great muscular power, stately and graceful in shape and movement; in his advancing years, of an aspect most venerable. His parishioners long remembered with pride how a certain famous and blustering hero from Andover, the mighty wrestler of all that region, once came down to Ipswich for the purpose of challenging their stalwart parson to a friendly trial of strength at wrestling; and how the parson, after much solicitation, at last reluctantly consented, but had scarcely wrapped his arms in iron hug around his antagonist, when the latter lay outstretched upon the earth, with his curiosity respecting the Reverend Mr. Wise completely satisfied.

The soul of this man was of the same large and indomitable make. He had a robust joy in nature and in human structure; the creed of a democrat, without fear and without truculence: to him the griefs of the oppressed and the aggressions of the oppressor were alike insupportable. In 1687, when Sir Edmund Andros sent down to Ipswich his lawless order for a province-tax, the young parson braved the tyrant's anger, by advising his people not to comply with that order; for which he was arrested, tried, deposed from the ministry, fined, and thrown into prison. In 1689, when Sir Edmund was overthrown, John Wise was back again in his parish; and, both there and in Boston, he was at the front among the bravest, who then sought to prevent the recurrence of such despotism, by making examples of the petty English despot and of his still pettier American accomplices. In 1690, when the new governor of Massachusetts, Sir William Phips, led an expedition against Canada, John Wise, by request of the colonial legislature, accompanied him as chaplain, distinguishing himself in the campaign by feats of heroism, endurance, and military skill, as well as by fidelity in preaching and praying.

Thus far in his life, he had been noted chiefly for traits of physical and moral greatness, a devout, benignant, valiant, and blameless manhood; but within a few years afterward, there came upon the country an event that made him famous for the exertion of intellectual powers, both in thought and speech, the most rugged, versatile, and splendid.

In the year 1705, on the fifth of November—ominous day!— there was issued at Boston a very shrewd document, without any signature attached, but purporting to have been framed by an association of ministers in and near that city. It was addressed to the churches and ministers of New England. It bore the unassuming title of "Questions and Proposals." Masked under the deferential and harmless phrases, it was really a project for taking away the power of the laity in all the churches of New England, for annulling the independence of each church, and for substituting in place of both the will of the clergy. The document was understood to have been the work of the two Mathers, backed by a coterie of clerical admirers, and representing an inclination widely cherished, even if concealed. The document had a meek look, innocuous, even holy; it sought only the glory of God and the good of man; it was not loud, peremptory, dogmatic; it only asked and suggested. But John Wise, from his rural study in Ipswich, saw its true character—a plot for an ecclesiastical revolution, and a revolution backward; and having given ample time for the scheme to work its way into general discussion, at last he lifted up his hand, and, at one blow, crushed it. His blow was a book, *The Churches' Quarrel Espoused,* published at Boston in 1710—a book that by its learning, logic, sarcasm, humor, invective, its consuming earnestness, its vision of great truths, its flashes of triumphant eloquence, simply annihilated the scheme which it assailed.

His introduction is planned with exceeding art to conciliate the reader, to rouse the suspicion of the public against the men who had proposed the revolutionary scheme, and to confirm the popular conviction that the order of church-government already established, had upon the whole worked satisfactorily: "The scheme seems to be the spectre . . . of Presbyterianism; . . . yet if I don't mistake, in intention there is something considerable of Prelacy in it. . . . There is also something in it which smells very strong of the infallible chair. . . . For the clergy to monopolize both the legislative and executive part of canon law, is but a few steps from the chair of universal pestilence; and by the ladder here set up, clergymen may, if they please, clamber thus high. . . . Who can limit their power, or shorten their arm in their executions? Their Bulls can now, upon any affront, bellow and thunder out a thousand terrible curses; and the poor affrighted and envassaled laity . . . must forfeit their salvation, if they don't tamely submit."

He then takes up, one by one, the several proposals; and exposes the danger and folly of each, with great power of logic, humor, and sarcasm. Thus, in commenting upon the proposed mode of receiving candidates into the ministry, he argues that it will surely lead to the evils of clerical corruption seen elsewhere: "How oft it is repeated that poor, sordid, debauched wretches are put into holy orders, whenas they were fitter to be put into the stocks, or sent to Bridewell for madmen, than to be sent with their testimonials to work in Christ's vineyard! How long have the Indies, the seas, the provinces, and many other parts of the empire, groaned under this damnable way of cheating God of his glory and the world of salvation!"

It was, however, objected that under the present system, candidates often got into the ministry too young. He replies: "What then? . . . If Christ be preached, all is well. . . . Despise not the day of small things. All men must have a beginning, and every bird which is pretty well fledged must begin to fly. And ours are not of the nest where Icarus was hatched, whose feathers were only glued on; but these belong to the angelic host, and their wings grow out from their essence; therefore, you may allow them with the lark now and then to dart heavenward, though the shell or down be scarce off their heads."

It was urged, likewise, that the scheme has quite a harmless look; and in reply, he shows that, in spite of that, it involves the possibility of great expansion into mischief: "Though it be but a calf now, yet in time it may grow—being of a thrifty nature—to become a sturdy ox that will know no 'whoa,' and, it may be, past the churches' skill then to subdue it. For if I am not much mistaken, . . . that great and terrible Beast with seven heads and ten horns . . . was nothing else, a few ages ago, but just such another calf as this is. It was, indeed, finely shaped and of neat limbs, . . . insomuch that the great potentates of the earth were much ravished with its aspect and features; some offered to suckle it on the choicest cows amongst all the herds of royal cattle, . . . hoping to stock their own countries with the breed; and when it was grown to a considerable magnitude, to render it more shapely and fair, they put iron tips on to its horns, and beset its stupendous bulk with very rich ornaments. . . . But alas, poor men! they have paid dear for their prodigality and fondness; for this very Creature, that was but a calf when they first begun to feed it, is now grown to be such a mad, furious, and wild Bull, that there is scarce a Christian monarch on earth . . . —the best horseman or huntsman of them all—that dare take this Beast by the horns, when he begins to bounce and bellow. Indeed the Emperor, within these few years, has recovered so much courage that he took him by the tail, to drive him out of his royal granges, being quite angry and weary with his cropping and browsing on the flowers of his imperial crown. But, otherwise, the Beast generally goes at large, and does what he will in all princes' dominions, and keeps them in awe. Therefore, to conclude, . . . 'Obsta principiis!' It is wisdom to nip such growths in the bud, and keep down by early slaughter such a breed of cattle."

The document that he is exposing, is dated "November the fifth." He does not let this incident slip; and having, with wonderful effectiveness, developed his argument that the scheme contained in that document is a treasonable conspiracy, he proceeds to give the authors of it a terrible thrust. Beginning with some "astrological remarks" upon the document, he says: "I find its nativity full of favorable aspects to English churches. The fifth day of November has been as a guardian angel to the most sacred interest of the empire; it has rescued the whole glory of church and state from the most fatal arrest of hell and Rome. . . . Had I been of the cabal . . . which formed these proposals, so soon as I had seen . . . the date, . . . I should have cried out, 'Miserere nostri Deus,'—the good Lord have mercy upon us. This is the 'gun-powder-treason day;' and we are every man ruined, being running Fawkes's fate! Why, gentlemen, have you forgot it? It is the day of the gun-powder-treason, and a fatal day to traitors. . . I have such an awe upon my mind of this very day, that I have made a settled resolution, that of all the days of the whole year, I will never conspire treason against my natural prince, nor mischief to the churches, on the fifth day of November. And so, farewell, gentlemen; for I dare not join with you in this conspiracy." But again, in the discussion, he returns to this date, and he addresses to it a fervid and brilliant apostrophe: "Blessed! thrice blessed day! uphold and maintain thy matchless fame in the calendar of time; and let no darkness or shadow of death stain thee; let thy horizon comprehend whole constellations of favorable and auspicious stars, reflecting a benign influence on the English monarchy; and upon every return, in thy anniversary circuits, keep an indulgent eye open and wakeful upon all the beauties, from the throne to the footstool, of that mighty empire! And when it is thy misfortune to conceive a Monster, which may threaten any part of the nation's glory, let it come crippled from the womb, or else travail in birth again, with some noble hero or invincible Hercules, who may conquer and confound it."

This noble passage is near the victorious close of the book; and having thus abundantly implied the infamous character of the conspiracy, he magnanimously tells the conspirators themselves that, for the present, and on their good behavior, they are safe; for he will not reveal their names: "Where the place was, or the persons who were present in this rendezvous, shall never be told by me, unless it be extorted by the rack. And though I have endeavored with freedom of argument to subvert the error, I will never stain their personal glory by repeating or calling over the muster-roll. Therefore, as Noah's sons cast a garment upon their father's nakedness, so . . . their names for me shall repose under a mantle of honorable pity and forgetfulness."

Upon the whole, this book has extraordinary literary merit. It is, of its kind, a work of art; it has a beginning, a middle, and an end—each part in fit proportion, and all connected organically. The author is expert in exciting and in sustaining attention; does not presume upon the patience of his readers; relieves the heaviness and dryness of the argument by gayety and sarcasm; and has occasional bursts of grand enthusiasm, of majestic and soul-stirring eloquence. In tone it is superior to its time; keen and urgent in its reasoning, showing no pity for opposing principles, it is full of forbearance and even of urbanity for opposing persons. It is a piece of triumphant logic, brightened by wit, and ennobled by imagination; a master-specimen of the art of public controversy.

The Churches' Quarrel Espoused is an exposition of the theory of democracy, in the Christian church, but the argument is developed according to the exigencies of a special occasion.

In 1717, seven years after the publication of that book, John Wise published a systematic treatise upon the same subject, expounding in a formal and didactic way the principles of ecclesiastical polity then adopted in New England. He entitled this work, *A Vindication of the Government of New England Churches.*

His theory of the best government for the church derives its character from his fundamental ideas of what is the best government for the state; and the treatment of the latter subject leads him into a broad discussion of the rights of man, the nature of civil obligation, and the various forms of civil polity.

He first deals with man in his natural state, "as a free-born subject under the crown of Heaven, and owing homage to none but God himself. . . . He is the favorite animal on earth, in that this part of God's image, namely, reason, is congenerate with his nature, wherein by a law immutable, enstamped upon his frame, God has provided a rule for men in all their actions, obliging each one to the performance of that which is right, . . . the which is nothing but the dictate of right reason founded in the soul of man. . . . The second great immunity of man is an original liberty enstamped upon his rational nature. . . . I shall waive the consideration of man's moral turpitude, but shall view him" as "the most august animal in the world. . . . Whatever has happened since his creation, he remains at the upper-end of nature." Man's natural liberty consists in three things: first, man has "a faculty of doing or omitting things according to the direction of his judgment"; second, "every man must be conceived to be perfectly in his own power and disposal, and not to be controlled by the authority of any other"; third, there is "an equality amongst men, which is . . . to be cherished and preserved to the highest degree, as will consist with all just distinctions amongst men of honor, and shall be agreeable with the public good. For man has a high valuation of himself, and the passion seems to lay its first foundation, not in pride, but really in the high and admirable frame and constitution of human nature. . . . Since, then, human nature agrees equally with all persons, and since no one can live a sociable life with another that does not own and respect him as a man, it follows as a command of the law of nature, that every man esteem and treat another as one who is naturally his equal, or who is a man as well as he. . . . The noblest mortal in his entrance on the stage of life is not distinguished by any pomp . . . from the lowest of mankind; and our life hastens to the same general mark. Death observes no ceremony, but knocks as loud at the barriers of the court as at the door of the cottage. . . . Nature having set all men upon a level and made them equals, no servitude or subjection can be conceived without inequality, and this cannot be made without usurpation in others, or voluntary compliance in those who resign their freedom and give away their degree of natural being."

In treating of man in a civil state, he shows that "the true and leading cause of forming governments and yielding up natural liberty, and throwing man's equality into a common pile . . . was . . . to guard themselves against the injuries men were liable to interchangeably; for none so good to man as man, and yet none a greater enemy. So that the first . . . original of civil power is the people. . . . The formal reason of government is the will of a community, yielded up and surrendered to some other subject, either of one particular person or more." He, then, speaks of "the three forms of a regular state"—democracy, aristocracy, and monarchy; and of the first he says: "This form of government appears in the greatest part of the world to have been the most ancient. . . . Reason seems to show it to be the most probable that when men . . . had thoughts of joining in a civil body, they would without question be inclined to administer their common affairs by their common judgment, and so must necessarily . . . establish a democracy."

Having thus spoken of each of these civil forms, he next deals with their analogous forms in church organization. He begins with the ecclesiastical monarchy, and of course finds this embodied in the Papacy: "It is certain his Holiness, either by reasonable pleas or powerful cheats, has assumed an absolute and universal sovereignty; this fills his cathedral chair, and is adorned with a triple crown." His claim is that "the Almighty has made him both key-keeper of heaven and hell, with the adjacent territories of purgatory, and vested in him an absolute sovereignty over the Christian world. . . . He therefore decks himself with the spoils of the divine attributes, styling himself, Our Lord God, 'Optimum, maximum, et supremum numen in terris'; a God on earth, a visible Deity, and that his power is absolute, and his wisdom infallible. And many of the great potentates of the earth have paid their fealty as though it was really so. . . . He has placed his holy foot on the monarch's profane neck, as crushing a vermin crawling out of the stable of his sovereignty; and others very frequently kiss his toes with profound devotion. . . . But the sad inquiry is, whether this sort of government has not plainly subverted the design of the gospel, and the end for which Christ's government was ordained, namely, the moral, spiritual, and eternal happiness of men. But I have no occasion to pursue this remark with tedious demonstrations. It is very plain; it is written with blood in capital letters, to be read at midnight by the flames of Smithfield and other such like consecrated fires,— that the governmen of this ecclesiastical monarch has, instead of sanctifying, absolutely debauched the world, and subverted all good Christianity in it. . . . Without the least show of any vain presumption, we may infer that God and wise Nature were never propitious to the birth of this Monster."

As regards the aristocratic form of church government, which he finds embodied in the Episcopacy, he thinks that Christianity "has been peeled, robbed, and spoiled" by it—"so doleful a contemplation is it to think the world should be destroyed by those men who by God were ordained to save it."

He then comes to the ecclesiastical democracy, and of course advocates it, doing so with calm, rational, and powerful arguments: "This is a form of government which the light of nature does highly value, and often directs to, as most agreeable to the just and natural prerogatives of human beings."

Throughout this entire work, the author shows abundant learning; but always he is the master of his learning, and not its victim. He lays out his propositions clearly and powerfully; marshals his arguments with tact and effect; is nowhere freakish, or extravagant; never fails in good temper, or in good sense.

Upon the whole, no other American author of the colonial time is the equal of John Wise in the union of great breadth and power of thought with great splendor of style; and he stands almost alone of our early writers for the blending of a racy and dainty humor with impassioned earnestness.

His force and brilliance in statement cannot be fully represented in sentences torn from their connection; yet on almost every page one meets terse and quotable sayings, here and there long passages grand for their nobility of feeling, their truth, and the music of their words. "Order," says he, "is both the beauty and safety of the universe. Take away the decorum whereby the whole hangs together, the great frame of nature is unpinned, and drops piece from piece; and out of a beautiful structure we have a chaos." "If men are trusted with duty," he exclaims, "they must trust that, and not events. If men are placed at helm to steer in all weather that blows, they must not be afraid of the waves or a wet coat."

Here is his stately and passionate chant of homage to religion: "Religion, in its infallible original, the wisdom and authority of God; in its Infinite Object, the ineffable Persons and Perfections of the Divine Essence; in its means, the gospel of salvation; in its inspired wakeful and capacious ministry; in its subject, the inestimable immortal soul of man; in its transcendent effects, in time the charming peace and joys of conscience, in eternity the joyful retreat and shouts of glory; —is the most incomparable gift of Palladium which ever came from heaven. Amongst all the favors of the Father of Lights, there is none parallel with this; when disclosed in its beauty, it ravisheth all the intellects of the universe; and challenge may be made that the prerogatives and glory belonging to all the crowned heads in the world, do bow and wait upon its processions through the earth, to guard it from its innumerable and inveterate enemies. . . . It is certain that the church of Christ is the pillar of truth, or sacred recluse and peculiar asylum of Religion; and this sacred guest, Religion, which came in the world's infancy from heaven to gratify the solitudes of miserable man, when God had left him, hath long kept house with us in this land, to sweeten our wilderness-state; and the renowned churches here are her sacred palaces. Then, certainly, it is not fair for her lovers, under pretence of maintaining her welcome in greater state, to desolate her pleasing habitations, though they stand somewhat low like the myrtle grove."

Perhaps even greater than the distinction he deserves for his brilliant writing, is the distinction due him for the prophetic clearness, the courage, and the inapproachable ability with which, in that unfriendly time, he, almost alone among Americans, avowed his belief in civil governments founded on the idea of human equality. He was the first great American democrat. In the earlier years of the eighteenth century, he announced the political ideas that, fifty years later, took immortal form under the pen of Thomas Jefferson. Indeed, in 1772, when the doctrine of human right had come to be a very urgent and very practical one among men, the two books of John Wise were called for in Boston by the Revolutionary leaders; they proved an armory of burnished weapons in all that stern fight. "The end of all good government is to cultivate humanity and promote the happiness of all, and the good of every man in all his rights, his life, liberty, estate, honor, and so forth, without injury or abuse to any." No wonder that the writer of that sentence was called up from his grave, by the men who were getting ready for the Declaration of Independence!

Not long before the Revolutionary War, a distinguished clergyman of Boston, Charles Chauncey, then an aged man, said, in a letter to President Stiles, that of all the eminent men he had known in New England, Jeremiah Dummer was "for extent and strength of genius" one of the three greatest. By all contemporary allusions it is evident that this man was regarded in his day as having extraordinary ability. Certainly no other American of that period began life with more brilliant promise; perhaps none ended it under sadder disappointment. He was born in Boston about 1679, of a family prominent and honorable in the country from its earliest settlement. He was graduated at Harvard College in 1699, where his student-life was long perpetuated in splendid tradition. Being at that time of a singularly devout spirit, he chose theology for his profession, and entered upon the study of it with his usual ardor and thoroughness. He soon went abroad for larger opportunities of instruction, taking his doctor's degree at the University of Utrecht; and upon his return to New England, probably in 1704, he brought with him testimonials to his industry and blameless life while in Europe. To his friends and to himself he now probably seemed fully ripe for the illustrious service among the churches of New England to which he had been destined. He began to preach in the pulpits of Boston; but somehow, in spite of all his genius and all his vast academic preparation, his preaching did not make any impression. It was without fault, and without effect. Thus, on the twenty-ninth of October, 1704, he preached "A Discourse on the Holiness of the Sabbath Day." It was immaculate for orthodoxy, fitting even the most ascetic Puritan variety of that article; it had an abundance of Biblical, theological, and classical learning in it; it was smooth and liquid in style; indeed, it had nearly every quality of a speech, except fitness for being spoken. It was simply a labored literary essay, quite too bookish, ornate, and fine to have any practical effect either on saints or sinners. The sermon, however, was at once published, under the high sanction of the venerable Increase Mather, who, in the preface, spoke of Dummer's unequalled success as a student at home and abroad, and of his personal excellence in creed and deed, but concluded with the alarming intimation that unless the churches of New England should make haste to possess themselves of this clerical prodigy, he would be very likely to with-draw into some other quarter of the universe.

The menace went unheeded. Dummer preached here and there for a time, but found no acceptable pulpit to which he was acceptable; and at last he gave up the quest. Five years later, 1709, he once more emerged into view. This time it was in London, in a new character, on a new theme. He had dropped his theological profession, and his theology, and, very likely, his religion; he had gone to England to be a politician, and to make for himself there a great career in secular life. He had arrived not long before the formation of the Tory ministry under Harley and St. John; and to the anguish of his friends in America, he soon allied himself with the latter powerful and profligate statesman; adopted his politics, and even his morals; served him in various secret negotiations; and had from him promises of high promotion. But, in 1714, the Queen died; Bolingbroke fled in disgrace to France; and poor Dummer, damned by such an alliance, found all his hopes of a political career in England blasted. It was impossible for him to confess his failure by a return to his native land; and in England he remained during the rest of his days, becoming a member of the Middle Temple, and indulging in certain respectable laxi-ties of conduct more suggestive of his later friends than of his earlier ones; at last, in 1739, he died, without ever grasping any of that glory in the world for which he had so laboriously qualified himself, almost unknown in the country which he had adopted, and long before forgotten in the country in which he was born.

Yet on behalf of Jeremiah Dummer it remains to be said, that whatever else, of true and good, he may have given up when he turned his back upon his own country, he never gave up his love for that country, or his passion to promote her wel-fare by his best labors. From 1710 to 1721, he served Massachu-setts as its agent in London; and when that office was taken from him, he continued to serve her still, without appointment and without pay, whenever he found occasion. However much of an Englishman he may have become, he never ceased to be an American. Whatever he wrote for the public, is upon American topics; and his letters to his friends in this country showed at times a pensive and affectionate regret for the land and the life that he could never return to.

His memory as a writer will rest upon two publications, both being proofs not only of his fine literary accomplishments, but of his vigilant and laborious zeal for his country. The first was printed, in London, in 1709, and is entitled, *A Letter to a Noble Lord concerning the late Expedition to Canada*, wherein he makes three points: first, that the conquest of Canada was of great importance to England; second, that the late expedition was wisely planned; third, that its failure cannot be charged upon New England. It is an able and convincing essay, written in urbane and graceful style, everywhere bright and readable. It contains some striking illustrations of the adroitness with which the French missionaries in Canada aided the political designs of France; for instance, teaching their Indian converts that "the Virgin Mary was a French lady, and that her Son, the Saviour of the world, was crucified by the English." The book also denotes how early and passionate among the English colonies in America was the dread of the American power of France; thus, even in 1709, he says that those colonies can never be easy or happy "whilst the French are masters of Canada."

But the second of Dummer's political publications is much the abler: *A Defence of the New England Charters*. It was published in London in 1728, at a time when there was danger of a bill passing the House of Commons, annulling the charters granted to the New England colonies. It opens with a fine sketch of the origin and growth of those colonies, and of the circumstances under which the charters were given to them; and then proceeds to establish these four propositions: first, that the charter-governments have a good right to their charters; second, that they have not forfeited them; third, that if they had, it would not be the interest of the crown to accept the forfeitures; and, fourth, that it is inconsistent with justice to disfranchise the charter-colonies by act of parliament. It is an admirable specimen of argumentative literature; strict in logic, strong in fact, clear, flowing, graceful, occasionally rising into noble enthusiasm, but always temperate, courteous, and cosmopolitan.

No one who would penetrate to the core of early American literature, and would read in it the secret history of the people in whose minds it took root and from whose minds it grew, may by any means turn away, in lofty literary scorn, from the almanac—most despised, most prolific, most indispensable of books, which every man uses, and no man praises; the very quack, clown, pack-horse, and pariah of modern literature, yet the one universal book of modern literature; the supreme and only literary necessity even in households where the Bible and the newspaper are still undesired or unattainable luxuries.

The earliest record of this species of literature in America carries us back to the very beginning of printed literature in America; for, next after a sheet containing "The Freeman's Oath," the first production that came from the printing-press in this country was *An Almanac calculated for New England, by Mr. Pierce,* and printed by Stephen Daye, at Cambridge, in 1639. Thenceforward for a long time, scarcely a year passed over that solitary printing-press at Cambridge, without receiving a similar salute from it. In 1676, Boston itself grew wise enough to produce an almanac of its own. Ten years afterward, Philadelphia began to send forth almanacs—a trade in which, in the following century, it was to acquire special glory. In 1697, New York entered the same enticing field of enterprise. The first almanac produced in Rhode Island, was in 1728; the first almanac produced in Virginia, was in 1731. In 1733, Benjamin Franklin began to publish what he called *Poor Richard's Almanac,* to which his own personal reputation has given a celebrity surpassing that of all other almanacs published anywhere in the world. Thus, year by year, with the multiplication of people and of printing-presses in this country, was there a multiplication of almanacs, some of them being of remarkable intellectual and even literary merit. From the first, they contained many of the traits that had become conventional in printed almanacs in Europe, ever since their first publication there in the fifteenth century; particularly astrological prophecies, or, as they were called, "prognostications," relating both to mankind and to the weather, and representing the traditional belief in the influence of the heavenly bodies upon mundane affairs. Gradually, to these were added other things—scraps of wisdom, crumbs of history, snatches of verse, proverbs, jests, all scattered through the little book according to the convenience of the printer and the supposed benefit of the reader. Throughout our colonial time, when larger books were costly and few, the almanac had everywhere a hearty welcome and frequent perusal; the successive numbers of it were carefully preserved year after year; their margins and blank pages were often covered over with annotations, domestic and otherwise. Thus, John Cotton, it will be remembered, used the blank spaces in his almanacs as depositories for his stealthy attempts at verse. So, also, the historian, Thomas Prince, recorded in his almanacs the state of his accounts with his hair-dresser and wig-maker. A writer of some note, born in Connecticut during the American Revolution, has left a vivid description of his own excitement, as a child, in reading again and again the literary treasures of the household, consisting, in large part, of a file of almanacs for fifty years.

One of the numerous myths still prevailing in the world with reference to Benjamin Franklin, describes him as the first founder of an almanac blending those qualities of shrewd instruction and keen mother-wit, that are to be seen in his famous series; a French encyclopaedist, for example, declaring that Franklin "put forth the first popular almanac which spoke the language of reason." In truth, much of the wisdom and wit introduced by Franklin into his almanac was borrowed from Bacon, Rabelais, Rochefoucauld, Steele, Swift, De Foe, and others: but even the idea of introducing into an almanac wit

and wisdom whether original or borrowed, had been thought of
and put into practice before Franklin's *Poor Richard* was born.
In 1728, five years before that event, Franklin's brother, James,
sent forth the first number of *The Rhode Island Almanac;* and
in its pages, year by year, one may find no little of that sagacity,
humor, and knack of phrase, that did so much for the fortunes
of his own runaway apprentice. But even three years before
James Franklin's almanac appeared, Nathaniel Ames, a physician and innkeeper of Dedham, Massachusetts, a man of original, vigorous, and pungent genius, began the publication of his
Astronomical Diary and Almanac; which he continued to publish till his death in 1764; which, under his management, acquired an enormous popularity throughout New England; and
which, from the first, contained in high perfection every type
of excellence afterward illustrated in the almanac of Benjamin
Franklin. Indeed, Ames's almanac was in most respects better
than Franklin's, and was, probably, the most pleasing representative we have of a form of literature that furnished so much
entertainment to our ancestors, and that preserves for us so
many characteristic tints of their life and thought.

Nathaniel Ames made his almanac a sort of annual cyclopae-
dia of information and amusement—a vehicle for the convey-
ance to the public of all sorts of knowledge and nonsense, in
prose and verse, from literature, history and his own mind, all
presented with brevity, variety, and infallible tact. He had the
instinct of a journalist; and, under a guise that was half-frolic-
some, the sincerity and benignant passion of public educator.
He carried into the furthest wildernesses of New England some
of the best English literature; pronouncing there, perhaps for
the first time, the names of Addison, Thomson, Pope, Dryden,
Butler, Milton; and repeating there choice fragments of what
they had written. Thus, eight years before Benjamin Franklin
had started his almanac, Nathaniel Ames was publishing one
that had all of its best qualities—fact and frolic, the wisdom of
the preacher without his solemnity, terse sayings, shrewdness,
wit, homely wisdom, all sparkling in piquant phrase.

As the public expected the almanac-maker to be a prophet,

Nathaniel Ames gratified the public; and he freely predicted future events, but always with a merry twinkle in his eye, and always ready to laugh the loudest at his own failure to predict them aright. He mixes, in delightful juxtaposition, absurd prognostications, curt jests, and aphorisms of profound wisdom, the whole forming a miscellany even now extremely readable, and sure, at that time, to raise shouts of laughter around thousands of fireplaces where food for laughter was much needed. Thus,

January 1. "About the beginning of the year expect plenty of rain or snow."
"Warm and clears off cold again."
May 22. "Some materials about this time are hatched for the clergy to debate on."
October 21. "He that lives by fraud is in danger of dying a knave."
November 9. "These aspects show violent winds and in winter storms of driving snow; mischiefs by Indians, if no peace; and among us, feuds, quarrels, bloody-noses, broken pates —if not necks."
November 24. "If there was less debating and more acting, 'twould be better times."
December 7-10.   "Ladies, take heed,
Lay down your fans,
And handle well
Your warming-pans."
December 15-18. "This cold, uncomfortable weather
Makes Jack and Gill lie close together."
December 20-22. "The lawyers' tongues—they never freeze,
If warmed with honest clients' fees."

Having been laughed at for his false predictions, he uses the almanac for 1729 to join in the laugh, and to turn the occasion of it into a witty and instructive home-thrust at every reader:

Man was at first a perfect, upright creature,
The lively image of his great Creator.
When Adam fell, all men in him transgressed;
And since that time they err that are the best.
The printer errs; I err,—much like the rest.
Welcome's that man for to complain of me,
Whose self and works are quite from errors free.

Sometimes, in a more serious tone, he gives his real opinion about this traditional department of the almanac, and helps to lift his readers above the demand for it: "He who has fore-ordained whatsoever comes to pass, knows, and he only knows with absolute certainty, what will come to pass. The Book of Fate is hid from all created beings. . . . Indeed, the Devil does not know so much of future events, as many expect an almanac-maker should foretell; although it must be owned that they are willing to allow him the help of the Devil for his information."

But everywhere it is plain enough that the author wears his mask of jester, only to hide a most earnest and friendly face; and having by his mirth gained admission to every New England cabin, he sits down with the family around the great crackling fire, and helps them to a wisdom that will enable them to keep on laughing. Thus, in the almanac for 1754, he has a preliminary address to the reader, uttered in the tone of a Cobbett or a Greeley—a born tribune of the people: "I have filled the two last pages with an essay on regimen. I don't pretend to direct the learned; the rich and voluptuous will scorn my direction, and sneer or rail at any that would reclaim them; but since this sheet enters the solitary dwellings of the poor and illiterate, where the studied ingenuity of the learned writer never comes, if these brief hints do good, it will rejoice the heart of your humble servant, Nathaniel Ames."

February 24-27. "If you fall into misfortunes, creep through those bushes which have the least briers."

March 21-23. "Expectation waits to know whether the mountain bears a mouse or no."

October 25-28. "There are three faithful friends—an old wife, an old dog, and ready cash."

November 6-8. "Were things done twice, many would be wise."

July 16-27. "Every man carries a fool in his sleeve; with some he appears bold, with some he only pops out now and then, but the wise keep him hid."

September 12-16. "To some men their country is their shame; and some are the shame of their country."

He sprinkles his pages with wholesome suggestions about health-getting and health-keeping. For September, 1762, he says: "This month is a proper season to recruit the unhealthy, by taking Dr. Horse and riding long journeys—though moderately." The gospel that he preaches is the gospel of health, virtue, economy, industry, content; he shows that always grumbling is either a vice or a disease, and that whichever it be, the first duty of every man is to rid himself of it:

> As for myself, whom poverty prevents
> From being angry at so great expense,
>
> .   .   .   .
>
> I choose to labor, rather than to fret;
> What's rage in some, in me goes off in sweat.
> If times are ill, and things seem never worse,
> Men, manners, to reclaim,—I, take my horse:
> One mile reforms 'em; or, if aught remain
> Unpurged—'tis but to ride as far again.
> Thus on myself in toils I spend my rage:
> I pay the fine, and that absolves the age.
> Sometimes, still more to interrupt my ease,
> I take my pen, and write such things as these;
> Which, though all other merit be denied,
> Show my devotion still to be employed.
>
> .   .   .   .
>
> And since midst indolence, spleen will prevail,
> Since who do nothing else, are sure to rail,
> Men should be suffered thus to play the fool
> To keep from hurt, as children go to school.

The almanac for 1736 ends with a brief prose essay, which is an amusing miscellany of physical learning and humor, all intended to interest the reader and to advertise the merits of a certain invaluable medicine—worm-seed for children; concluding with this paragraph worthy of the shrewdness of Poor Richard himself: "Some nurses are so superstitious that they dare not give their children worm-seed without pounding and sifting it, affirming that every seed that escapes being bruised in the mortar will become a live worm in the bowels of the child.

But, by the by, it is an excellent medicine for the purpose, and they need not be afraid to use it; for, if they will prove that it can breed worms in children, I can as easily prove that it can breed children in women; and so those unhappy persons who have had the ill-luck to have children without fathers, need not lie under the imputation of scandal, if they can produce sufficient evidence that they have taken worm-seed."

His pages are sprinkled with verses from the English poets and from his own pen—the latter often of great vigor and sprightliness. For 1736, he spreads over the almanac a poem of twelve stanzas, one stanza being prefixed to each month. The subject of the poem is the Day of Judgment, and is so vivid and powerful in its descriptions, and is so blended with ominous references to the stars and to the warring elements, that it must have carried awe into many impressible minds, as if the omniscient almanac-maker intended actually to announce the coming of the awful day that very year. This is the stanza for January:

> The muses tremble with a faltering wing,
> While nature's great catastrophe they sing;
> For Helicon itself, their sacred throne,
> Must to the womb of chaos back return.
> The cheerful region of the earth and air
> Is filled with horror, darkness, and despair.

So, with fascinating gloom opens the year; and thus it proceeds, with variations of poetic horror, month by month. In March, we have this mystic and dreadful description of the moon and stars:

> No more she rules as regent of the night,
> But fills her orb with blood instead of light;
> And dissolution reigns both near and far,
> Through heaven's wide circuit round. Each shining star
> His intricate nocturnal mazes stops,
> And from his place assigned in heaven down drops.

In the following month things grow rapidly worse. The stars, it will be remembered, have fallen:

> Their light extinct, nature in darkness ends,
> Except what light hell's horrid bosom sends
> Around the sky; her baneful torches come
> To light dissolving nature to her tomb.
> The earth with trembling agonies doth roll,
> As though she mixed her centre with the pole.

In May,

> The seas do roar; and every peaceful lake
> And wandering rivers horrid murmurings make;
> The rocks explode, and trembling mountains nod,
> And valleys rise at the approaching God;
> From heaven's high court angelic throngs descend;
> Myriads this great solemnity attend.

It must have given some relief to sensitive readers to cast the eye further down the page, and to read in the author's prose his cheerful prophecies concerning the course of the weather for that very month; for he assures them of "a fine pleasant air, with gentle gales," and of "fair, pleasant, growing weather." And although there is an ominous threat of combustibility during the last week—"This week will afford heat and thunder"—yet the prospect is redeemed by the subsequent promise of "now and then a sprinkling of rain"—which, of course, must defer the general conflagration. The stanza for July concludes with this couplet:

> A rending sound from the expanded skies
> Commands the dead, the sleepy dead, to rise;

which harmonizes admirably with the weather probabilities for the same time; "The month ends with thunder and hot weather."

The almanac for 1749, the year succeeding the close of King George's War, has a fine literary tone, and its poetic motto, on the title-page, is a noble prophecy of peace in the world:

> No heroes' ghosts, with garments rolled in blood,
> Majestic stalk; the golden age renewed,
> No hollow drums in Flanders beat; the breath
> Of brazen trumpets rings no peals of death.

The milder stars their peaceful beams afford,
And sounding hammer beats the wounding sword
To ploughshares now; Mars must to Ceres yield,
And exiled Peace returns and takes the field.

The essay at the end of the almanac for 1758, is of unusual merit for thought and vivacity of expression. It is a fine specimen of what we now call a leading editorial article—terse, epigrammatic, vigorous, formed to catch and to hold the attention; and it is a very credible example of literary style. It was written in the midst of the struggle between France and England for the empire of America. It is upon "America—its Past, Present, and Future State." With reference to the Past, he says: "Time has cast a shade upon this scene. Since the creation, innumerable accidents have happened here, the bare mention of which would create wonder and surprise; but they are all lost in oblivion. The ignorant natives, for want of letters, have forgot their stock, and know not from whence they came, or how, or when they arrived here, or what has happened since." Then glancing at the events that have happened in America since the arrival of the Europeans, he describes the magnificent territory of the North-West then in dispute: "Time was when we might have been possessed of it; at this time two mighty kings contend for this inestimable prize. Their respective claims are to be measured by the length of their swords. The poet says, 'the Gods and Opportunity ride post'; that you must take her by the forelock, being bald behind. Have we not too fondly depended upon our numbers? Sir Francis Bacon says, 'The wolf careth not how many the sheep be.' But numbers, well-spirited, with the blessing of heaven, will do wonders when by military skill and discipline the commanders can actuate, as by one soul, the most numerous bodies of armed people. Our numbers will not avail till the colonies are united. . . . If we do not join heart and hand in the common cause against our exulting foes, but fall to disputing amongst ourselves, it may really happen as the governor of Pennsylvania told his assembly, 'We shall have no privilege to dispute about, nor country to dispute in.' "

His treatment of the Future State of America shows a remarkable grasp of facts relating to the physical resources of the continent, and an unusual power of reason in constructing the possibilities of civil and material development, especially in the West: "Here we find a vast stock of proper materials for the art and ingenuity of man to work on,—treasures of immense worth, concealed from the poor, ignorant, aboriginal natives. . . . As the celestial light of the gospel was directed here by the finger of God, it will doubtless finally drive the long, long night of heathenish darkness from America. . . . So arts and sciences will change the face of nature in their tour from hence over the Appalachian Mountains to the Western Ocean; and as they march through the vast desert, the residence of wild beasts will be broken up, and their obscene howl cease forever. Instead of which, the stones and trees will dance together at the music of Orpheus, the rocks will disclose their hidden gems, and the inestimable treasures of gold and silver be broken up. Huge mountains of iron ore are already discovered; and vast stores are reserved for future generations. This metal, more useful than gold and silver, will employ millions of hands, not only to form the martial sword and peaceful share alternately, but an infinity of utensils improved in the exercise of art and handicraft amongst men. . . . Shall not then these vast quarries that teem with mechanic stone,—those for structure be piled into great cities, and those for sculpture into statues, to perpetuate the honor of renowned heroes—even those who shall now save their country?" He then closes with this appeal to posterity: "O ye unborn inhabitants of America! should this page escape its destined conflagration at the year's end, and these alphabetical letters remain legible when your eyes behold the sun after he has rolled the seasons round for two or three centuries more, you will know that in Anno Domini, 1758, we dreamed of your times."

THE *wilderness was a constant in our colonial history; in one way or another it touched every man, woman, and child. Yet from the very beginning the colonies developed distinctive sectional characteristics. Each colony was founded by different people and often for widely different reasons, and paradoxically, the very wilderness that provided a common experience also made communication and cooperative development very difficult.*

Life and thought were not the same in colonial Massachusetts and New York and Pennsylvania. Peter Kalm, who traveled through the colonies from 1748 to 1751, "was astonished at the isolation of each in laws, in moneys, in military plans, in social usages." Tyler, well over a century later, understood and described the differences between the colonies.

Literature in the Middle Colonies

NEAR the middle of the year 1664, the Dutch town of New Amsterdam was suddenly transformed into the English town of New York—being then just forty-one years old, and having a population of fifteen hundred souls, The whole province, of course, shared the new name and the new mastership that had overtaken its chief town.

The Dutch, who founded both town and province, had thriven there from the beginning, according to the habit of their race—a patient, devout, labor-loving, wealth-getting, stolid community. Though popular education was neglected, and intellectual life ran sluggish and dull, there were among them many men of strong brains and scholarly attainments: Van der Donck, Megapolensis, and DeVries, who wrote history; Stuyvesant, Beeckman, and Van Rensselaer, whose letters show considerable learning; Van Dincklagen and Van Schelluyne, who were wise in the law; Jacob Steendam, Henricus Selyns, and Nicasius De Sillè, who wrote poetry; and besides these, several theologians and physicians who were well-read in their own sciences.

History of American Literature, Vol. II, chap. 16, pp. 205–34, 241–53.

Though the prevailing race in New Amsterdam was Dutch, from an early day the town had been an attractive one to men of other races. Twenty-one years before it fell into the hands of the English, it had, within it and near it, a population speaking eighteen different languages. After it fell into the hands of the English, its attractiveness to men of many languages certainly did not diminish; and it became, what its best historian calls it, "the most polygenous of all the British dependencies in North America." In the first twenty-four years of its existence under English sway, its population was nearly quadrupled; and by the end of the colonial time, it had increased almost twenty-fold. A community of many tongues, of many customs, of many faiths—there was, doubtless, in that fact a prophecy of metropolitan largeness and generosity, in store for it somewhere in the future.

Nevertheless, we shall greatly err if we imagine that, during the larger part of the colonial time, New York was much more than a prosperous and drowsy Dutch village, perplexed by polyglot interference and the menace of intellectual illumination; the scene of a petty life; ravaged by sectarian and provincial bigotries, and by vulgar competitions in society and in politics; very slowly moving toward the discovery that, in all the world, there is any other pursuit so noble as the pursuit of wealth. The historian, William Smith, writing in 1757, mentions that, for a long time, his own father and James De Lancey "were the only academics" in the province; and that, as late as 1745, there were only thirteen more. "What a contrast," he exclaims, "in everything respecting the cultivation of science, between this and the colonies first settled by the English!" "Our schools are of the lowest order—the instructors want instruction; and through a long and shameful neglect of all the arts and sciences, our common speech is extremely corrupt; and the evidences of bad taste, both as to thought and language, are visible in all our proceedings, public and private."

The history of literature in such a community, at such a period, must be the record, not of any concentrated and continuous literary activity, but of the occasional efforts of cultivated men to express themselves, for practical purposes, in some literary form.

Daniel Denton, the son of a minister in Connecticut, removed in 1644 into the province of New York, where he rose to distinction both as a land-owner and as a politician. In 1670, apparently with the view of attracting immigration to that province, he published, in London, *A Brief Description of New York*—a book of twenty-two pages, uncommonly graphic and animated. He kept closely to the facts that had come under his own eyes, prudently declining to say anything about those portions of the province that lay "to the northward yet undiscovered," or in "the bowels of the earth not yet opened." Even on the basis of literal and visible fact, however, he had enough, both useful and beautiful, to justify his enthusiasm for the land which he sought to make known to English emigrants. He gives an account of its fitness for all sorts of industrial success; not forgetting to describe its natural charms, as in May, when "you shall see the woods and fields so curiously bedecked with roses, and an innumerable multitude of delightful flowers, . . . that you may behold nature contending with art, and striving to equal if not excel many gardens in England"; and "divers sorts of singing-birds, whose chirping notes salute the ears of travellers with an harmonious discord; and in every pond and brook, green, silken frogs, who, warbling forth their untuned tunes, strive to bear a part in this music." Having given a sufficient account of the natural and social advantages of the province, he seeks to win inhabitants for it by appealing to the English love of personal independence and domestic thrift: "If there be any terrestrial happiness to be had by people of all ranks, especially of an inferior rank, it must certainly be here. Here any one may furnish himself with land, and live rent-free; yea, with such a quantity of land that he may weary himself with walking over his fields of corn and all sorts of grain. . . . Here those which Fortune hath frowned upon in England to deny them an inheritance amongst their brethren, or such as by their utmost labors can scarcely procure a living, . . . may procure here inheritances of lands and possessions, stock themselves with all sorts of cattle, enjoy the benefit of them whilst they live, and leave them to the benefit of their children when they die. Here you need not trouble the shambles for meat, nor bakers and brewers for beer and bread, nor run to a linen-draper for a supply. . . . If there be any terrestrial Canaan, 'tis surely here, where the land floweth with milk and honey. The inhabitants are blessed with peace and plenty, blessed in their country, blessed in their fields, blessed in the fruit of their bodies, in the fruit of their grounds, in the increase of their cattle, horses, and sheep, blessed in their basket and in their store; in a word, blessed in whatsoever they take in hand, or go about, the earth yielding plentiful increase to all their painful labors."

Precisely fifteen years after the publication of Daniel Denton's winsome sketch of the province of New York, Thomas Budd, of New Jersey, a worthy Quaker, and a man of much importance in his own neighborhood, published, likewise at London, a little book entitled *Good Order established in Pennsylvania and New Jersey in America.* The purpose of this book, like that of Daniel Denton, was to catch the eye of emigrants; and for that purpose it perhaps did not need, as certainly it did not have, much literary merit.

Another book belonging to this pioneer period of literature in New York and its neighborhood, is a very curious one: *News of a Trumpet sounding in the Wilderness; or, The Quakers' ancient testimony revived, examined, and compared with itself, and also with their new doctrine—whereby the ignorant may learn wisdom and the wise advance in their understandings;* published by William Bradford in 1697, and written by Daniel Leeds, once a Quaker and an early settler in Pennsylvania. This man, having quarrelled with his brethren there, abandoned them and finally their province, and established himself in New York, probably in 1693, where, for about thirty years, he continued in his famous almanacs that warfare against the Quakers which he had begun in his book.

Lewis Morris, born in 1671, on the paternal estate of Morrisania, lived a long and vigorous life as colonial politician in New York and New Jersey; was, for more than twenty years, chief-justice of the former province, and died, in 1746, as royal governor of the latter; a man of large inherited wealth, of high social consideration, of bold and somewhat unscrupulous talent; a natural intriguer. Though he settled into manhood sufficiently sedate, his youth was uncommonly vivacious, and sparkled long afterward in a trail of amusing traditions. Being left an orphan in his infancy, he came under the care of an uncle, who seems to have found the boy hard to tame into industry and propriety. At one time, he had for his tutor an enthusiastic Quaker, one Hugh Coppathwaite, who enjoyed much of the divine presence through various inward and outward communications. The boy conceived the happy thought of helping his preceptor to a new revelation, and himself to a holiday; and, accordingly, hiding in the branches of a tree under which the Quaker was used to walk, the lad called out to him in solemn tones, and commanded him to go away at once, and preach the gospel among the Mohawks. The good man accepted the mandate as the very voice of heaven, and was on the point of setting out to obey it, when, unluckily for the boy, the trick was discovered, and his studies were not interrupted. Subsequently, breaking away from all restraints, he roamed into Virginia to see the world, thence to the West Indies, picking up a living as best he could; after some years, the vagabond came home, was pardoned by his uncle, married, and entered soon upon his distinguished public career. He was an able speaker; loved power over men, and the arts by which it is gained; and though his own contact with books must have been casual and irregular, he greatly enjoyed literature and the society of literary men. There remains a letter of his to his London bookseller, for the year 1739, containing a list of books which he desired, and indicating that, even at the age of sixty-eight, his mind was reaching out toward new studies, as well as old ones: law books, political treatises, theological writings, histories, a Hebrew grammar, an Arabic grammar, and an edition of John Milton.

He wrote nothing that he thought of as literature; but the brightness and vigor of his mind are shown in his correspondence, and in his state-papers. He appears to have been not incapable even of sportive rhymes on occasion. For instance, in 1709, in sending to the governor of New York, Lord Lovelace, a memorial for the board of trade, he added a private address on his own account, beginning with these lines:

> As kings at their meals sit aione at a table,
> Not deigning to eat with the lords of the rabble,
> So that great Lewis Morris presents an address
> By himself, all alone, not one else of the mess.

In 1735, he went to England, to make complaint to the parliament and ministry respecting the conduct of William Cosby, at that time governor of New York, under royal appointment; and his letters to friends at home are good examples of the sprightliness of his mind. The visit of this American politician to the metropolis, appears to have been the means of a rough disenchantment, robbing him of many beautiful provincial illusions respecting the tender and paternal care with which English statesmen were supposed to deal with Americans and their affairs: "You have very imperfect notions of the world on this side of the water—I mean that world with which I have to do. They are unconcerned at the sufferings of the people in America. . . . It may be you will be surprised to hear that the most nefarious crime a governor can commit is not, by some, counted so bad, as the crime of complaining of it; the last is an arraigning of the ministry that advised the sending of him." "We talk in America of applications to parliaments. Alas! my friend, parliaments are parliaments everywhere; here, as well as with us, though more numerous. We admire the heavenly bodies which glitter at a distance; but should we be removed into Jupiter or Saturn, perhaps we should find it composed of as dark materials as our own earth. . . . We have a parliament and ministry, some of whom, I am apt to believe, know that there are plantations and governors—but not quite so well as we do. Like the frogs in the fable, the mad pranks of a plantation governor is sport to them, though death to us; and [they] seem less concerned in our contests than we are at those between crows and kingbirds. Governors are called the king's representatives; and when by repeated instances of avarice, cruelty, and injustice, they extort complaints from the injured, in terms truly expressive of the violence committed and injuries suffered, it must be termed a flying in the face of government; the king's representative must be treated with softness and decency; the thing complained of is nothing near so criminal in them, as the manner of complaint in the injured. And who is there that is equal to the task of procuring redress? Changing the man is far from an adequate remedy, if the thing remains the same; and we had as well keep an ill, artless governor we know, as to change him for one equally ill, with more art, that we do not know. One of my neighbors used to say that he always rested better in a bed abounding with fleas after they had filled their bellies, than to change it for a new one equally full of hungry ones; the fleas having no business there but to eat. The inference is easy."

Cadwallader Colden was the son of a Presbyterian minister in Scotland, but was himself accidentally born in Ireland. He was educated at the University of Edinburgh; after studying medicine there and in London, he emigrated to America in 1710, and settled at Philadelphia for the practice of his profession. In 1718, at the friendly solicitation of General Robert Hunter, the governor of New York, he removed to that province, where he received the office of surveyor-general; became proprietor of a large estate in lands; was made a member of the king's council, and in the latter part of his life, lieutenant-governor, with frequent exercise of the duties of governor; and died, in September, 1776, aged eighty-eight, a loyalist to his king, and bitterly hated by the people whom he had served so long, but whose later movements toward revolution he had felt it his duty to resist.

Thus, the life of Cadwallader Colden, though it had a patriarchal length, had not the patriarchal quietude; it was a life of manifold outward occupation, and latterly of political turmoil and rancor; and yet, so valiant and craving was his spirit, that he found time, during all those busy lustrums of his, to be not only a cultivator of various learning, but one of the leaders of mankind in its cultivation. A monument of his industry and of his versatility, remains to us in the vast mass of his writings, published and unpublished, which deal, acutely and philosophically, with almost every great topic of human interest—divinity, ethics, metaphysics, politics, mathematics, history, geology, botany, optics, zoology, medicine, agriculture, and even certain improvements in the mechanic arts, as stereotypy.

The one production of his that most nearly approaches a purely literary effort, is *The History of the Five Indian Nations*. Of this work, the first part, bringing the narrative down to 1688, was originally published in New York, in 1727; and the second part, continuing the narrative to the peace of Ryswick, 1697, was published in London, in 1747. The book is principally a sketch of five powerful allied Indian tribes then residing in the northern part of the province of New York—their forms of government, their wars with hostile tribes, their conflicts and treaties with Frenchmen, Dutchmen, and Englishmen; upon the whole, a very slender, not altogether accurate, and not in the least interesting account of sundry parcels of savages, of their steady employment in scalping and in getting scalped, mitigated by occasional interludes of palaver with one another and with white men. Though the author writes with ease, and generally with verbal correctness, it is impossible for him to redeem his book from the curse of being a history of what deserves no history. A single episode, giving the exploits of the Algonquin chief, Piscaret, has some dramatic vividness, even though also the flavor of palpable myth; while the best piece of writing in the book, is its dedication to William Burnet, the governor of New York—particularly, the passage wherein the author celebrates the austere virtues of the savages whose history he records: "The Five Nations are a poor, barbarous people, under the darkest ignorance; and yet a bright and noble genius shines through these black clouds. None of the greatest Roman heroes have discovered a greater love to their country, or a greater contempt of death, than these barbarians have done, when life and liberty came in competition. Indeed, I think our Indians have outdone the Romans in this particular; for some of the greatest Romans have murdered themselves, to avoid shame or torments; whereas our Indians have refused to die, meanly, with the least pain, when they thought their country's honor would be at stake by it, but gave their bodies willingly up to the most cruel torments of their enemies, to show that the Five Nations consisted of men whose courage and resolution could not be shaken."

The hope that these vivacious sentences awaken in us, of some broad and fine human interest connected with the history of the author's nude patriots and stoics, is not fulfilled.

In the year 1722, there was published in London a book respecting America, which deserved the deep attention of English and American statesmen at that time, and which, on one account, is still worthy of remembrance by us. It bore this formidable title: *A Description of the English Province of Carolana, by the Spaniards called Florida, and by the French La Louisiane; as also the great and famous river, Meschacebe or Mississippi, the five vast navigable lakes of fresh-water, and the parts adjacent; together with an account of the commodities, of the growth and production of the said province; and a preface containing some considerations on the consequences of the French making settlements there.*

The author was Daniel Coxe, a man of wealth, and of high social and political influence in New Jersey, who had inherited from his father a claim to the vast territory described in his book. It is the preface of the book, however, that is now of special interest to us; for in that preface, the author discussed, at great length and with great ability, the condition and the perils of the English colonies in America, the legal right of the English to the interior of the continent, and especially, the strategy to be pursued by enlightened statesmanship in realizing that right in opposition to the competing claims of the Spanish and the French. The chief element in the strategy proposed by him, is described in one word—union. Thus, in 1722, Daniel Coxe publicly explained and advocated a plan of union among the American colonies—the details of which closely resemble those brought forward by Franklin, thirty-two years afterward, at the famous congress of Albany: "That all the colonies . . . be united under a legal, regular, and firm establishment; over which . . . a lieutenant or supreme governor may be . . . appointed to preside on the spot, to whom the governors of each colony shall be subordinate"; that the council or assembly of each province elect annually two delegates "to a great council or general convention of the estates of the colonies"; that the latter "consult and advise for the good of the whole." "A coalition or union of this nature," adds Daniel Coxe, in his earnest argument for it, "tempered with and grounded on prudence, moderation, and justice, and a generous encouragement given to the labor, industry, and good management of all sorts and conditions of persons, . . . will, in all probability, lay a sure and lasting foundation of dominion, strength, and trade, sufficient not only to secure and promote the prosperity of the plantations, but to revive and greatly increase the late flourishing state and condition of Great Britain."

Jonathan Dickinson was born at Hatfield, Massachusetts, in 1688; and was graduated at Yale College, in 1706. In 1708, he went to Elizabethtown, New Jersey; and there, for the subsequent thirty-nine years, he lived a most energetic life, as minister, physician, educator, and author, displaying great ability in all these spheres, and acquiring a commanding influence through the whole land. He was a leader in ecclesiastical politics in the middle colonies; he was a fascinating and mighty pulpit-orator; he was the principal founder of the College of New Jersey, and its first president; in person he was of so saintly and impressive an aspect, "that the wicked seemed to tremble in his presence"; his long life was so pure, consistent, and noble, that "the memory of it is still fragrant on the spot where he lived," and the descendants "of those who knew and loved him cherish an hereditary reverence for his name and his grave."

He was a voluminous author, his chief distinction pointing toward skill in theological controversy. He had the talent of a logician; he was an intrepid debater; as a protagonist for Calvinism, he stood in reputation among American theologians of his time, next to Jonathan Edwards; and a great Scottish divine testified that even "the British Isles had produced no such writers on divinity in the eighteenth century," as were these two men—both born on the confines of the New England forests, and both bred at Yale College.

Perhaps the most interesting specimen of his literary and dialectical gifts, is his *Familiar Letters to a Gentleman, upon a Variety of seasonable and important Subjects in Religion*; in which are these sentences, portraying the logical difficulties to be assumed by any one who shall reject the historical verity of the New Testament: "If this history be not true, then all the known laws of nature were changed; all the motives and incentives to human actions, that ever had obtained in the world, have been entirely inverted; the wickedest men in the world have taken the greatest pains and endured the greatest hardship and misery, to invent, practise, and propagate the most holy religion that ever was; and not only the apostles and first preachers of the gospel, but whole nations of men and all sorts of men, Christian, Jew, and pagan, were—nobody can imagine how or why—confederated to propagate a known cheat, against their own honor, interest, and safety; and multitudes of men, without any prospect of advantage, here or hereafter, were brought most constantly and tenaciously to profess what they knew to be false, to exchange all the comforts and pleasures of life for shame and contempt, for banishments, scourgings, imprisonments, and death; in a word, voluntarily to expose themselves to be hated both of God and man, and that without any known motive whatsoever."

In the year 1747, was published in New York a little book entitled *Philosophic Solitude; or, The Choice of a Rural Life*—a poem of nearly seven hundred lines, announcing itself as the production of "a gentleman educated at Yale College." This gentleman proved to be William Livingston, then twenty-four years old, just beginning the practice of the law in New York, and destined to a long and illustrious career as a statesman in the era of the Revolution. During his whole life, he was absorbed in stormy and agitating public movements; yet he found time to retain an uncommon intimacy with the best literature, and to exercise in many ways his own remarkable aptitude for literary work. This poem is obviously the effort of a rhyming apprentice, still in bondage to the methods of his master, Alexander Pope; yet he catches the knack of his master with a cleverness proving the possibility of original work, on his own account, by and by. It illustrates, likewise, a trait of human nature, that this young lawyer and politician, having given himself to a practical career in the thick of the world's affairs, and one made tumultuous by his own aggressive spirit, should have begun it by depicting, in enthusiastic verse, his preference for a life of absolute retirement and serene meditation:

> Let ardent heroes seek renown in arms,
> Pant after fame, and rush to war's alarms;
> To shining palaces, let fools resort,
> And dunces cringe to be esteemed at court:
> Mine be the pleasures of a rural life,
> From noise remote, and ignorant of strife;
> Far from the painted belle, the white-gloved beau,
> The lawless masquerade and midnight show;
> From ladies, lapdogs, courtiers, garters, stars,
> Fops, fiddlers, tyrants, emperors, and czars.

He then pictures for us the situation of the home in the country, in which he would spend his tranquil life—its furniture, its surroundings; he sings over again his love of solitude; he mentions the sort of friends whom he would have within call; he portrays the frame of devotion and calm contemplation which should abide with him. His hermitage should be far from

> Prime-ministers, and sycophantic knaves,
> Illustrious villains, and illustrious slaves.

There he would

> live retired, contented, and serene,
> Forgot, unknown, unenvied, and unseen.

He would have books for his most intimate friends; he would have Virgil as prince of the classic bards; he would be surrounded by Milton, Pope, Dryden, and "the gentle Watts"; also, by Locke, Raleigh, Denham; among philosophers, he would give the place of honor to Newton. Moreover, he would alleviate his solitude by the presence of a wife. This being should be none of those "ideal goddesses" who

> to church repair,
> Peep through the fan, and mutter o'er a prayer;
> .   .   .   .
> Or, deeply studied in coquettish rules,
> Aim wily glances at unthinking fools.

She is to be not an ideal goddess, but a literal one, an absolutely faultless being, who having accepted his addresses becomes he says,

> Imparadised within my eager arms.

He then reaches the climax of his poem by depicting the crowning experience of his "philosophic solitude"—a solitude the peculiar rigors of which would not seem to have required a vast exertion of philosophy to endure:

> With her I'd spend the pleasurable day,
> While fleeting minutes gayly danced away:
> .   .   .   .

I'd reign the happy monarch of her charms;
Oft in her panting bosom would I lay,
And, in dissolving raptures, melt away;
Then lulled by nightingales to balmy rest,
My blooming fair should slumber at my breast.

The voluptuous languors of this poem, report a quality in the author that did not control him; and henceforward, through nearly half a century, his real life was a battle for stern and great ideas. He was of Scottish ancestry; and if he had within him the romantic intensity of his race, he had likewise its intellectual ruggedness, its iron grasp of conviction, its unsubmissiveness, its onrushing and most fervid pleasure in strife, its nerve of invincible endurance—a double strain sent down to him from the old Scottish ballad-makers and from the old Scottish covenanters. The practice of his profession did not consume his energy; he was felt, as a pamphleteer and as a journalist, in all the topics that came up for debate in the colony in those years, especially those connected with the denominational control of King's College, with military operations, and with the establishment of an American Episcopate. He was a resolute member of the Reformed Dutch Church. By his newspaper articles against the efforts of the Episcopalians to obtain the mastery of King's College, he had brought upon himself the charges of atheism, deism, and Presbyterianism; and with reference to these imputations, he retorted upon his opponents with his usual wit and vigor, in a travesty on the Thirty-nine Articles: "1. I believe the Scriptures of the Old and New Testament, without any foreign comments or human explanations but my own; for which I should, doubtless, be honored with martyrdom, did I not live in a government which restrains that fiery zeal which would reduce a man's body to ashes, for the illumination of his understanding. . . . 5. I believe that the word orthodox is a hard, equivocal, priestly term that has caused the effusion of more blood than all the Roman emperors put together. . . . 7. I believe that to defend the Christian religion is one thing, and to knock a man on the head for being of a different opinion is another thing. . . . 11. I believe that he who feareth God and worketh righteousness, will be accepted of Him, even though he refuse to worship any man or order of men into the bargain. . . . 13. I believe that riches, ornaments, and ceremonies were assumed by churches for the same reason that garments were invented by our first parents. . . . 15. I believe that a man may be a good Christian, though he be of no sect in Christendom. . . . 17. I believe that our faith, like our stomachs, may be overcharged, especially if we are prohibited to chew what we are commanded to swallow. . . . 38. I believe that the virulence of some of the clergy against my speculations, proceeds not from their affection to Christianity, which is founded on too firm a basis to be shaken by the freest inquiry, and the divine authority of which I sincerely believe,—without receiving a farthing for saying so; but from an apprehension of bringing into contempt their ridiculous claims and unreasonable pretensions, which may justly tremble at the slightest scrutiny, and which I believe I shall more and more put into a panic, in defiance of both press and pulpit."

His most serious effort as a prose writer, during this period of our literary history, was *A Review of the Military Operations in North America*, from 1753 to 1756. This work is in the form of a letter addressed to a nobleman, and was first published, without the author's name, in London, in the year 1756. Its historical value is considerable—principally, as embalming the fury of partisanship that raged, at that time, between the great families of the colony of New York, and that drew within its folds the reputations of Sir William Johnson on the one hand, and of Governor William Shirley on the other. As a literary work, the book rises far above the mob of political pamphlets. Though somewhat lacking in concentration, it is written with much elegance; and it is especially remarkable for its elaborate portraits of the great men of the day. The painter of these portraits makes no pretence of impartiality, but tints his canvas at will with the frankness of his love or of his hate.

It is not disagreeable to be reminded, once more, of the ten-

der and gallant vein that streaked the nature of this robust
political combatant; and to find that, even amid the rancors of
his strenuous career, there were moods in which he could dash
off verses so graceful and so sprightly as these:

> Soon as I saw Eliza's blooming charms,
> I longed to clasp the fair one in my arms.
> Her every feature proved a pointed dart
> That pierced with pleasing pain my wounded heart;
> And yet, this beauty—it transcends belief—
> This blooming beauty is an arrant thief.
> Attend: her numerous thefts I will rehearse
> In honest narrative and faithful verse.
>
> From the bright splendor of the noonday sky,
> She stole the sparkling lustre of her eye.
> Her cheeks, though lovely red, still more to adorn,
> She filched the blushes of the orient morn.
> To embalm her lips, she robbed the honey-dew;
> To increase their bloom, the rose-bud of its hue.
> .   .   .   .
> Her voice, enchanting to the dullest ears,
> She pillaged from the music of the spheres;
> To make her neck still lovelier to the sight,
> She robbed the ermine of its spotless white;
> From Virgil's Juno, Jove's fictitious mate,
> She stole the queen-like and majestic gait.
> Of all her charms, she robbed the Cyprian queen,
> And, still insatiate, stripped the Graces of their mien.
>
> But now, to perfect an harmonious whole,
> With those internal charms that can't be stole,
> Kind Heaven, without her thieving, took delight
> To grant supernal grace, and inward light:
> To charms angelic, it vouchsafed to impart
> Angelic virtues, and an angel heart.
> Thus fair in form, embellished thus in mind,
> All beauteous outward, inward all refined,
> What could induce Eliza still to steal,
> And make poor plundered me her theft to feel?
> For, last, she stole (if with ill-purposed art
> I'll ne'er forgive the theft) she stole—my heart;
> Yes, yes, I will, if she will but incline
> To give me half of hers, for all the whole of mine.

William Smith was the son of an eminent lawyer of New York, where he was born in 1728. He was graduated at Yale College, in 1745. Devoting himself to the professions of law and of politics, he speedily rose to distinction in both. During the Revolutionary War, he was a loyalist; in 1783, he went to England, and three years later, was rewarded for his fidelity to the crown, by the appointment of chief-justice of Canada. In Canada, he died in 1793.

While still a very young man, he gave great attention to the legal and political records of his native province,—an experience that led him to write a *History of New York, from the First Discovery to the Year 1732*. This work, which was first published in London, in 1757, is a strong and clear piece of work, with the tone of a scholar and a gentleman, somewhat dashed by provincialism. Himself a New York politician, and the son of one, it was not easy for him, in dealing with the story of New York politics, wholly to suppress his partisan prejudices; and his narrative, as he admitted, "deserves not the name of a history." It is an able and sturdy historical pamphlet, aggravated by vast public documents quoted in bulk. Although he believed that in his book the laws of truth had not been infringed, either "by positive assertions, oblique, insidious hints, wilful suppressions, or corrupt misrepresentations," and that in his writing of it he had chosen "rather to be honest and dull than agreeable and false," he was charged by a contemporary, Cadwallader Colden, with having "wilfully misrepresented" some things; while in our own time, the ablest of the historians of New York, John Romeyn Brodhead, has declared that, in several instances, William Smith gave utterance to "fabulous" statements.

In his book, it is interesting to note the tokens of American sensitiveness, even in that age, to the infinite and serene ignorance prevalent among the people of England concerning their own plantations in America: "The main body of the people conceive of these plantations under the idea of wild, boundless, inhospitable, uncultivated deserts; and hence, the punishment of transportation hither, in the judgment of most, is thought

not much less severe than an infamous death." His portraits of
the long line of royal governors who had in succession preyed
upon the province, are drawn with the vivacity of genuine feeling; in the ardor of his filial pride and affection, he has painted
a glowing picture of the learning and eloquence of his own
father; and his sketches of society in New York in his time, particularly of the steady preference there of the pursuits of wealth
to those of mere knowledge, have a courageous authenticity,
perhaps not altogether obsolete even yet.

In the year 1765, was published *The History of the Colony of
Nova Caesarea, or New Jersey;* the author being Samuel Smith,
an honest, solid Quaker, a native of the region that he wrote
about, himself then forty-five years old. His book is a dry,
ponderous performance, a compilation of dull documents and
dull facts; the whole written, doubtless, with great patience,
and only to be read by an abundant exercise of the same
virtue.

A sagacious English student of American history has said
that "the most remarkable of the American colonies after the
New England group, is Pennsylvania." In spite of all outward
differences, of all mutual dislikes, there was an inward kinship
between the Quakers of Pennsylvania and the Puritans of New
England. "I came for the Lord's sake," said William Penn, in
1682. "Our business here in this new land," said one of the first
Pennsylvanians, "is not so much to build houses, and establish
factories, and promote trade and manufactures that may enrich
ourselves, . . . as to erect temples of holiness and righteousness,
which God may delight in; to lay such lasting foundations of
temperance and virtue, as may support the superstructures of
our future happiness, both in this and the other world."

The society that these men founded in Pennsylvania was, of
course, serious, laborious, economic, monotonous, prim, especially pained by the pleasures of existence. Thomas Chalkley
abhorred music as a thing "of evil consequence"; he denounced
cards "as engines of Satan"; and of dancing he said, that "as

many paces or steps as the man or woman takes in the dance, so many paces or steps they take toward hell."

On the other hand, William Penn was a man of great intellectual foresight, and swayed by a passion to be both just and humane; and he began by inoculating his young commonwealth with the idea of civic generosity: "We have, with reverence to God and good conscience to men, to the best of our skill contrived and composed the frame of this government to the great end of all government,—to support power in reverence with the people, and to secure the people from the abuse of power." "Whoever is right," said he, "the persecutor must be wrong." From the beginning, a part of the fundamental law of Pennsylvania was the law of liberty for the souls of men. Through every turnpike in that province, ideas travelled toll-free.

But were there, in that province, any ideas inclined to travel? The founder of Quakerism, being himself able to get all necessary wisdom by the facility of an inward flash, quite naturally despised those who had to get it by the slow process of study; he despised books, also, and schools; and he declared that "God stood in no need of human learning." William Penn, however, and many of his associates in the settlement of Pennsylvania, had never yielded to that barbaric mood of their religious teacher; and being themselves men of considerable learning, they at once devised means for the spread of learning among others. "Before the pines had been cleared from the ground," they "began to build schools and set up a printing-press." It was their noble ambition, "inter silvas quaerere verum." The first school in Pennsylvania was founded during the first year of the existence of Pennsylvania; and in the sixth year of its existence, there was in Philadelphia an academy at which even those who had no money, might get knowledge without price.

The first impulse to the production of any sort of literature in Pennsylvania was given by a desire to publish through the world the advantages of that commonwealth. Very soon, the fierceness of religious controversy set other pens to work— though with results too crude and too brutal to be called literature. Science, also and the slavery-question, and the Indian-question prompted others to write. Near the end of the first quarter of the eighteenth century—about the time that Benjamin Franklin commenced his career there—Philadelphia, though still dominated by the Quakers, had become the seat of a large population who were not Quakers; it had something of the liberal tone of a metropolis—where men of cultivation, of vivacity, of literary aptitude, had begun to realize the presence of one another, and of a common literary purpose. By the close of the colonial age, Philadelphia had grown to be the centre of a literary activity more vital and more versatile than was to be seen anywhere else upon the continent, except at Boston. In the ancient library of Philadelphia, there are "four hundred and twenty-five original books and pamphlets that were printed in that city before the Revolution."

In 1681, in the first ship that sailed from England to the great American province of William Penn, was the pleasant Quaker, Gabriel Thomas, who, for the next seventeen years, lent a strong and willing hand to the task of building up there a generous drab commonwealth; and who returning to England in 1698, probably for a brief visit, carried with him and published in London, in that year, *An Historical and Geographical Account of the Province and Country of Pennsylvania and of West New Jersey*. The book, which is written with Quaker-like frankness and simplicity, and with an undercurrent of playfulness not exactly Quaker-like, is full of information for the guidance of the poor in the old world to a good refuge in the new; and in the author's opinion, no better spot could be found anywhere along the vast American coast than that happily obtained by William Penn: "For though this country has made little noise in story or taken up but small room in maps, yet, . . . the mighty improvements . . . that have been made lately there, are well worth communicating to the public. . . . This noble spot of earth will thrive exceedingly." "The air here is very delicate, pleasant, and wholesome; the heavens serene, rarely o'ercast, bearing mighty resemblance to the better part of France." In delineating the natural characteristics of the country, he passes now and then into a semi-facetious intensity, into a droll largeness of statement, from which even the demureness of his sect did not save him, and which thus early show themselves as traits of American humor; saying, for example, that the bullfrog in Pennsylvania "makes a roaring noise hardly to be distinguished from that well known of the beast from whom it takes its name." His pictures of the new social conditions formed there, have elements of uncommon attractiveness; as when he remarks: "Of lawyers and physicians I shall say nothing, because this country is very peaceable and healthy. Long may it so continue, and never have occasion for the tongue of the one nor the pen of the other, both equally destructive of men's estates and lives."

Once again, also, we catch in this book the tender American note of sympathy with men and women in Europe who have a hard lot there; a cheery voice from this side of the Atlantic sounding out clear above the countless laughter of its billows, and telling all who need a new chance in life that at last they can have it: "Reader, what I have here written is not a fiction, flam, whim, or any sinister design, either to impose upon the ignorant or credulous, or to curry favor with the rich and mighty; but in mere pity and pure compassion to the numbers of poor laboring men, women, and children in England—half-starved visible in their meagre looks—that are continually wandering up and down, looking for employment without finding any, who here need not lie idle a moment, nor want due encouragement or reward for their work, much less vagabond or drone it about. Here are no beggars to be seen, . . . nor, indeed, have any here the least occasion or temptation to take up that scandalous lazy life."

A desire to bear public testimony to the delights and benefits of life in Pennsylvania, took possession of several others among its first inhabitants; and unfortunately, in some cases, this testimony sought utterance in verse. Thus, Richard Frame, probably a Quaker, published at Philadelphia, in 1692, *A Short Description of Pennsylvania; or, A relation what things are known, enjoyed, and like to be discovered in the said province.* So, also, John Holme, who came to Pennsylvania in 1686, and died there about the year 1701, wrote *A True Relation of the Flourishing State of Pennsylvania.* Both of these works are very slight as specimens of descriptive literature; and as examples of verse, they scarcely rise to the puerile—they approach the idiotic.

A piece of narration and description, happily in honest prose, and having the merit of being uncommonly interesting, is *God's Protecting Providence Man's surest Help and Defence in Times of greatest Difficulty and most eminent Danger,* by Jonathan Dickenson, an English Quaker of property and education, who, after some sojourn in Jamaica, sailed thence, in 1696, for Pennsylvania, having with him his wife, an infant child, and several negro servants. On the voyage, they were cast away on the coast of Florida, and after suffering almost incredible hardships, not only "from the devouring waves of the sea" but "also from the cruel, devouring jaws of the inhumane cannibals of Florida," they made their way to Philadelphia. Of this frightful and most afflictive experience, Dickenson wrote an account, under the title already given—telling his story in a modest, straight-forward, manly way, like a hero and a Christian. He remained in Pennsylvania the rest of his life, became chief-justice of the province, and died there in 1722.

In 1699, when William Penn was on the point of sailing for the second time to his province, he became deeply interested in a young Irishman of Scottish descent, named James Logan, who, though highly educated, and with strong aptitudes for literary and scientific pursuits, had recently embarked in trade at Bristol. Penn saw in this young man one whom he could safely lean upon, and whom he greatly needed; and after urgent solicitation, Logan gave up his own plans, and putting his fate into Penn's keeping, went with him to America. There he remained all the rest of his days; and there he died in 1751, at the age of seventy-seven.

That second visit of William Penn to Pennsylvania proved, also, to be his last; and when, in 1701, he went on board the ship that was to carry him away from the province forever, he wrote these words to the man whom he had commissioned to stand there in his place: "I have left thee in an uncommon trust, with a singular dependence on thy justice and care, which I expect thou wilt faithfully employ in advancing my honest interests. . . . For thy own services I shall allow thee what is just and reasonable. . . . Serve me faithfully as thou expects a blessing from God, or my favor, and I shall support thee to my utmost, as thy true friend." Thenceforward, James Logan's letters to his patron and to his patron's family, are the letters of a man who deserved such trust; for he served them with flawless fidelity.

His office proved to be a most laborious and vexatious one. Year by year his troubles as Penn's agent thickened. In 1704, he wrote to his master: "I wish thou could be here thyself, for I cannot bear up under all these hardships; they break my rest, and I doubt will sink me at last. . . . I have been so true to thee, that I am not just to myself; and had I now a family, it would appear that there has scarce been a greater knave in America to another's affairs, than I have been to my own."

But though James Logan was through all his life thus faithful to the proprietors of Pennsylvania, he was never unfaithful to the people of Pennsylvania. He held in succession the leading offices in the province; from 1736 to 1738, as president of the council, he was really governor; and while, at times, he drew upon himself great unpopularity, he served the people better than they knew, in all their highest interests, in peace and even in war.

His long life and his great influence went especially for the public enlightenment; and in all possible ways he helped to build up good literature in Pennsylvania. His own intellectual accomplishments were extraordinary. Almost from childhood he had been familiar with the principal languages, ancient and modern; at the age of sixteen he began that enthusiastic study of the higher mathematics which he prosecuted all his life; and there seemed to be no topic in science or literature that did not have his attention. He carried on an extensive correspondence with the most illustrious scholars in Europe and America; and in these letters as well as in the mass of private papers that he left behind him, he discussed, with originality and precision, the leading subjects that then engaged the minds of learned men. "Sometimes Hebrew or Arabic characters and algebraic formulas roughen the pages of his letter-books. Sometimes his letters convey a lively Greek ode to a learned friend; and often they are written in the Latin tongue."

The larger part of his writings still remain unprinted; but during his lifetime were published, besides several Latin treatises by him upon scientific subjects, his *Translation of Cato's Distichs into English Verse,* and his more celebrated translation of *M. T. Cicero's Cato Major; or, Discourse on Old Age*— works that not only denoted his own elegant literary taste, but also tended to develop such taste in others. His correspondence with the Penn family, from 1700 to 1750, has been recently made public; and though much of it is taken up with uninteresting details respecting business and politics, it is also a great storehouse of information respecting men and manners in Pennsylvania during that period. Everywhere this correspondence reveals the carefulness and the intellectual breadth of James Logan; and occasionally one finds in it a passage of general discussion, in which the clear brain and the noble heart of the writer utter themselves in language of real beauty and force.

In 1751, the very year in which James Logan died, there came to America another man of the same Scottish stock, and of the same Scottish vigor for various intellectual work, who, in the middle colonies, and especially in Pennsylvania, was to carry forward, during the second half of the eighteenth century, many of the wholesome scientific and literary influences with which the life of James Logan had been identified, during the first half of that century. This man was William Smith, born at Aberdeen about 1726, and graduated at its university in 1747. In New York, where he spent the first two years after his arrival in America, he found the leading men greatly occupied with the project of founding a college there; and in the discussion of this subject he skilfully participated by publishing *A General Idea of the College of Mirania,* a sort of educational romance, written in graceful style, and unfolding with much vigor the author's notions of what a college in America should be.

A copy of the book soon fell under the eye of Benjamin Franklin, who was, at that time, also deeply engaged in plans for a college at Philadelphia; and was even then looking about for some one competent to take charge of it. Not long afterward, the ambitious young Scotchman was invited to Philadelphia for that purpose. He immediately went to England for holy orders; and returning to Philadelphia in 1754, he entered upon his duties at the head of the institution which, in the following year, took the name of a college. From that time onward until his death in 1803, William Smith, as educator, politician, clergyman, and man of letters, was a tireless, facile, and powerful representative in Philadelphia of the higher intellectual interests of society. Under his care the little college grew apace; and by his own example as an eloquent writer, by his enthusiasm for good literature, and by his quick and genial recognition of literary merit in the young men who were growing up around him, he did a great work for the literary development of his adopted country. . . .

Probably the most brilliant pulpit-orator produced in the colonial time, south of New England, was Samuel Davies, born in Newcastle County, Delaware, in 1723. His classical education was obtained chiefly at the famous school founded by Samuel Blair, at Fogg's Manor, in Chester County; and there, also, he pursued the study of theology. He began to preach in 1746; and in the following year, he visited Virginia, where his earnestness, his imaginative rhetoric, and his impassioned elocution won for him a sudden and extensive popularity. In 1748, he accepted an invitation to settle in that colony; and during the subsequent five years, what before was popularity deepened into fame and a most benign influence, and filled the whole country. In 1753, in the company of Gilbert Tennent, he went to England to solicit aid for the College of New Jersey. He remained there about eleven months, having great success in his mission, and winning for himself high reputation as an orator. On his return, he resumed his labors in Virginia. In 1759, he succeeded Jonathan Edwards as president of the College of New Jersey; and upon him there fell the fate of speedy death, which, for a time, seemed to be the inevitable portion of those who should accept that office. He died in 1761.

During his life, many of his sermons were published, and were widely diffused. One of them, preached in Virginia, in 1755, shortly after the defeat of General Braddock, is remarkable for its prophetic allusion to the destiny of George Washington: "I may point out to the public that heroic youth, Colonel Washington, whom I cannot but hope Providence has hitherto preserved in so signal a manner, for some important service to his country." Not long after his death, a collection of his sermons was published in three large volumes; and these have been repeatedly printed since that time.

A glance at any page of these discourses reveals the fact that the author of them was, above all other things, an orator. He prepared his sermons with the utmost care; for he "always thought it to be a most awful thing to go into the pulpit and there speak nonsense in the name of God." What he prepared, however, was meant for the ear rather than for the eye. He had all the physical qualifications for oratory—voice, gesture, temperament; and in appearance he was so commanding that "he looked like the ambassador of some great king." As uttered by himself, these discourses must have been vivid and thrilling orations; but they suffer from the revelations of type. The thought is often loose; the imagery is sometimes confused; the sentences are frequently swollen into verbosity.

As we read, however, some of his eloquent sentences—for example, these from his sermon on "The General Resurrection"—we may easily imagine ourselves in the presence of the orator himself, and borne away beyond criticism, on the tide of his heroic faith and his passionate declamation: "They shall come forth. Now methinks I see, I hear, the earth heaving, charnel-houses rattling, tombs bursting, graves opening. Now the nations under ground begin to stir. There is a noise and a shaking among the dry bones. The dust is all alive, and in motion, and the globe breaks and trembles, as with an earthquake, while this vast army is working its way through and bursting into life. The ruins of human bodies are scattered far and wide, and have passed through many and surprising transformations. A limb in one country, and another in another; here the head and there the trunk, and the ocean rolling between. Multitudes have sunk in a watery grave, been swallowed up by the monsters of the deep, and transformed into a part of their flesh. Multitudes have been eaten by beasts and birds of prey, and incorporated with them; and some have been devoured by their fellow-men in the rage of desperate hunger, or of unnatural cannibal appetite, and digested into a part of them. Multitudes have mouldered into dust, and this dust has been blown about by winds, and washed away with water, or it has petrified into stone, or been burnt into brick to form dwellings for their posterity; or it has grown up in grain, trees, plants, and other vegetables, which are the support of man and beast, and are transformed into their flesh and blood. But through all these various transformations and changes, not a particle that was essential to one human body has been lost, or incorporated with another human body, so as to become an essential part of it. . . . The omniscient God knows how to collect, distinguish, and compound all those scattered and mingled seeds of our mortal bodies. And now, at the sound of the trumpet, they shall all be collected, wherever they are scattered; all properly sorted and united, however they were confused; atom to its fellow-atom, bone to its fellow bone. Now methinks you may see the air darkened with fragments of bodies flying from country to country to meet and join their proper parts. . . . Then, my brethren, your dust and mine shall be reanimated and organized. . . . And what a vast improvement will the frail nature of man then receive? Our bodies will then be substantially the same; but how different in qualities, in strength, in agility, in capacities for pleasure or pain, in beauty or deformity, in glory or terror, according to the moral character of the person to whom they belong! . . . The bodies of the saints will be formed glorious, incorruptible, without the seeds of sickness and death. . . . Then will the body be able to bear up under the exceeding great and eternal weight of glory; it will no longer be a clog or an incumbrance to the soul, but a proper instrument and assistant in all the exalted services and enjoyments of the heavenly state. The bodies of the wicked will also be improved, but their improvements will all be terrible and vindictive. Their capacities will be thoroughly enlarged, but then it will be that they may be made capable of greater misery; they will be strengthened, but it will be that they may bear the heavier load of torment. Their sensations will be more quick and strong, but it will be that they may feel the more exquisite pain. They will be raised immortal that they may not be consumed by everlasting fire, or escape punishment by dissolution or annihilation. In short, their augmented strength, their enlarged capacities, and their immortality, will be their eternal curse; and they would willingly exchange them for the fleeting duration of a fading flower, or the faint sensations of an infant. The only power they would rejoice in is that of self-annihilation."

Upon the fascinating pages of Franklin's *Autobiography*, one meets several times the name of an ingenious and philosophical glazier of Philadelphia, named Thomas Godfrey.

It was this glazier and his family, who, upon Franklin's return
to Philadelphia after his first pilgrimage to London, shared
with the economical young printer the space and the expense of
his hired house "near the market"; it was the wife of this
glazier, who, with much feminine diplomacy, tried to make a
match between Franklin and one of her own relations, and was
so offended at Franklin's intractableness in the affair, that she
and her family removed from his house; again, it was the glazier
himself who, in 1744, was enrolled as "a mathematician" among
the nine original members of the American Philosophical
Society.

Among the children of this astute and worthy man, was a
son, likewise named Thomas, who left such proofs of poetic
genius, that his name will always have a prominent place in
the story of our colonial literature. The expression of his genius,
however, was inadequate; for he had three misfortunes—
stinted education, poverty, an early death. He was born at
Philadelphia, in 1736. Being left an orphan at the age of thirteen, he was soon taken from school and apprenticed to a watch-
maker—a trade that he did not like. His heart was in music,
and especially in poetry; and to these he gave whatever time he
could purloin from the business that was to him a servitude.
In 1758, having reached his majority, he became a lieutenant
in the Pennsylvania militia and served through the campaign
that resulted that year in the capture by the English of Fort
Duquesne. In 1759, he went to North Carolina, and remained
there under engagement as a factor for three years. At the end
of that time, being still unsettled, he made journeys to Philadelphia and to New Providence; then returned to North Carolina; and there, on the third of August, 1763, he suddenly died.
Two years after his death, his writings, collected and edited
by another young poet, Nathaniel Evans, were published at
Philadelphia under this title: *Juvenile Poems on Various Subjects; with the Prince of Parthia, a Tragedy.*

The poems called "juvenile," doubtless deserve that term.
They have no original manner or matter; they are merely ten-

tative and preparatory; those of them that failed to receive correction from his scholarly friends, reveal, in their imperfect metre, false accent, and false syntax, his own lack of scholarship. The topics are the usual ones in the case of poetic fledglings: "A Cure for Love"; "Ode on Friendship"; "A Dithyrambic on Wine." There are also some pastorals, and as many as seven or eight love-songs; and besides these, an ambitious and not discreditable poem in pentameter couplets, entitled "The Court of Fancy," obviously suggested by Chaucer and Pope.

These alone would not have gained for Thomas Godfrey any remembrance. There is in the volume, however, a tragedy—the first drama, probably, ever produced in this country—that has very considerable merit, and assures us of the presence in him of a constructive genius in poetry from which, very likely, great things would have come, had the stars befriended him.

This poem is in blank verse. It is an oriental story of love and lust, of despotism, ambition, and jealousy. A certain king of Parthia, Artabanus, has three sons. The eldest, Arsaces, is a military hero and an idol of the populace; he is also the object of consuming envy on the part of the second son, Vardanes, and of loyal affection on the part of the third son, Gotarzes. The first scene is in the temple of the sun, and represents the joy of this youngest son, over a great victory recently gained by the Prince Arsaces in a battle with the Arabians. The second scene represents the envious brother, Vardanes, and his friend Lysias, as talking together of the rage they both felt at the success of Arsaces and at his enormous popularity. In the course of this conversation, it appears that Vardanes is in love with a beautiful Arabian captive, named Evanthe, who, however, is betrothed to Arsaces. The third scene introduces the queen, Thermusa, who reveals to an attendant her hatred of Arsaces and her desire for his destruction; likewise, her wrath at the beautiful captive, Evanthe, with whom the king himself has fallen in love. In the fourth scene, Evanthe herself appears, and talks with her maid, Cleone, of the popular enthusiasm for her beloved Arsaces, and of her own eagerness for his return:

How tedious are the hours which bring him
To my fond, panting heart! For oh, to those
Who live in expectation of the bliss,
Time slowly creeps, and every tardy minute
Seems mocking of their wishes. Say, Cleone,—
For you beheld the triumph,—midst his pomp,
Did he not seem to curse the empty show,
The pageant greatness—enemy to love—
Which held him from Evanthe? Haste to tell me,
And feed my greedy ear with the fond tale.

In this conversation, while waiting for her lover, Evanthe
tells the story of her early life and of her captivity. Her father,
a high officer at court, and a great general,

                              was reputed,
Brave, wise, and loyal; by his prince beloved.
Oft has he led his conquering troops, and forced
From frowning Victory her awful honors.

One day, while

                    bathing in Niphate's silver stream,
Attended only by one favorite maid,
As we were sporting on the wanton waves,
Swift from the wood a troop of horsemen rushed;
Rudely they seized and bore me trembling off.
In vain Edessa with her shrieks assailed
The heavens; for heaven was deaf to both our prayers.

Her captor, a cruel and lustful wretch, was afterward killed
in battle by Arsaces, and thus Evanthe fell into his gallant
keeping. In this scene, hearing that other Arabian captives had
been brought in from the recent battle, she desires to get news
of her father. The fifth scene presents the king in state, surrounded by his princes and officers, and in the act of reproach-
ing a brave Arabian captive, named Bethas, who is before him
in chains. To the king's hard words, Bethas answers:

True I am fallen, but glorious was my fall;
The day was bravely fought; we did our best;
But victory's of heaven. Look o'er yon field.
See if thou findest one Arabian back
Disfigured with dishonorable wounds!

No, here, deep on their bosoms, are engraved
The marks of honor! 'Twas through here their souls
Flew to their blissful seats. Oh! why did I
Survive the fatal day? To be this slave—
To be the gaze and sport of vulgar crowds;
Thus, like a shackled tiger, stalk my round,
And grimly lower upon the shouting herd.
Ye Gods!—

KING
Away with him to instant death.

ARSACES
Hear me, my lord. Oh, not on this bright day—
Let not this day of joy blush with his blood;
Nor count his steady loyalty a crime;
But give him life. Arsaces humbly asks it,
And may you e'er be served with honest hearts.

The king grants the request of his eldest son, and Bethas is
sent to prison. Thus closes the first Act. The second Act opens
with a scene wherein the malignant brother, Vardanes, is contriving with Lysias a plot to destroy Arsaces. Their plan is to
induce the king to believe that Arsaces is intending to slay him
and to win the throne, and that the intercession of the prince
on behalf of Bethas was for the purpose of securing the help of
that great soldier. The talk of the two conspirators is by night,
and in the gloomy prison, of which Lysias has charge; and it
proceeds in the midst of a fearful storm:

VARDANES
Heavens! what a night is this!

LYSIAS
'Tis filled with terror;
Some dread event beneath this horror lurks,
Ordained by fate's irrevocable doom,—
Perhaps Arsaces' fall; and angry heaven
Speaks it in thunder to the trembling world.

VARDANES
Terror indeed! It seems as sickening Nature
Had given her order up to general ruin:

The heavens appear as one continued flame;
Earth with her terror shakes; dim night retires,
And the red lightning gives a dreadful day,
While in the thunder's voice each sound is lost.
Fear sinks the panting heart in every bosom;
E'en the pale dead, affrighted at the horror,
As though unsafe, start from their marble jails,
And howling through the streets are seeking shelter.

.   .   .   .

LYSIAS

I saw a flash stream through the angry clouds,
And bend its course to where a stately pine
Behind the garden stood; quickly it seized
And wrapped it in a fiery fold; the trunk
Was shivered into atoms, and the branches
Off were lopped, and wildly scattered.

VARDANES

Why rage the elements? They are not cursed
Like me! Evanthe frowns not angry on them;
The wind may play upon her beauteous bosom,
Nor fear her chiding; light can bless her sense,
And in the floating mirror she beholds
Those beauties which can fetter all mankind.

.   .   .   .

LYSIAS

My lord, forget her; tear her from your breast.
Who, like the Phoenix, gazes on the sun,
And strives to soar up to the glorious blaze,
Should never leave ambition's brightest object,
To turn, and view the beauties of a flower.

VARDANES

O Lysias, chide no more, for I have done.
Yes, I'll forget the proud disdainful beauty;
Hence with vain love:—ambition, now, alone,
Shall guide my actions. Since mankind delights
To give me pain, I'll study mischief too,
And shake the earth, e'en like this raging tempest.

LYSIAS

A night like this, so dreadful to behold,—
Since my remembrance' birth, I never saw.

VARDANES

E'en such a night, dreadful as this, they say,
My teeming mother gave me to the world.
Whence by those sages who, in knowledge rich,
Can pry into futurity, and tell
What distant ages will produce of wonder,
My days were deemed to be a hurricane.

.   .   .   .

LYSIAS

Then, haste to raise the tempest.
My soul disdains this one eternal round,
Where each succeeding day is like the former.
Trust me, my noble prince, here is a heart
Steady and firm to all your purposes;
And here's a hand that knows to execute
Whate'er designs thy daring breast can form,
Nor ever shake with fear.

It is on this conspiracy, hatched by night and amid the
storm, that the plot turns. From that point, the action moves on
swiftly; the entanglements and cross-purposes and astute vil-
lanies are well presented; Bethas proves to be the father of
Evanthe; the conspirators nearly succeed; they murder the
king and are about to murder Arsaces and Bethas, and they
have Evanthe in their power, when suddenly, the youngest
brother arrives with a great army. A battle is fought in the
streets of the city. Evanthe sends Cleone to a tower to see
how the contest is going, and especially, to ascertain the fate of
Arsaces. Cleone sees a hero slain, whom she mistakes for
Arsaces, and rushes down with the dreadful news. Upon this,
Evanthe takes poison; Arsaces, who has won the battle, rushes
in, and the beautiful maiden dies in his arms. At once he kills
himself; and the kingdom passes to the loyal and loving brother,
Gotarzes.

The whole drama is powerful in diction and in action. Of
course, there are blemishes in it—faults of inexperience and of
imperfect culture: but it has many noble poetic passages; the
characters are firmly and consistently developed; there are
scenes of pathos and tragic vividness; the plot advances with

rapid movement and with culminating force. Thomas Godfrey was a true poet; and "The Prince of Parthia" is a noble beginning of dramatic literature in America.

On the tenth of May, 1762, David Hume writing from Edinburgh to Benjamin Franklin in London, uses these words: "I am very sorry that you intend soon to leave our hemisphere. America has sent us many good things—gold, silver, sugar, tobacco, indigo, and so forth; but you are the first philosopher, and indeed the first great man of letters, for whom we are beholden to her." Even eight years before that time, an eminent French scholar, in sending to Franklin, at Philadelphia, the greetings of Buffon, Fonferrière, Marty, and the other great savans of Paris, had added this testimony—"Your name is venerated in this country."

Thus, before the close of its colonial epoch, America had produced one man of science and of letters who had reached cosmopolitan fame. Yet, within the period here treated of, the renown of Franklin was that of a great scientific experimenter, rather than of a great writer. He had, indeed, very early in life acquired that mastery of style—that pure, pithy, racy, and delightful diction—which he never lost, and which makes him still one of the great exemplars of modern English prose. He had, likewise, before 1765, written many of his best productions—essays on politics, commerce, education, science, religion, and the conduct of life; multitudes of wise and witty scraps of literature for his newspaper, his almanacs, and his friends; anecdotes, apologues, maxims; above all, many of those incomparable letters for his private correspondents, to the reading of which, since then, the whole world has been admitted, greatly to its advantage in wisdom and happiness. Nevertheless, all his writings had been composed for some immediate purpose, and if printed at all, had been first printed separately, and as a general thing without the author's name. In 1751, however, a partial collection of his writings was published in London without his knowledge—the book consisting of the papers on electricity sent by him to his friend, Peter Collinson. But these papers, valuable and even celebrated as they were as contributions to science, could give to the public no idea of the various and the marvellous powers of Franklin as a contributor to literature.

At the close of our colonial epoch, Benjamin Franklin, then fifty-nine years of age, was the most illustrious of Americans, and one of the most illustrious of men; and his renown rested on permanent and benign achievements of the intellect. He was, at that time, on the verge of old age; his splendid career as a scientific discoverer and as a citizen seemed rounding to its full; yet there then lay outstretched before him—though he knew it not—still another career of just twenty-five years; in which his political services to his country and to mankind were to bring him more glory than he had gained from all he had done before; and in which he was to write one book—the story of his own life—that is still the most famous production in American literature, that has an imperishable charm for all classes of mankind, that has passed into nearly all the literary languages of the globe, and that is "one of the half-dozen most widely popular books ever printed." It will be most profitable for us to defer our minute study of the literary character of this great writer, until, in a subsequent volume of this work, we can view his literary career as a whole.

COLONIAL *New England produced Thomas Hooker and John Wise; Pennsylvania produced James Logan and Benjamin Franklin. But it remained for Maryland to produce the caustic wit of the author of* The Sot-Weed Factor *who could say of Maryland as he left her shores:*

> *May wrath divine then lay these regions waste,*
> *Where no man's faithful, and no woman's chaste.*

Out of Virginia came that polished gentleman, William Byrd of Westover, who observed that the settlers of Jamestown "like true Englishmen . . . built a church that cost no more than fifty pounds, and a tavern that cost five hundred."

Maryland, Virginia, and the South

A VEIN of genuine and powerful satire was struck in Maryland in the early part of the eighteenth century by a writer calling himself "Ebenezer Cook, Gentleman." Who he was, what he was, whence he came, whither he went— are facts that now baffle us. His book is an obvious extravaganza; and the autobiographic narrative involved in the plot, is probably only a part of its robust and jocular mirth. It is entitled, *The Sot-Weed Factor; or, A Voyage to Maryland,—a satire, in which is described the laws, government, courts, and constitutions of the country, and also the buildings, feasts, frolics, entertainments, and drunken humors of the inhabitants in that part of America.*

The author pretends to be an Englishman, under doom of emigrating to America:

> Condemned by fate to wayward curse
> Of friends unkind and empty purse,—
> Plagues worse than filled Pandora's box,—
> I took my leave of Albion's rocks;
> With heavy heart concerned, that I

Was forced my native soil to fly,
And the old world must bid good-bye.

.   .   .   .

Freighted with fools, from Plymouth sound
To Maryland our ship was bound.

After a three months' voyage, they arrived in Maryland.
Intending "to open store," he brought on shore his goods, and
at once the "sot-weed factors," or tobacco agents, swarmed
around him:

In shirts and drawers of Scotch cloth blue,
With neither stockings, hat, nor shoe,
These sot-weed planters crowd the shore,
In hue as tawny as a Moor.
Figures so strange, no god designed
To be a part of human kind;
But wanton nature, void of rest,
Moulded the brittle clay in jest.

He wonders who and what they are:

At last a fancy very odd
Took me, this was the land of Nod;
Planted at first when vagrant Cain
His brother had unjustly slain;
Then conscious of the crime he'd done,
From vengeance dire he hither run;

.   .   .   .

And ever since his time, the place
Has harbored a detested race,
Who when they could not live at home
For refuge to these worlds did roam;
In hopes by flight they might prevent
The devil and his full intent,
Obtain from triple-tree reprieve,
And heaven and hell alike deceive.

He thinks it best to give an account of his entertainment,

That strangers well may be aware on
What homely diet they must fare on,
To touch that shore where no good sense is found,
But conversation's lost and manner's drowned.

He crosses the river in a canoe; after some trouble, he finds
in a cottage lodging and rough but cordial hospitality. This
leads him to describe his host, the furniture, the customs of the
house, and his own futile attempts at sleeping that night—
pestered by mosquitoes and so forth. After breakfast, he is
kindly sent on his journey, and goes to a place called Battle-
town. On his way he meets an Indian:

> No mortal creature can express
> His wild fantastic air and dress.
>
> .   .   .   .
>
> His manly shoulders, such as please
> Widows and wives, were bathed in grease
> Of cub and bear.

He proceeds on his journey, discussing with his companion
the origin of Indians; and at last he reaches a place where court
is in session, and a great crowd of strange people are assembled:

> Our horses to a tree we tied,
> And forward passed among the rout
> To choose convenient quarters out;
> But being none were to be found,
> We sat like others on the ground,
> Carousing punch in open air,
> Till crier did the court declare.
> The planting rabble being met,
> Their drunken worships being likewise set,
> Crier proclaims that noise should cease,
> And straight the lawyers broke the peace.
> Wrangling for plaintiff and defendant,
> I thought they ne'er would make an end on't
> With nonsense, stuff, and false quotations,
> With brazen lies and allegations;
> And in the splitting of the cause,
> They used such motions with their paws,
> As showed their zeal was strongly bent
> In blows to end the argument.

A mêlée ensues, in which judges, jury, clients and all take a
hand; and thus the court breaks up for that session:

> The court adjourned in usual manner,
> With battle, blood, and fractious clamor.

The poet then describes the scenes of riot, debauchery, fighting, and robbery that filled the next night; tells how he lost his shoes, his stockings, his hat, and wig, how his friend was also stripped, and how after getting supplied anew, he and his friend rode away in disgust to the home of the latter:

> There with good punch and apple-juice
> We spent our hours without abuse,
> Till midnight in her sable vest
> Persuaded gods and men to rest.

After various other experiences, he thinks it time to sell his wares:

> To this intent, with guide before,
> I tripped it to the Eastern Shore.
> While riding near a sandy bay,
> I met a Quaker, yea and nay;
> A pious, conscientious rogue,
> As e'er wore bonnet or a brogue;
> Who neither swore nor kept his word,
> But cheated in the fear of God;
> And when his debts he would not pay,
> By Light Within he ran away.

By this drab scoundrel the poet is basely swindled; and in his rage he goes to a lawyer, who was also a doctor,

> an ambidexter quack
> Who learnedly had got the knack
> Of giving glisters, making pills,
> Of filling bonds, and forging wills,
> And with a stock of impudence,
> Supplied his want of wit and sense;
> With looks demure amazing people;
> No wiser than a daw in steeple.

To this versatile gentleman the poet offers a great fee:

> And of my money was so lavish,
> That he'd have poisoned half the parish,

And hanged his father on a tree,
For such another tempting fee.

In the litigation which followed, the author is cheated by his lawyer even worse than he had been by the Quaker; and at last, mad with rage, he hurries away from the country, leaving this curse upon it as his legacy:

May cannibals, transported over sea,
Prey on these shores as they have done on me;
May never merchant's trading sails explore
This cruel, this inhospitable shore;
But left abandoned by the world to starve,
May they sustain the fate they well deserve.
May they turn savage; or, as Indians wild,
From trade, converse, and happiness exiled,
Recreant to heaven, may they adore the sun,
And into pagan superstitions run,
For vengeance ripe;
May wrath divine then lay these regions waste,
Where no man's faithful, and no woman's chaste.

This work was published in London, a quarto of twenty-one pages, in 1708. Twenty-two years afterward, a writer, professing to be the same rough satirist, published at Annapolis another poem, entitled *Sot-Weed Redivivus; or, The Planter's Looking-Glass, in burlesque verse, calculated for the meridian of Maryland*—a quarto of twenty-eight pages. The first poem has, indeed, an abundance of filth and scurrility, but it has wit besides; the second poem lacks only the wit.

Probably no other man in the colonial time did so much for the intellectual life of Virginia, as did the sturdy and faithful clergyman, James Blair, who came into the colony in 1685, and who died there in 1743, having been a missionary of the Church of England fifty-eight years, the commissary of the Bishop of London fifty-four years, the president of the College of William and Mary fifty years, and a member of the king's council fifty years.

Born in Scotland in 1656, and graduated at the University

of Edinburgh in 1673, he was rector of Cranston until the year
1682, when he went into England in the hope of finding preferment there; but was induced by the Bishop of London to
give up his life to the service of God and of man in Virginia.

On his arrival there, he was pained not only at the disorderly
and ineffective condition of the church, but at the almost universal neglect of education. Henceforward, the story of his
life is a story of pure and tireless labors for the rectification of
both these evils. He was a man of great simplicity and force of
character, very positive, very persistent, with an abundance
of Scottish shrewdness as well as of Scottish enthusiasm, actuated by a lofty, apostolic determination to be useful to his fel-
low-creatures—whether, at the moment, they liked it or not.
"He could not rest until school-teachers were in the land"; and
he did not rest until there was a college in the land, also. For the
latter, he toiled mightily, and with invincible hopefulness.
First, he induced the Virginians themselves to put their names
to subscriptions for a college, to the amount of twenty-five hundred pounds sterling. Next, having secured for the plan of a
college the approbation of the colonial assembly, he crossed
the ocean, and against all official resistance gained for it the
approbation of the monarchs of England also—in whose honor
the little college was named William and Mary. Then, returning to Virginia in 1693, with a royal charter for the college and
a royal endowment, the indefatigable man laid its foundations, and he served it with dauntless fidelity the next fifty
years. In the year 1700, the Commencement was celebrated
there with much éclat: "There was a great concourse of people. Several planters came thither in coaches, and others in
sloops from New York, Pennsylvania, and Maryland,—it being a new thing in that part of America to hear graduates perform their exercises. The Indians themselves had the curiosity,
some of them, to visit Williamsburg upon that occasion; and
the whole country rejoiced as if they had some relish of learning."

Thus, James Blair may be called the creator of the healthiest and the most extensive intellectual influence that was felt in the southern group of colonies before the Revolution. Moreover, his direct contributions to American literature were by no means despicable. He was, probably, the principal writer of a book upon the title-page of which the names of Henry Hartwell and Edward Chilton are joined with his own, and which was published in London in 1727: *The Present State of Virginia and the College.* It is expertly written; is neat and vigorous in style; abounds in facts respecting the condition of civilization in the colony at that time; and is not lacking in the courage of plain speech: "As to all the natural advantages of a country," Virginia "is one of the best, but as to the improved ones, one of the worst, of all the English plantations in America. When one considers the wholesomeness of its air, the fertility of its soil, the commodiousness of its navigable rivers and creeks, the openness of its coast all the year long, the conveniency of its fresh-water runs and springs, the plenty of its fish, fowl, and wild beasts, the variety of its simples and dyeing-woods, the abundance of its timbers, minerals, wild vines, and fruits, the temperature of its climate; . . . in short, if it be looked upon in all respects as it came out of the hand of God, it is certainly one of the best countries in the world. But, on the other hand, if we enquire for well-built towns, for convenient ports and markets, for plenty of ships and seamen, for well-improved trades and manufactures, for well-educated children, for an industrious and thriving people, or for an happy government in church and state, and in short for all the other advantages in human improvements, it is certainly, for all of these things, one of the poorest, miserablest, and worst countries in all America, that is inhabited by Christians."

But James Blair's chief claim to remembrance in our literary history is based upon a series of one hundred and seventeen discourses on *Our Saviour's Divine Sermon on the Mount,* which were twice published in London during the author's lifetime, and which received public applause from the great English theologian, Daniel Waterland. In these discourses the range of topics is as wide as that of the wonderful discourse upon which they are founded. The thought is fully wrought out; the divisions are sharp and formal; each discourse is short and to the point. The tone of the author's mind is moderate, judicial, charitable, catholic; he is not brilliant; his style is smooth, simple, honest, earnest; there is no display; he is trying to make people good. The drift of his argument is steadily toward practical results. "An error in morals," he says, "is more dangerous than a mere speculative error. . . . It is only the practical errors, the transgressions of morality, which our Saviour degrades into the lowest rank. . . . Speculative errors, which have no influence on the life and conversation, cannot be near so dangerous as those errors which lead men out of the way of their duty. As in a voyage at sea, the master and seamen and passengers may chance to see several objects, and very friendly and innocently may differ in their opinions about the names, and natures, and colors, and shapes, and properties of them; and yet none of all these opinions, the most true or the most erroneous, either furthers or hinders their voyage. But if they should be in an error in using a bad compass, or in not knowing the tides and currents, the rocks and shelves; if they should run rashly on the shore in the night-time, by not keeping a right reckoning, thinking themselves far enough from land;—these are errors of fatal consequence, such as may endanger the ship and voyage. Just so it is in errors of opinion."

While he insists upon the highest excellence in outward conduct, he shows that all moral significance attaches to the inward state of a man: "It is the great secret of Christian morals, which our Saviour drives at in all duties whatsoever, and is the principal thing which distinguishes the righteousness of a good Christian, from the righteousness of the Scribes and Pharisees." "Particularly, has Christ interpreted the law in a more spiritual sense, killing vice in the seed, and strictly forbidding the feeding the very thoughts and imaginations with it. Then, let us employ a great part of our care in the good government of our heart and thoughts, that when wicked fancies or imaginations start up in our minds, or are thrown in by the Devil, we may take care not to harbor them, but to throw them quickly out, before they sprout out into bad resolutions and designs, or ripen into wicked actions and evil habits."

Virginia had been in existence a hundred years before it produced an historian of its own. This was Robert Beverley, of an ancient family in England, himself born in Virginia. His father, likewise Robert Beverley, a man of considerable fortune at Beverley in Yorkshire, had removed to the colony in time to become a prominent politician in 1676, acting resolutely, amid the tumults of that year, on the side of Sir William Berkeley against Nathaniel Bacon. The young Beverley was sent to England for his education; and early in life seems to have been employed by his father and an elder brother as assistant in charge of the colonial records. This circumstance turned his thoughts toward the study of his country's history. Happening to be in London in 1703, his bookseller told him of a new work just then in press,—Oldmixon's *British Empire in America*—and gave him for inspection, the sheets relating to Virginia and Carolina. These sheets the young Virginian began to read, with his pen in hand for the purpose of jotting down any corrections that might be necessary; but he soon gave up that task in despair—the new book being quite beyond the reach of correction. Prompted by this experience, and having with him his own memoranda of studies upon the subject, Beverley at once undertook to write a history of his native colony. This was first published in London, in 1705; was published in a Franch translation, both at Paris and at Amsterdam, in 1707; and was brought out in London in a second English edition, much enlarged and improved, in 1722.

The traits of the man confront us on every page of this book. He had large wealth in lands, in houses, and in slaves, high social position, intense affection for Virginia, a sturdy pride in it; and he was as independent in mind as he was in circumstances. The robust virtues—simplicity, thrift, industry, enterprise, economy—had not died out of him in the soft air of Virginia. He lived upon his great estate with Spartan plainness; and in his book he never misses the opportunity of rasping his countrymen for their luxury, their supineness, and the indolent use they were making of the overflowing bounties of nature. He gives first the history of the colony, then an account of the country itself, then a description of the Indians, finally a picture of the political and industrial condition of the colony in his own time. He writes not like a book-man or a theorist, but like a country-gentleman and a man of affairs. He speaks out plainly what he thinks; he has respect to limits, never loses himself in pedantries or long stories; he interprets all things, past and present, with shrewd, practical sense. In his style there is no flavor of classical study, or even of modern letters; yet it has the promptness, lucidity, and raciness of real talk among educated men of the world. It continues to be interesting. In some places, his history degenerates into a partisan pamphlet; for he inherited his father's hate of the Virginia governors— Lord Culpepper and the Earl of Effingham—having also a plenty of hate on his own account for Francis Nicholson. He is not heedless of accuracy; yet he has not a few errors. He knew the Indians well: in fact, in his first edition he identified himself with them by playfully calling himself an Indian; and the portion of his book devoted to them is written with love of the subject and full mastery of it. All his notices of natural objects also, are sharp and full. His eye was quick to see the characteristics of all sorts of dumb creatures, in the midst of whose haunts he passed his manly life; as may be illustrated in his graphic and amusing stories of the snake in the act of charming and swallowing a hare, and of the fish-hawk pursued by a bald eagle.

The whole work is fresh, original; not weighed down by documents; the living testimony of a proud and generous Virginian. Without apparent effort, he often hits upon strong and happy phrases, as when he speaks of "the almighty power of gold"—anticipating the more famous expression of Washington Irving. There is a tonic enjoyment in his under-flavor of humor and in his crisp sarcasms. He expresses a sort of contemptuous surprise at the "prodigious phantasms" with respect to Virginia, which he found cherished among the English; as, "that the servants in Virginia are made to draw in cart, and plough as horses and oxen do in England, and that the country turns all people black who go to live there." As to his own country, he has a smile of quiet ridicule for its military development: "The militia are the only standing forces in Virginia. They are happy in the enjoyment of an everlasting peace, which their poverty and want of towns secure to them." But if their military power was small, their hospitality certainly was not small; and he speaks of it with satisfaction: "The inhabitants are very courteous to travellers, who need no other recommendation but the being human creatures. A stranger has no more to do but to inquire upon the road where any gentleman or good housekeeper lives; and there he may depend upon being received with hospitality. This good nature is so general among their people, that the gentry when they go abroad order their principal servant to entertain all visitors with everything the plantation affords. And the poor planters who have but one bed will often sit up, or lie upon a form or couch all night, to make room for a weary traveller to repose himself after his journey. If there happen to be a churl that, either out of covetousness or ill nature, won't comply with this generous custom, he has a mark of infamy set upon him, and is abhorred by all." The author exults in the fact that "nobody is poor enough to beg or want food"; but checks himself with the confession, that "they have abundance of people that are lazy enough to deserve it. I remember the time when five pounds was left by a charitable testator to the poor of the parish he lived in; and it lay nine years before the executors could find one poor enough to accept of this legacy; but at last it was given to an old woman." When he thinks of the charms of the climate of Virginia, he is indignant at the calumnies heaped upon it by those English merchants who had visited it, but who, with insular obstinacy, persisted there in all the habits that they were used to in a very different climate: "Many of the merchants and others that go thither from England, make no distinction between a cold and hot country; but wisely go sweltering about in their thick clothes all the summer, because forsooth they used to do so in their northern climate; and then unfairly complain of the heat of the country. They greedily surfeit with their delicious fruits, and are guilty of great intemperance therein, through the exceeding plenty thereof, and liberty given by the inhabitants; by which means they fall sick, and then unjustly complain of the unhealthiness of the country. In the next place, the sailors, for want of towns there, were put to the hardship of rolling most of the tobacco a mile or more to the water-side; this splinters their hands sometimes, and provokes them to curse the country. Such exercise and a bright sun made them hot, and then they imprudently fell to drinking cold water, or perhaps new cider, which in its season they found in every planter's house; or else they greedily devour the green fruit and unripe trash they met with, and so fell into fluxes, fevers, and the bellyache; and then, to spare their own indiscretion, they in their tarpaulin language cry, God d—n the country."

In 1724, there came out in London a book of a hundred and fifty-one pages, entitled *The Present State of Virginia.* Its author was a Virginia clergyman, Hugh Jones, born in England, but naturalized in the new world by a life of versatile and energetic usefulness there; rector of Jamestown, mathematical professor in William and Mary College, and chaplain to the colonial assembly. He was one of the earliest Americans to appease the demand for elementary text-books in our schools, serving well the advancing generations by his *English Grammar,* his *Accidence to Mathematics,* and his *Accidence to Christianity.* His book on Virginia, which appears to have been published during some visit of the author to the mother-country, evidently had a philanthropic intention. He sets forth the condition of Virginia up to the latest dates, in the hope of arousing and directing a more intelligent cooperation in England with the efforts of good men in the new world who were trying to build up there a prosperous and benign commonwealth. His book is that of an earnest, downright, and rather original man, intent on getting some good done in his part of the world, and having clear views as to the methods of doing it. He describes frankly the sort of material then extant in Virginia to make a nation of—Indians, negroes, Englishmen; its next door neighbors, also—the North Carolinians and the Marylanders; likewise, the schemes he had formed for promoting learning, religion, and trade in those regions. It is a book of solid facts and solid suggestions, written in a plain, positive style, just sufficiently tinctured with the gentlemanly egotism of a Virginian and of a Churchman.

His eulogiums upon his adopted colony are not incapable of a sarcastic edge when turned toward the other colonies in America: "If New England be called a receptacle of dissenters, and an Amsterdam of religion, Pennsylvania the nurse of Quakers, Maryland the retirement of Roman Catholics, North Carolina the refuge of runaways, and South Carolina the delight of buccaneers and pirates, Virginia may be justly esteemed the happy retreat of true Britons and true Churchmen."

Yet he is nowhere blind to the blemishes of his own noble colony and its people; he particularly sees its weakness in the great matters of popular education, individual discipline, public spirit, industry, and the like. The Virginians themselves, he tells us, "have good natural notions and will soon learn arts and sciences; but are generally diverted, by business or inclination, from profound study and prying into the depth of things. . . . Through their quick apprehension they have a sufficiency of knowledge and fluency of tongue, though their learning for the most part be but superficial. They are more inclinable to read men by business and conversation, than to dive into books." "As for education, several are sent to England for it." "The common planters, leading easy lives, don't much admire labor or any manly exercise except horse-racing, nor diversion except cock-fighting. . . . This easy way of living and the heat of the summer makes some very lazy, who are then said to be climate-struck." "They are such lovers of riding, that almost every ordinary person keeps a horse; and I have known some spend the morning in ranging several miles in the woods to find and catch their horses, only to ride two or three miles to church, to the court-house, or to a horse-race."

He laments the poverty and consequent ineffectiveness of the College of William and Mary: "For it is now a college without a chapel, without a scholarship, and without a statute; there is a library without books, comparatively speaking; and a president without a fixed salary till of late."

He makes valuable suggestions for the religious improvement of Virginia, and draws portraits of the sort of clergymen who are needed there: not "quarrelsome and litigious ministers who would differ with their parishioners about insignificant trifles," nor "mere scholars and stoics," nor "zealots too rigid in outward appearance," but pure, devout, sensible, and friendly men, fitted to deal successfully with a warm-hearted and high-spirited people who "are for moderate views neither high nor low," and who "never refuse to shout,

> God bless the church, and George its defender,
> Convert the fanatics, and balk the Pretender."

Perhaps the most accomplished and the wittiest Virginian of the colonial time was William Byrd of Westover, a man of princely fortune and of princely ways. He was born in the colony in 1674, and died there in 1744. His father, having the same name, had come to Virginia in early life; had founded a great estate there; during the latter part of the seventeenth century, had been conspicuous in public affairs; and finding this son to be endowed with every personal quality corresponding to the great position that awaited him in life, had given him the amplest training in the schools and in the society of Europe. He was educated in England, under the particular care of Sir

Robert Southwell; "was called to the bar in the Middle Temple; studied for some time in the Low Countries; visited the court of France; and was chosen Fellow of the Royal Society." In England, he had "the acquaintance of many of the first persons of the age for knowledge, wit, virtue, birth, or high station, and, particularly, contracted a most intimate and bosom friendship with the learned and illustrious Charles Boyle, Earl of Orrery."

On returning to his native land, he entered upon a long career of public and private usefulness. He was made receiver-general of the king's revenues; for thirty-seven years he was a member of the council, and at last its president; three times he was sent as the agent of Virginia to the court of England; he founded the two famous cities of Richmond and Petersburg; as the proprietor of tracts of land vast enough for a royal domain, he was active in the development of the agricultural and mineral resources of the colony; best of all, he was "the constant enemy of all exorbitant power, and hearty friend to the liberties of his country." His course in private life was equally brilliant and attractive. On his estate at Westover he lived in a style of great magnificence. He was a student of science, a man of wit, of letters, of elegant tastes; and he had "the best and most copious collection of books" in that part of America.

Of course, such a man, absorbed by manifold engagements, and living in a whirl of gayety and of hospitable pleasures, was not likely to devote himself to any deliberate literary work. Yet his mind was an active and fertile one; and stirred by outward incidents, he dashed off two or three bits of writing that have extraordinary merit—representing the geniality of his nature, his wit, and the facility and grace of his style.

In the early part of the year 1729, in obedience to an appointment by the governor of Virginia, William Byrd joined an expedition for fixing the dividing line between that colony and North Carolina. The party consisted of two other commissioners for Virginia, the commissioners for North Carolina, a chaplain, several surveyors, and numerous attendants and laborers. The expedition occupied six weeks in the spring of that year; it was then abandoned on account of hot weather; and being resumed in the autumn, it occupied ten weeks more. Beginning at a point on the sea-coast, the line was run westward six hundred miles, through the Great Dismal Swamp, through "marshes . . . and great (waters," "over steep hills, craggy rocks, and thickets hardly penetrable." Of the two expeditions that accomplished this labor, William Byrd kept a journal, which, after lying in manuscript upwards of a century, was first published in 1841, under the title given to it by its author—*The History of the Dividing Line.*

In the peculiar qualities that distinguish this little book, it is almost unique in our colonial age; and it is, without question, one of the most delightful of the literary legacies which that age has handed down to ours. Here we have the off-hand, daily jottings of a very clever Virginia gentleman of the early time, who has travelled much, read much, been long in the best company; and who, with a gayety that will not yield to any hardship or vexation, travels for several weeks through a wilderness, accompanied by a little army of very miscellaneous and very queer people, encountering Indians, semi-savage whites, wild beasts, insects, reptiles, every sort of fatigue and discomfort, the horrors and the grandeurs of nature in its wildest state.

As he is to record the story of a definite partitionment from Virginia of land that once belonged to it, he begins with a sparkling sketch of the history of Virginia up to that time; particularly showing how all English America was once Virginia, and how all other English colonies have been formed by being "carved out of Virginia." He sets off, with much humor, the traits of the first inhabitants of Virginia; saying that the original colony consisted of "about an hundred men, most of them reprobates of good families"; and that at Jamestown, "like true Englishmen, they built a church that cost no more than fifty pounds, and a tavern that cost five hundred." He points out the great mistake made by the first colonists in not intermarrying with the Indians: "Morals and all considered, I can't think the Indians were much greater heathens than the first adventurers, who, had they been good Christians, would have had the charity to take this only method of converting the natives to Christianity. For, after all that can be said, a sprightly lover is the most prevailing missionary that can be sent amongst these, or any other infidels. Besides, the poor Indians would have had less reason to complain that the English took away their land, if they had received it by way of portion with their daughters. . . . Nor would the shade of the skin have been any reproach at this day; for if a Moor may be washed white in three generations, surely an Indian might have been blanched in two." "I may safely venture to say, the Indian women would have made altogether as honest wives for the first planters, as the damsels they used to purchase from aboard the ships. It is strange, therefore, that any good Christian should have refused a wholesome, straight bedfellow, when he might have had so fair a portion with her, as the merit of saving her soul."

Very much of his journal, especially the earlier portion of it, is taken up with sarcastic comments upon North Carolina—its backwardness in civilization, the idleness, ignorance, and poverty of its inhabitants; he heaps innumerable jokes upon them. Some of the people, he says, were sunk into absolute savagery. He tells of a poor wretch on the South Shore—"a Marooner, that modestly called himself a hermit, though he forfeited that name by suffering a wanton female to cohabit with him. His habitation was a bower covered with bark after the Indian fashion. . . . Like the ravens, he neither ploughed nor sowed, but subsisted chiefly upon oysters, which his handmaid made a shift to gather from the adjacent rocks. Sometimes, too, for change of diet, he sent her to drive up the neighbors' cows, to moisten their mouths with a little milk. But as for raiment, he depended mostly upon his length of beard, and she upon her length of hair, part of which she brought decently forward, and the rest dangled behind quite down to her rump, like one of Herodotus's East Indian Pigmies. Thus did these wretches

live in a dirty state of nature, and were mere Adamites, innocence only excepted."

He had many sarcasms on the irreligion of North Carolina:
" 'Tis natural for helpless man to adore his Maker in some form
or other; and were there any exception to this rule, I should
suspect it to be among the Hottentots of the Cape of Good Hope
and of North Carolina." The religious service held there by the
chaplain of the Virginia party, "was quite a new thing to our
brethren of North Carolina, who live in a climate where no
clergyman can breathe, any more than spiders in Ireland."
"They account it among their greatest advantages that they
are not priestridden, not remembering that the clergy is rarely
guilty of bestriding such as have the misfortune to be poor."
"One thing may be said for the inhabitants of that province, that they are not troubled with any religious fumes,
and have the least superstition of any people living. They do
not know Sunday from any other day, any more than Robinson
Crusoe did; which would give them a great advantage, were
they given to be industrious. But they keep so many Sabbaths
every week, that their disregard of the seventh day has no
manner of cruelty in it, either to servants or cattle." He suggests that, once in two or three years, the clergy of Virginia
should "vouchsafe to take a turn among these gentiles. . . .
'Twould look a little apostolical; and they might hope to be
requited for it hereafter,—if that be not thought too long to
tarry for their reward."

He has occasion to speak of Edenton, the capital of North
Carolina, which he describes as consisting of "forty or fifty
houses, most of them small and built without expense. A citizen
here is counted extravagant if he has ambition enough to aspire
to a brick-chimney. Justice herself is but indifferently lodged,
the court-house having much the air of a common tobacco-
house. I believe this is the only metropolis in the Christian or
Mohammedan world, where there is neither church, chapel,
mosque, synagogue, or any other place of public worshp, of any
sect or religion whatsoever." In North Carolina, "they pay no
tribute, either to God or to Caesar."

As to food, "provisions here are extremely cheap, and extremely good; so that people may live plentifully at a trifling expense. Nothing is dear but law, physic, and strong drink, which are all bad in their kind, and the last they get with so much difficulty, that they are never guilty of the sin of suffering it to sour upon their hands." He does, however, criticise their excessive use of pork: "The truth of it is, the inhabitants of North Carolina devour so much swine's flesh, that it fills them full of gross humors. . . . They are commonly obliged to eat it fresh, and that begets the highest taint of scurvy." This disease often develops into a worse one—"the yaws, called there very justly the country-distemper. . . . First it seizes the throat, next the palate, and lastly shows its spite to the poor nose, of which 'tis apt, in a small time, treacherously to undermine the foundation. This calamity is so common and familiar here, that it ceases to be a scandal; and in the disputes that happen about beauty, the Noses have in some companies much ado to carry it. Nay, 'tis said that once, after three good pork years, a motion had like to have been made in the house of burgesses, that a man with a nose should be incapable of holding any place of profit in the province; which extraordinary motion could never have been intended without some hopes of a majority."

He amuses himself, likewise, over the indolence of the people. He speaks of "the Carolina felicity of having nothing to do." Drones are common in North Carolina, but they are all men; the women "spin, weave, and knit, all with their own hands, while their husbands, depending on the bounty of the climate, are slothful in everything but getting of children, and in that only instance make themselves useful members of an infant-colony." The men "make their wives rise out of their beds early in the morning, at the same time that they lie and snore, till the sun has run one-third of his course, and dispersed all the unwholesome damps. Then, after stretching and yawning for half an hour, they light their pipes, and under the protection of a cloud of smoke venture out into the open air; though, if it happens to be never so little cold, they quickly return shivering into the chimney corner. When the weather is mild, they stand leaning with both their arms upon the cornfield fence, and gravely consider whether they had best go and take a small heat at the hoe, but generally find reasons to put it off till another time. Thus, they loiter away their lives, like Solomon's sluggard, with their arms across, and at the winding up of the year scarcely have bread to eat."

As the expedition moves westward, the author's attention is taken up by other things than the drolleries of North Carolina society; and he jots down admirable notices of rare plants and animals, racy sketches of Indian character, amusing stories of forest-adventure, a learned digression upon music, and vivacious pictures of the country through which they pass. He becomes a great enthusiast over the virtues of the plant, ginseng: "Though practice will soon make a man of tolerable vigor an able footman, yet, as a help to bear fatigue, I used to chew a root of ginseng as I walked along. This kept up my spirits, and made me trip away as nimbly in my half jack-boots as younger men could in their shoes. This plant is in high esteem in China, where it sells for its weight in silver. . . . Indeed, it is a vegetable of so many virtues, that Providence has planted it very thin in every country that has the happiness to produce it. Nor, indeed, is mankind worthy of so great a blessing, since health and long life are commonly abused to ill purposes. . . . Its virtues are, that it gives an uncommon warmth and vigor to the blood, and frisks the spirits beyond any other cordial. It cheers the heart even of a man that has a bad wife, and makes him look down with great composure on the crosses of the world. It promotes insensible perspiration, dissolves all phlegmatic and viscous humors that are apt to obstruct the narrow channels of the nerves. It helps the memory, and would quicken even Helvetian dulness. 'Tis friendly to the lungs, much more than scolding itself. It comforts the stomach, and strengthens the bowels, preventing all colics and fluxes. In one word, it will make a man live a great while, and very well while he does. And what is more, it will make even old age amiable, by rendering it lively, cheerful, and good humored."

Three years after these journeys across the debatable ground between Virginia and North Carolina, the author made another journey, of much less difficulty and of much less public importance, the leading incidents of which he has chronicled in some very piquant and charming memoranda, entitled *A Progress to the Mines*. In the autumn of the following year, 1733, with a party of four gentlemen, five woodmen, four negroes, and three Indians, he made a journey to a vast tract of land owned by him, near the River Dan in North Carolina. His diary of this expedition is called *A Journey to the Land of Eden*, the latter phrase being the somewhat ironical name of the region referred to. Both of these narratives are full of merriment; nearly every sentence has some jovial touch; and pervading all, is the perfect and ingrained gentlemanliness of the writer. One day, he arrived at a place where were two mills belonging to himself: "I had the grief to find them both stand as still for the want of water, as a dead woman's tongue, for want of breath." At one house he was detained for a day or two on account of bad weather; and in his account of the way in which he and his friends amused themselves during their imprisonment, by reading the second part of *The Beggars' Opera*, which he found in that remote Virginia mansion, we catch a glimpse of the early presence of the Queen Anne writers even in our American forests, as well as of William Byrd's familiar acquaintance with the current literary gossip of London. Continuing that journey under a promise of better weather, he mentions his arrival at "the homely dwelling of the Reverend Mr. Marij," by "a path as narrow as that which leads to heaven, but much more dirty." Further on, he tells how, one night, himself and another gentleman, after positively declaring against it, were induced by the ladies of the house to eat a hearty supper—upon which he has this comment: "So very pliable a thing is frail man, when women have the bending of him." He was a devout Churchman, and a faithful friend of the clergy of Virginia; and for the latter he shows his good-will by never missing an opportunity of playfully remarking upon their personal and professional characteristics. Thus, of a visit one Sunday to Brunswick church: "Mr. Betty, the parson of the parish, entertained us with a good, honest sermon; but whether he bought it, or borrowed it, would have been uncivil in us to inquire. Be that as it will, he is a decent man, with a double chin that fits gracefully over his band, and his parish, especially the female part of it, like him well. . . . When church was done, we refreshed our teacher with a glass of wine, and then receiving his blessing, took horse and directed our course to Major Embry's."

William Stith, who was born in Virginia in 1689 and died in 1755, began late in his life to write the history of that colony; being particularly moved to the task by noticing "how empty and unsatisfactory" was everything at that time published upon the subject, excepting, as he said, "the excellent but confused materials" of Captain John Smith. He had been a busy person in his day—clergyman, master of the grammar school of William and Mary College, chaplain of the house of burgesses, president of the college, and man of public utility in general. Being related to several of the most eminent families in Virginia, and in constant association with its leading men, he was from his youth familiar with all its historical traditions; he had access to many rare manuscripts relating to its past; and, finally, he had won for himself "perfect leisure and retirement." All things seemed to favor his ambition to give to Virginia what it greatly needed—a history of itself. "Such a work," said he, "will be a noble and elegant entertainment for my vacant hours, which it is not in my power to employ more to my own satisfaction, or the use and benefit of my country." Accordingly, in 1747, he published at Williamsburg, in a volume of three hundred and thirty-one pages, the first part of *The History of the First Discovery and Settlement of Virginia*, carrying the narrative down only to the year 1624. Though he lived eight years longer, this first part of his history proved to be also its last part. The book is not ill-written. It is, indeed, projected upon a scale too large for its subject; it fills up the canvas with small incidents; it seeks to give historical memory to the petty doings of politicians, pioneers, and savages, that carry in themselves the necessity of being forgotten. Nevertheless, while the interest of the story is often swamped in a deluge of details, and the whole book is a sin against artistic proportion and the limits of human life, the reader will be likely to pronounce unjust the verdict of Thomas Jefferson, who says that Stith, though "very exact," had "no taste in style," and that his writing is "inelegant." The author founds his work chiefly upon the narratives of Captain John Smith, in whom he confides with a blissful faith that is now amusing: "I take him to have been a very honest man and a strenuous lover of truth." The historian protests his own impartiality: "I declare myself to be of no party, but have labored solely with a view to find out and relate the truth." Yet his account of the early governor, Samuel Argall, is so hostile that he has been accused of yielding unduly to partisan documents against that personage, and even of adding "bitter and groundless accusations of his own." Against King James the First, who vexed the affairs of the colony by his ceaseless and senseless interference, the historian speaks with a frankness of contempt that leaves an unwonted animation upon his pages: "If more than a century is not enough to un-Solomonize that silly monarch, I must give up all my notions of things. . . . I take it to be the main part of the duty and office of an historian, to paint men and things in their true and lively colors; and to do that justice to the vices and follies of princes and great men after their death, which it is not safe or proper to do whilst they are alive. And herein, as I judge, chiefly consist the strength and excellency of Tacitus and Suetonius. Their style and manner are far inferior to Livy's, and the writers of the Julian and Augustan ages; but they have more than painted and exposed alive to view the greatest train of monsters that ever disgraced a throne, or did dishonor to human nature. . . . King James the First fell, indeed, far short of the Caesars' superlative wickedness and supremacy in vice. He was at best only very simple and injudicious, without any steady principle of justice and honor; which was rendered the more odious and ridiculous by his large and constant pretensions to wisdom and virtue. And he had, in truth, all the forms of wisdom,—forever erring very learnedly, with a wise saw or Latin sentence in his mouth; for he had been bred up under Buchanan, one of the brightest geniuses and most accomplished scholars of that age, who had given him Greek and Latin in great waste and profusion—but it was not in his power to give him good sense. That is the gift of God and nature alone, and is not to be taught; and Greek and Latin without it only cumber and overload a weak head, and often render the fool more abundantly foolish. I must, therefore, confess that I have ever had, from my first acquaintance with history, a most contemptible opinion of this monarch; which has perhaps been much heightened and increased by my long studying and conning over the materials of this history. For he appears in his dealings with the company to have acted with such mean arts and fraud, and such little tricking, as highly misbecome majesty. And I am much mistaken if his arbitrary proceedings and unjust designs will appear from any part of his history more fully than from these transactions with the company and colony. . . . I think and speak of him with the same freedom and indifferency that I would think and speak of any other man long since dead; and therefore I have no way restrained my style in freely exposing his weak and injurious proceedings."

A good example of Stith's descriptive manner is his account of the dreadful massacre of the white people in Virginia by the Indians, in 1622—a passage of genuine dignity, pathos, and graphic power.

"In the year 1700," writes a genial and enterprising young Englishman named John Lawson, "when people flocked from all parts of the Christian world to see the solemnity of the grand jubilee at Rome, my intention at that time being to travel, I accidentally met with a gentleman who had been abroad and was very well acquainted with the ways of living in both Indies; of whom having made inquiry concerning them, he assured me that Carolina was the best country I could go to, and that there then lay a ship in the Thames in which I might have my passage. I laid hold on this opportunity, and was not long on board before we fell down the river and sailed to Cowes, where having taken in some passengers we proceeded on our voyage." Thus a very useful and notable man found his way to the new world, arriving at Charleston, South Carolina, early in September, 1700. Of this place and its people, just as they appeared to him in that closing year of the seventeenth century, he has left us a goodly picture: "The town has very regular and fair streets, in which are good buildings of brick and wood; and since my coming thence, has had great additions of beautiful, large brick buildings, besides a strong fort and regular fortifications made to defend the town. The inhabitants, by their wise management and industry, have much improved the country, which is in as thriving circumstances at this time as any colony on the continent of English America. . . . They have a considerable trade both to Europe and to the West Indies, whereby they become rich. . . . Their cohabiting in a town has drawn to them ingenious people of most sciences, whereby they have tutors amongst them, that educate their youth alamode. . . . All enjoy at this day an entire liberty of their worship; . . . it being the lord-proprietors' intent that the inhabitants of Carolina should be as free from oppression as any in the universe. . . . They have a well-disciplined militia. . . . Their officers, both infantry and cavalry, generally appear in scarlet mountings, and as rich as in most regiments belonging to the crown, which shows the richness and grandeur of this colony. They are a frontier, and prove such troublesome neighbors to the Spaniards, that they have once laid their town of St. Augustine in ashes, and drove away their cattle. . . . The merchants of Carolina are fair, frank traders. The gentlemen seated in the country are very courteous, live very noble in their houses, and give very genteel

entertainment to all strangers and others that come to visit
them."

After staying in this delightful community nearly four
months, the young immigrant determined, for some reason, to
seek his fortune in North Carolina; and on the third day after
Christmas, 1700, he began his voyage thither along the coast,
going in a large canoe, and having in his company five white
men and four Indians. Upon this journey, he went by sea only
as far as the Santee river; he then struck inland and wandered
in zigzag fashion toward the north, paddling up rivers or
wading across them, pushing through the highlands and mo-
rasses, among savages, serpents, wild beasts, and white pioneers, and encountering in good humor all manner of hardships and perils. This long strain of travel in those woods, in
those times, proved altogether a revelation to John Lawson,
fresh and tender from the beatitudes of a civilized English
home; and he had the good sense to keep a faithful record of it.
He put down on paper what he saw and experienced day by
day as he went along: mishaps, prosperities; descriptions of
the country, rivers, plants, trees, animals; their own talk by
the way; their occasional entertainment in the hovels of
white settlers and of Indians; especially such traits of the latter
as seemed to him novel, picturesque, or amusing. He is particularly minute and facetious in his account of the Indian
women they met; telling some broad stories of the intrigues of
his own party with these tawny beauties—wherein the supposed distinction in morals between Christian and pagan seems
to become effaced, or, if possible, to be in favor of the pagan.
At last, however, after "a thousand miles' travel among the
Indians," he and his associates arrive safe in North Carolina;
"where," he says, "being well received by the inhabitants and
pleased with the goodness of the country, we all resolved to
continue."

A man of John Lawson's intelligence was of course a boon
to that colony. He was especially useful by his ability to sur-
vey land. Accordingly, they soon made him their surveyor-

general; and for the next twelve years he was kept busy in that function, going in every direction through the wilderness, and having his eyes open all the time for information about man and nature—much of which he carefully noted down in his journal. He had some skill in natural history, and compiled minute descriptions of birds, fishes, beasts, minerals, and the flora of the country. The country itself, however, its beauty and fertility, and the charms of its climate, bred in him an enthusiasm. Its coast, he tells us, in fine imagery, is "a chain of sand-banks, which defends it from the violence and insults of the Atlantic ocean; by which barrier a vast sound is hemmed in, which fronts the mouths of the navigable and pleasant rivers of this fertile country, and into which they disgorge themselves." He gives a picture of the spot where the first hapless colonists sent by Sir Walter Raleigh had their fatal residence; and he adds to it this sweet and poetic story "that passes for an uncontested truth amongst the inhabitants of this place, . . . that the ship which brought the first colonists does often appear amongst them, under sail, in a gallant posture, which they call Sir Walter Raleigh's ship."

As to North Carolina, it is "a delicious country, being placed in that girdle of the world which affords wine, oil, fruit, grain, and silk, with other rich commodities, besides a sweet air, moderate climate, and fertile soil. These are the blessings, under Heaven's protection, that spin out the thread of life to its utmost extent, and crown our days with the sweets of health and plenty, which, when joined with content, renders the possessors the happiest race of men upon earth. The inhabitants of Carolina, through the richness of the soil, live an easy and pleasant life; the land being of several sorts of compost; . . . one part bearing great timbers; others being savannahs or natural meads, where no trees grow for several miles, adorned by nature with a pleasant verdure and beautiful flowers, . . . yielding abundance of herbage for cattle, sheep, and horses. The country in general affords pleasant seats, the land, except in some few places, being dry and high banks, parcelled out into most convenient necks by the creeks; . . . whereby, with a small trouble of fencing, almost every man may enjoy to himself an entire plantation, or rather park. . . . I may say the universe does not afford such another."

In his office of colonial surveyor he often had to live a rough and solitary life in the far-off woods; and his experience was fruitful in adventures, instructive and amusing for him and for us. Thus, in giving a description of the alligator, he narrates this incident, which occurred at an early period of his residence in North Carolina, and before he had become intimately acquainted with the playful ways of that interesting monster: "This animal in these parts sometimes exceeds seventeen feet long. It is impossible to kill them with a gun, unless you chance to hit them about the eyes, which is a much softer place than the rest of their impenetrable armor. They roar and make a hideous noise against bad weather, and before they come out of their dens in the spring. I was pretty much frightened with one of these once. . . . I had built a house about a mile from an Indian town on the fork of Neuse River, where I dwelt by myself, excepting a young Indian fellow, and a bull dog that I had along with me. I had not then been so long a sojourner in America as to be thoroughly acquainted with this creature. One of them had got his nest directly under my house, which stood on pretty high land and by a creek side, in whose banks his entering-place was, his den reaching the ground directly on which my house stood. I was sitting alone by the fireside, about nine o'clock at night, sometime in March, the Indian fellow being gone to the town to see his relations, so that there was nobody in the house but myself and my dog; when, all of a sudden, this ill-favored neighbor of mine set up such a roaring, that he made the house shake about my ears. . . . The dog stared as if he was frightened out of his senses; nor indeed could I imagine what it was. . . . Immediately again I had another lesson, and so a third. Being at that time amongst none but savages, I began to suspect they were working some piece of conjuration under my house, to get away my goods. . . . At last my man came in, to whom when I had told the story, he laughed at me and presently undeceived me."

Of course he had great opportunities of studying the Indians, whom he always speaks of with a sort of gentle liking, especially their women. Among the latter, he says, "it seems impossible to find a scold; if they are provoked or affronted by their husbands or some other, they resent the indignity offered them in silent tears, or by refusing their meat. Would some of our European daughters of thunder set these Indians for a pattern, there might be more quiet families found amongst them." "When young and at maturity, they are as fine-shaped creatures . . . as any in the universe. They are of a tawny complexion; their eyes are very brisk and amorous; their smiles afford the finest composure a face can possess; their hands are of the finest make with small, long fingers, and as soft as their cheeks; and their whole bodies of a smooth nature. They are not so uncouth . . . as we suppose them, nor are they strangers or not proficients in the soft passion. . . . As for the report that they are never found unconstant, like the Europeans, it is wholly false; for were the old world and the new one put into a pair of scales, in point of constancy, it would be a hard matter to discern which was the heavier." "The woman is not punished for adultery; but 'tis the man that makes the injured person satisfaction. . . . The Indians say that the woman is a weak creature and easily drawn away by the man's persuasion; for which reason, they lay no blame upon her, but the man (that ought to be master of his passion) for persuading her to it."

At one time he saw this prodigy amongst the Indians—"the strangest spectacle of antiquity I ever knew, it being an old Indian squaw, that, had I been to have guessed at her age by her aspect, old Parr's head (the Welsh Methusalem) was a face in swaddling clouts to hers. Her skin hung in reaves, like a bag of tripe. By a fair computation, one might have justly thought it would have contained three such carcasses as hers then was. . . . By what I could gather she was considerably above one hundred years old, notwithstanding she smoked tobacco and eat her victuals, . . . as heartily as one of eighteen."

He tells in another place of an interview with the king of the Santee Indians, who came to him attended by his conjuror, or doctor—the latter being a shrewd quack remarkably successful, like his brethren in Christendom, in living upon the credulity of his victims. This doctor himself had in former times been afflicted with a certain dangerous and disreputable disease; and in order to treat himself for it in secret, he had withdrawn into the woods, having with him but a single companion, who was suffering from the same distemper. The conjuror succeeded in effecting a cure for both of them, but only at the expense of the noses of both; and, at last, "coming again amongst their old acquaintance so disfigured, the Indians admired to see them metamorphosed after that manner, inquired of them where they had been all that time, and what were become of their noses. They made answer that they had been conversing with the white man above—meaning God Almighty; . . . he being much pleased with their ways, . . . had promised to make their capacities equal with the white people in making guns, ammunition, and so forth; in retaliation of which, they had given him their noses. The verity of which they yet hold."

The author greatly admired the dignity and self-contained power of the Indians: "Their eyes are commonly full and manly, and their gait sedate and majestic. They never walk backward and forward as we do, nor contemplate on the affairs of loss or gain, the things which daily perplex us. They are dexterous and steady, both as to their hands and feet, to admiration. They will walk over deep brooks and creeks on the smallest poles, and that without any fear or concern. Nay, an Indian will walk on the ridge of a barn or house, and look down the gable end, and spit upon the ground, as unconcerned as if he was walking on terra firma."

The fate of this admirable observer was sufficiently mournful. Continuing his career as public surveyor of North Carolina as late as 1712, he went out in that year upon an expedition into the wilderness, in the company of a Swiss nobleman, Baron de Graffenried, who had plans for bringing a colony thither. They fell into the hands of hostile Indians, who burned Lawson at the stake, and permitted the escape of the baron only upon his payment of a ransom. But John Lawson, though slain thus miserably, had made good use of his time in the Carolinas; and three years before his death, he had published in London a quarto volume embodying the story of his adventures and observations in the new world, under the rather inapt title of *The History of North Carolina*—an uncommonly strong and sprightly book.

There were in South Carolina in the eighteenth century three distinguished men of the name of Alexander Garden; one a physician and naturalist; another, his son, an officer in the Revolutionary War, and the author of a book of anecdotes respecting that contest; the third, perhaps not related to the other two, an Episcopal clergyman, who died in Charleston in 1756, after a service of thirty-four years as the rector of St. Philip's in that city. This man, a native of Scotland, came to South Carolina about the year 1720, being then not far from thirty-five years old; and besides his rectorship in Charleston, he held for the larger part of his life the office of commissary to the Bishop of London, for the Carolinas, Georgia, and the Bahama islands. He was a person of extraordinary influence in his day. All his opinions were sharply defined; and in the expression of them he was absolutely without fear. He stood for the authority of his church in all things; he was an austere disciplinarian, orderly, energetic, neither taking nor granting any relaxation from the letter of ecclesiastical law. For example, he would never perform the ceremony of marriage in Lent, or on any fast day, or in any manner deviating in the smallest particular from that prescribed in the Prayer-book; for marriage-fees, he would receive not one penny less or more than the law allowed; and exactly one-tenth of his income was measured out with arithmetical precision as charity to the poor.

In the year 1740, alarmed and disgusted by the proceedings of the great preacher, George Whitefield, who was a clergyman of the Church of England, Garden not only prosecuted him vigorously in the ecclesiastical court, but pursued him with energy and wit in the wider court of public opinion. He preached, and then published, two sermons entitled "Regeneration and the Testimony of the Spirit," based upon the text, "They who have turned the world upside down have come hither also"; and referring caustically to Whitefield as a preacher whose sermons are "a medley of truth and falsehood, sense and nonsense, served up with pride and virulence, and other like saucy ingredients." He likewise published a series of six letters to Whitefield, which are sprightly and pungent, and which the New England divine, Thomas Prince, described as "full of mistake, misconstruction, misrepresentation, cavil, ill nature, ill manners, scorn, and virulence." Three years afterward, in the year 1743, Garden himself reviewed the tremendous controversy, and justified his own course in it, doing this in a letter to a friend, some sentences of which may sufficiently represent to us the rather tart and spicular quality of his style. All his efforts, he says, have been directed solely in defence of "the cause of truth against the frantics gone forth amongst us. . . . I could now indeed wish that my pen against Whitefield had run in somewhat smoother a style. But had you been here on the spot to have seen the frenzy he excited among the people, the bitterness and virulence wherewith he raved against the clergy of the Church of England in general, and how artfully he labored to set the mob upon me in particular, I dare say you would have thought the provocation enough to ruffle any temper, and a sufficient apology for the keenest expressions I have used against him. . . . As to the state of religion in this province, it is bad enough, God knows. Rome and the Devil have contrived to crucify her 'twixt two thieves,—Infi-

delity and Enthusiasm. The former, alas, too much still prevails; but as to the latter, thanks to God, it is greatly subsided,
and even at the point of vanishing away. We had here trances,
visions, and revelations both 'mong blacks and whites, in abundance. But ever since the famous Hugh Brian, sousing himself
into the River Jordan, in order to smite and divide its waters,
had his eyes opened, and saw himself under the delusion of the
Devil, those things have dwindled into disgrace, and are now
no more. Bad also is the present state of the poor orphan-house
in Georgia,—that land of lies, and from which we have no
truth but what they can neither disguise nor conceal. The
whole colony is accounted here one great lie, from the beginning to this day; and the orphan-house, you know, is a part
of the whole—a scandalous bubble."

The story usually given concerning the original settlement,
in 1733, of the youngest of the American colonies, reads like a
chapter from some political romance, in which the hero, General James Oglethorpe, appears to be a compound of Solon,
Achilles, Don Quixote, and the Man of Ross. The commonwealth of Georgia makes a prompt and rather brilliant entrance
into American literature, by virtue of a little book written just
seven years after the colony was founded—the joint production
of Patrick Tailfer, Hugh Anderson, David Douglass, and other
primitive inhabitants of the colony. These men, apparently of
considerable literary culture, had quarrelled with Oglethorpe,
and had been worsted; and having escaped to Charleston in
1740, they continued the fight by publishing in that year, both
there and in London, an artful and powerful book against Oglethorpe, called *A True and Historical Narrative of the Colony
of Georgia.*

Within a volume of only one hundred and twelve pages, is
compressed a masterly statement of the authors' alleged grievances at the hands of Oglethorpe. The book gives a detailed
and even documentary account of the rise of the colony, and of
its quick immersion in suffering and disaster, through Ogle-

thorpe's selfishness, greed, despotism, and fanatic pursuit of social chimeras. It charges his deputy, Thomas Causton, with a long course of brutal tyranny and cruelty, in which he was sustained by his master. Its summary of "the causes of the ruin and desolation of the colony," contains these seven particulars, —delusive reports in England of the natural advantages of Georgia, restrictions upon the tenure and use of its lands, enormous quit-rents, paralysis of agriculture through Oglethorpe's refusal to admit negro-labor, the cruel abuse of authority by Oglethorpe and his subordinates, their neglect of manufactures, finally, Oglethorpe's perversion of moneys entrusted to him in Christian charity for the erection of churches and schools.

Whatever may be the truth or the justice of this book, it is abundantly interesting; and if any one has chanced to find the prevailing rumor of Oglethorpe somewhat nauseating in its sweetness, he may here easily allay that unpleasant effect. Certainly, as a polemic, it is one of the most expert pieces of writing to be met with in our early literature. Its mastery of the situation is everywhere maintained, through the perfect mastery on the part of the authors, of their own temper. It never blusters or scolds. It is always cool, poised, polite, and merciless; and it passes back and forth, with fatal ease, between dreadful fact and equally dreadful invective and raillery. For example, it accuses Oglethorpe of caring more for the prosperity of his political hobbies, than for the happiness of his colonists: "Alas, our miseries could not alter his views of things." It contrasts the brave and beautiful fictions about Georgia that were sown broadcast over England, with the sorrowful and terrible realities: "Thus, while the nation at home was amused with the fame of the happiness and flourishing of the colony, . . . the poor miserable settlers and inhabitants were exposed to as arbitrary a government as Turkey or Muscovy ever felt. Very looks were criminal; and the grand sin of withstanding . . . authority . . . was punished without mercy." After spreading before the world the whole horrible story, the book concludes with this powerful and pathetic sentence: "By these and many other such hardships, the poor inhabitants of Georgia are scattered over the face of the earth,—her plantations a wild, her towns a desert, her villages in rubbish, her improvements a byword, and her liberties a jest, an object of pity to friends, and of insult, contempt, and ridicule to enemies."

The above description of the contents of the book may prepare the reader to appreciate the most artistic and amusing part of it—the dedication. With exquisite mockery, the book is inscribed to Oglethorpe himself. It places his name in full at the head of the address, prefixing and affixing all his sonorous titles, military, political, literary, and feudalistic; it addresses him always, with feigned reverence, as "your Excellency"; and it forms altogether a most laughable burlesque upon laudatory dedications in general, and an elegant and most caustic satire upon what the authors call the vanity and hypocrisy of Oglethorpe in particular. Referring to the confusion, the poverty and wretchedness into which the colony had fallen, and veiling this deadly meaning under the forms of utmost urbanity and compliment, it thus salutes him: "May it please your Excellency, As the few surviving remains of the colony of Georgia find it necessary to present the world, and in particular Great Britain, with a true state of that province, from its first rise to its present period, your Excellency, of all mankind, is best entitled to the dedication, as the principal author of its present strength and affluence, freedom and prosperity. And though incontestable truths will recommend the following narrative to the patient and attentive reader, yet your name, Sir, will be no little ornament to the frontispiece, and may possibly engage some courteous reader a little beyond it."

It then delicately taunts Oglethorpe with the elaborate and nauseous flattery in prose and verse to which he was accustomed, and which he seemed to encourage: "That dedication and flattery are synonymous, is the complaint of every dedicator, who concludes himself ingenious and fortunate, if he can discover a less trite and direct method of flattering than is usually practised; but we are happily prevented from the least intention of this kind, by the repeated offerings of the muses and news-writers to your Excellency, in the public papers. 'Twere presumptuous even to dream of equalling or increasing them. We therefore flatter ourselves that nothing we can advance will in the least shock your Excellency's modesty, not doubting but your goodness will pardon any deficiency of elegance and politeness, on account of our sincerity, and the serious truths we have the honor to approach you with."

With the most deferential tones they then proceed to compliment him on the principal traits of novelty in his arrangements for Georgia, every item mentioned as an encomium being, in fact, a thrust of deadly sarcasm: "We have seen the ancient custom of sending forth colonies, for the improvement of any distant territory or new acquisition, continued down to ourselves; but to your Excellency alone it is owing that the world is made acquainted with a plan highly refined from those of all former projectors. They fondly imagined it necessary to communicate to such young settlements the fullest rights and properties, all the immunities of their mother-countries, and privileges rather more extensive. By such means, indeed, these colonies flourished with early trade and affluence. But your Excellency's concern for our perpetual welfare could never permit you to propose such transitory advantages for us. You considered riches, like a divine and a philosopher, as the 'irritamenta malorum,' and knew that they were disposed to inflate weak minds with pride, to hamper the body with luxury, and introduce a long variety of evils. Thus have you 'protected us from ourselves,' as Mr. Waller says, by keeping all earthly comforts from us. You have afforded us the opportunity of arriving at the integrity of the primitive times, by entailing a more than primitive poverty on us. The toil that is necessary to our bare subsistence, must effectually defend us from the anxieties of any further ambition. As we have no properties to feed vainglory and beget contention, so we are not puzzled with any

system of laws to ascertain and establish them. The valuable
virtue of humility is secured to us by your care to prevent our
procuring, or so much as seeing, any negroes, . . . lest our simplicity might mistake the poor Africans for greater slaves than
ourselves. And that we might fully receive the spiritual benefit
of those wholesome austerities, you have wisely denied us the
use of such spirituous liquors as might in the least divert our
minds from the contemplation of our happy circumstances.

"Be pleased, . . . Great Sir, to accompany our heated imaginations in taking a view of this colony of Georgia,—this child
of your auspicious politics,—arrived at the utmost vigor of its
constitution at a term when most former states have been struggling through the convulsions of their infancy. This early maturity, however, lessens our admiration that your Excellency
lives to see (what few Founders ever aspired after) the great
decline and almost final termination of it. So many have finished their course during the progress of the experiment, and
such numbers have retreated from the phantoms of poverty
and slavery which their cowardly imaginations pictured to
them, that you may justly vaunt with the boldest hero of them
all,

Like Death you reign
O'er silent subjects and a desert plain.

"Yet must your enemies (if you have any) be ready to confess that no ordinary statesman could have digested, in the like
manner, so capacious a scheme, such a copious jumble of power
and politics. We shall content ourselves with observing that
all those beauteous models of government which the little states
of Germany exercise, and those extensive liberties which the
boors of Poland enjoy, were designed to concentre in your
system; and were we to regard the modes of government, we
must have been strangely unlucky to have missed of the best,
where there was an appearance of so great a variety. For, under
the influence of our Perpetual Dictator, we have seen something like aristocracy, oligarchy, as well as the triumvirate,

decemvirate, and consular authority of famous republics, which have expired many ages before us. What wonder, then, we share the same fate? Do their towns and villages exist but in story and rubbish? We are all over ruins; our public-works, forts, wells, highways, light-houses, stores, and water-mills, and so forth, are dignified like theirs with the same venerable desolation. The log-house, indeed, is like to be the last forsaken spot of your empire; yet even this, through the death or desertion of those who should continue to inhabit it, must suddenly decay; the bankrupt jailor himself shall soon be denied the privilege of human conversation; and when this last moment of the spell expires, the whole shall vanish like the illusion of some eastern magician.

"But let not this solitary prospect impress your Excellency with any fears of having your services to mankind, and to the settlers of Georgia in particular, buried in oblivion; for if we diminutive authors are allowed to prophesy,—as you know poets in those cases formerly did,—we may confidently presage, that while the memoirs of America continue to be read in English, Spanish, or the language of the Scots Highlanders, your Excellency's exploits and epocha will be transmitted to posterity.

"Should your Excellency apprehend the least tincture of flattery in anything already hinted, we may sincerely assure you, we intended nothing that our sentiments did not very strictly attribute to your merit; and in such sentiments we have the satisfaction of being fortified by all persons of impartiality and discernment.

"But not to trespass on those minutes which your Excellency may suppose more significantly employed on the sequel, let it suffice at present to assure you that we are deeply affected by your favors; and though unable of ourselves properly to acknowledge them, we shall embrace every opportunity of recommending you to higher powers, who, we are hopeful, will reward your Excellency according to your Merit!"

PROFESSOR TYLER *concluded the two volumes from which the preceding selections were taken by describing the period between 1607 and 1765 as years of "colonial isolation." These volumes are a history of American letters as it developed in the various colonies and geographical sections; for his last two volumes, Tyler shifted the theme from colonial diversity to national unity. During the revolutionary years between 1763 and 1783 a nation was born.*

It may be that the first seed of the American Revolution was sown at Jamestown, Virginia, in the summer of 1619 when the first representative assembly to meet in America convened. Or, perhaps the seed was sown in 1763 when the Peace of Paris drove the French out of North America and led the British into a series of attempts to force the colonies to assume part of the financial burden of the expanded empire.

The Revenue Act of 1764 levied additional duties on sugar and other commodities and gave customs officers the power to issue writs of assistance. James Otis in his arguments against the use of these writs raised many of the legal and theoretical issues of the Revolution.

Then, on March 22, 1765, Parliament passed the Stamp Act.

The Stamp Act and Political Discussion

ALL students of the American Revolution, who have been accustomed to view the passage of the Stamp Act, in March, 1765, as the initial event in a famous series that became sufficiently long and tragic, are likely to find some difficulty in accounting for the seeming suddenness with which the American people then sprang up, from what is thereby assumed to have been a previous condition of profound colonial content, into one of universal alarm and anger, as well as of clearly-defined and highly-matured constitutional opposition. In truth, however, there never was in America that previous condition of profound colonial content, although, until the removal, through the

Peace of Paris in 1763, of the greater danger from France, the American colonists had submitted with as much reticence as possible to the lesser danger from England. Ever since their earliest settlements here, which began in the reigns of the first James and the first Charles, these Englishmen in America had retained and exercised their hereditary race-qualities: they had always been sensitive to the encroachments of prerogative, and they had always been political grumblers. Moreover, the specimens of American political literature which have thus far received our attention, all show the peculiar alertness of political suspicion which had been awakened among them for at least two years before the passage of the Stamp Act, as well as the clear development of their political philosophy and political purpose touching those extraordinary constitutional dangers which, during the same two years, had been steadily gathering head.

Within the last few weeks of the year 1764—that year of premonition to the American colonies—was first published, in London, Goldsmith's poem of "The Traveller"; and among the ten closing lines of it, written, as is well known, by Dr. Johnson, are these two:

> How small, of all that human hearts endure,
> That part which laws or kings can curse or cure!

The events which occurred both in England and in America, during the subsequent twelve months, furnish a rather derisive comment on the limited range of the poet's vision when he wrote this sonorous couplet, and especially on his entire unconsciousness of the vast and bitter burdens, for millions of human hearts, actually to be created by laws just then under consideration in London—an unconsciousness in which, probably, Samuel Johnson was surpassed by no other great man in England, excepting always his good friend, the King.

Among the most striking of the literary responses to the news that, in disregard of all appeals from America, the Stamp Act had become a law, was one by a writer of extraordinary vigor in

argument, of extraordinary affluence in invective, who chose to
view the whole problem as having logical and historical relations far more extensive than had then been commonly supposed—relations far more serious to mankind in general, than
would attach to a mere dispute in Anglo-American politics.
This writer was John Adams, then but thirty years old, a rising
member of the bar of Massachusetts, already known in that
neighborhood for his acuteness, fearlessness, and restless energy as a thinker, and for a certain truculent and sarcastic
splendor in his style of speech. To the very end of his long life,
even his most offhand writings, such as diaries and domestic
letters, reveal in him a trait of speculative activity and boldness: they show that his mind teemed and bubbled and
sparkled with ideas; that he was all the time building theories
of society, government, religion, literature, education, conduct;
that he was for ever piercing with his virile and dauntless intelligence the past, present, and future, the qualities and relation-
ships of all beings in time and eternity, in heaven, and earth,
and hell. Moreover, his ideas are never cool, never colorless.
His brain was not insulated from his heart; nay his heart, and
even his conscience, poured their warm streams through his
brain, and gave to his words a moral and emotional thoughtfulness which is at least stimulating, often wholesome and refreshing. This quality makes John Adams's writings interesting
—which, of course, is not always a test of value, or of real impressiveness. With the exception of Jefferson, he is the most
readable of the statesmen of the Revolutionary period. While
his intellect was ever alert, active, and coruscating, it was not
high enough or calm enough to look all around any subject,
and to take in the whole case as a serious quest for truth. Never
could he have been a great judge, or a great historian, or a supreme statesman, or a supreme thinker. He was by nature an
orator and an advocate; his frankest discussions of a subject always have the note of partisanship and sophistication.

What, then, to John Adams was the meaning of this incipient rupture between England and America in 1765, over

the imposition of the Stamp Act? To him it seemed but one passage in that ancient, world-wide, inappeasable feud which ever rages among men between corporate authority on the one hand, and individualism on the other. Particularly since the advent of Christianity, corporate authority has, according to John Adams, found its most perfect development in the canon and the feudal law—words which he uses as synonyms for "ecclesiastical and civil tyranny." "By the former of these, the most refined, sublime, extensive, and astonishing constitution of policy that ever was conceived by the mind of man, was framed by the Romish clergy for the aggrandizement of their own order." "In the latter, we find another system, similar in many respects to the former; which, although it was originally formed, perhaps, for the necessary defense of a barbarous people against the inroads and invasions of her neighboring nations, yet for the same purposes of tyranny, cruelty, and lust which had dictated the canon law, it was soon adopted by almost all the princes of Europe, and wrought into the constitutions of their government." The climax of misfortune to mankind was reached when, between the two systems of tyranny above described, a confederacy was established. "It seems to have been even stipulated between them, that the temporal grandees should contribute everything in their power to maintain the ascendency of the priesthood, and that the spiritual grandees in their turn should employ their ascendency over the consciences of the people, in impressing on their minds a blind, implicit obedience to civil magistracy. Thus, as long as this confederacy lasted and the people were held in ignorance, liberty, and with her, knowledge and virtue too, seem to have deserted the earth, and one age of darkness succeeded another, till God in his benign providence raised up the champions who began and conducted the Reformation."

It was, then, the uprising of individualism against corporate authority which gave us the Reformation, even as it was the Reformation which peopled North America with Englishmen

—with Englishmen, that is, who were champions of individualism. "I always consider the settlement of America with reverence and wonder, as the opening of a grand scene and design in Providence for the illumination of the ignorant, and the emancipation of the slavish part of mankind all over the earth." These Englishmen in America "formed their plan both of ecclesiastical and civil government, in direct opposition to the canon and the feudal systems." "Tyranny in every form, shape, and appearance was their disdain and abhorrence." "They saw clearly that popular powers must be placed as a guard, a control, a balance, to the powers of the monarch and the priest, in every government, or else it would soon become the man of sin, the whore of Babylon, the mystery of iniquity, a great and detestable system of fraud, violence, and usurpation. . . . They saw clearly, that of all the nonsense and delusion which had ever passed through the mind of man, none had ever been more extravagant than the notions of absolutions, indelible characters, uninterrupted successions, and the rest of those fantastical ideas derived from the canon law, which had thrown a glare of mystery, sanctity, reverence, and right reverend eminence and holiness, around the idea of a priest, as no mortal could deserve, and as always must, from the constitution of human nature, be dangerous in society. For this reason, they demolished the whole system of diocesan episcopacy; and, deriding, as all reasonable and impartial men must do, the ridiculous fancies of sanctified effluvia from episcopal fingers, they established sacerdotal ordination on the foundation of the Bible and common sense." In like manner, they organized their governments in disdain of the feudal law. They "had an utter contempt of all that dark ribaldry of hereditary, indefeasible right,—the Lord's anointed,—and the divine, miraculous original of government, with which the priesthood had enveloped the feudal monarch in clouds and mysteries, and from whence they had deduced the most mischievous of all doctrines—that of passive obedience and non-resistance. They knew that government was a plain, simple, intelligible thing, founded in nature and reason, and quite comprehensible by common sense." They knew that "nothing could preserve their posterity from the encroachments of the two systems of tyranny . . . but knowledge diffused generally through the whole body of the people." And the Stamp Act—what is it but a master stroke on behalf of ecclesiastical and civil tyranny, another effort of aggression on the part of the confederated enemies of mankind, a device expressly framed "to strip us in a great measure of the means of knowledge, by loading the press, the colleges, and even an almanac and a newspaper, with restraints and duties; and to introduce the inequalities and dependencies of the feudal system, by taking from the poorer sort of people all their little subsistence, and conferring it on a set of stamp officers, distributors, and their deputies."

Therefore, in taking our stand against the enforcement of the Stamp Act, we are but placing ourselves in that mighty line of heroes and confessors and martyrs who since the beginning of history have done battle for the dignity and happiness of human nature against the leagued assailants of both. Herein, let no one dare to accuse us of being overbold. Nay, "the true source of our sufferings has been our timidity. We have been afraid to think. We have felt a reluctance to examining into the grounds of our privileges, and the extent in which we have an indisputable right to demand them, against all the power and authority on earth." Nor may we be told that this attitude of ours toward Great Britain is unbecoming the children of a fond mother: "Is there not something exceedingly fallacious in the commonplace images of mother country and children colonies? Are we the children of Great Britain, any more than the cities of London, Exeter, and Bath? Are we not brethren and fellow subjects with those in Britain, only under a somewhat different method of legislation, and a totally different method of taxation? But, admitting we are children, have not children a right to complain when their parents are attempting to break their limbs, to administer poison, or to sell them to enemies for slaves? Let me entreat you to consider, will the mother be

pleased when you represent her as deaf to the cries of her children,—when you compare her to the infamous miscreant who
lately stood on the gallows for starving her child,—when you
resemble her to Lady Macbeth in Shakespeare (I cannot think
of it without horror) who

> Had given suck, and knew
> How tender 't was to love the babe that milked her,

but yet who could,

> even while 't was smiling in her face,
> Have plucked her nipple from the boneless gums,
> And dashed the brains out.

"Let us banish for ever from our minds, my countrymen, all
such unworthy ideas of the king, his ministry, and parliament.
. . . Let us presume, what is in fact true, that the spirit of liberty
is as ardent as ever among the body of the nation, though a few
individuals may be corrupted. Let us take it for granted, that
the same great spirit which once gave Caesar so warm a reception, which denounced hostilities against John till Magna
Charta was signed, which severed the head of Charles the First
from his body, and drove James the Second from his kingdom,
the same great spirit (may Heaven preserve it till the earth
shall be no more) which first seated the great-grandfather of
his present most gracious majesty on the throne of Britain, is
still alive and active and warm in England; and that the same
spirit in America, instead of provoking the inhabitants of that
country, will endear us to them for ever, and secure their good-
will."

Such was the teaching, and such the temper, of a series of
four essays by John Adams, which were first published, though
without his name and without any descriptive title, in the
Boston Gazette, in August, 1765. By their wide range of allusion, their novelty, audacity, eloquence, by the jocular savagery
of their sarcasms on things sacred, they easily and quickly produced a stir, and won for themselves considerable notoriety. At
the instigation of Thomas Hollis, they were almost immedi-

ately reproduced in the *London Chronicle*; and in 1768, also by Hollis's act, they were welded together into a single document, and as such were published in London under the somewhat misleading title of *A Dissertation on the Canon and the Feudal Law*.

On the sixth of September, 1765, there appeared in a newspaper published in New London the first of a series of five essays addressed "To the Freemen of the Colony of Connecticut," and traversing in grave tone and with masterful intelligence the troublesome matters thrust upon public attention by the Stamp Act. "It is the most critical season," said the writer, "that ever this colony of America saw,—a time when everything dear to us in this world is at stake." Certainly, if parliament may now begin to encroach upon those ancient rights which were secured to us by royal grants and charters—these being in reality compacts entered into for a valid consideration —at what point can the encroachments of parliament be expected to end? If they "have a right to impose a stamp tax, they have a right to lay on us a poll tax, a land tax, a malt tax, a cider tax, a window tax, a smoke tax; and why not tax us for the light of the sun, the air we breathe, and the ground we are buried in? If they have a right to deny us the privilege of trial by juries, they have as good a right to deny us any trials at all, and to vote away our estates and lives at pleasure." Thus, in plain, pungent fashion, level to the common mind, this writer argues against the constitutionality of the Stamp Act as well as of every other form of colonial taxation by the British parliament, exposing at every turn the enormous menace it involves to the most valued rights of Americans—to their very existence, in fact, in any civil rank higher than that of slaves.

Though the authorship of these trenchant essays was at first carefully concealed, they were soon known as the work of a Congregational pastor in Connecticut, Stephen Johnson, sprung from the oldest and best stock in that colony, a graduate of Yale in the class of 1743, a man of pure life, of humane and active sympathy, a sturdy thinker, a strong writer, and of a patriotism so rugged as to show itself on the battlefields of the Revolution as well as in those intellectual combats which led to them. With a boldness which perhaps no other American writer had then equalled, twice in that year, 1765, this Connecticut pastor gave sharp warning to the mother country that if the policy then in vogue should be persisted in, a bloody revolution would follow, and England would suffer "the loss of two millions of the best affected subjects." "We cannot think it within any power to make our rights no rights." "The American colonies can't be enslaved and ruined but by their own folly, consent, or inactivity."

On the fourteenth of October, 1765, while the members of the Stamp Act Congress were in the midst of their labors upon the great problem of the hour, there came from a printing office in Annapolis a pamphlet, of portly dimensions, dealing with the same problem, and doing so with a degree of legal learning, of acumen, and of literary power, which gave to it, both in America and in England, the highest celebrity among the political writings of this period. It was entitled "Considerations on the Propriety of Imposing Taxes in the British Colonies, for the Purpose of Raising a Revenue by Act of Parliament." The pamphlet was without the author's name; and, still further to obscure its origin, it bore on the title-page, for the place of publication, merely the words "North America." Moreover, the preface was dated "Virginia"—another device for throwing the reader off the true scent; for, in reality, Maryland was the colony to which its author belonged, and in which, undoubtedly, his pamphlet was written.

All this machinery for self-occultation failed to accomplish its purpose. The marks which the pamphlet bore of its author's individuality, were too definite and too unusual to permit him to remain long undiscovered. The men then living in the colonies who were capable of handling such a problem in such a manner, were not many and could not be obscure; and, before

very long, it was everywhere known as the work of Daniel
Dulany, then the foremost lawyer of Maryland, for many years
the secretary of the province, and one of its most accomplished
and influential citizens. Born in Maryland in 1721, Daniel
Dulany had been sent to England for his education, which he
received at Eton College, at Clare Hall, Cambridge, and at the
Temple. Returning in due time to his native colony, he was admitted to the bar in 1747, his own father being at that time one
of its most eminent members. It was not many years before his
own extraordinary abilities and his lofty personal character
raised him to the very head of his profession not only in Maryland but in the middle colonies. His authority was so great that
the courts of his own province were accustomed to submit to
him the most difficult questions which came before them; his
opinion was also sought from England upon abstruse matters of
law; while in some parts of Virginia it was no unusual thing for
cases to be withdrawn from their own courts, and even from the
hands of the Lord Chancellor in England, in order to leave
them to him for settlement. Finally, his great gifts for the understanding of the law, were accompanied by those which contribute to its persuasive exposition—powerful oratory, felicity
of literary allusion, and a fine and gracious personality. William Pinkney, who could have known Dulany only in his later
years and who had a familiar acquaintance also with the great
orators of England near the close of the eighteenth century, is
said to have been of the opinion "that even amongst such men
as Fox, Pitt, and Sheridan," was no one superior to this barrister in an American province.

The logical expertness of Dulany as a debater is apparent in
the skill with which, at the beginning of his pamphlet, he fixes
the true issue. For, in the very preamble of the Stamp Act, he
finds an assumption which seems to him to lie at the bottom
of every question in dispute between the colonies and the
mother country: it is the assumption whereon parliament
undertakes to "give and grant" certain portions of the property

of the people of America. "What right had the commons of Great Britain to be thus munificent at the expense of the commons of America?" Upon one point, at least, all parties are agreed, namely, that nowhere can British subjects be taxed except "with their own consent given by their representatives." Are, then, the commons of Great Britain the representatives of the people of America? It is not pretended that we have ever elected any members of the house of commons. How, then, can the members of that house be our representatives? The answer is, that this is a case of virtual representation—precisely such representation as subsists between the house of commons and the vast majority of the people of Great Britain itself, who likewise have no votes for members of that body. Now, this non-voting majority of the people of Great Britain, though not actually represented in the house of commons, are understood to be virtually represented by that house; and they accept the relation as a valid, even if imperfect, compliance with the old constitutional maxim, and submit themselves, accordingly, to such taxes as are imposed upon them by parliament. But, as regards the privilege of voting for members of parliament, the situation of those British subjects in Great Britain is the same as that of all British subjects in America; and, consequently, though the latter are not actually, they are virtually, represented by the house of commons; hence, they also should accept this virtual representation as a valid compliance with the old constitutional maxim, and should submit themselves to the taxes that may be laid upon them by the imperial legislature, which represents them and their interests as truly as it does the vast non-voting population of the mother country.

This imposing analogy between the situation, and therefore between the obligations, of the non-voting people of Great Britain and the non-voting people of America, it is the chief purpose of Dulaney's pamphlet to break down and destroy—as resting on an argument which, in his opinion, "is totally defective," since "it consists of facts not true, and of conclusions inadmissible." "I shall," he says, "undertake to disprove the supposed similarity of situation, whence the same kind of representation is deduced of the inhabitants of the colonies, and of the British non-electors; and if I succeed, the notion of a virtual representation of the colonies must fail—which, in truth, is a mere cobweb spread to catch the unwary, and to entangle the weak." Accordingly, he goes on to point out a number of particulars in which the situation of the American non-electors is radically different from that of the British non-electors. Thus, in Great Britain, the interests "of the non-electors, the electors, and the representatives, are individually the same, to say nothing of the connection among neighbors, friends, and relations. The security of the non-electors against oppression is that their oppression will fall also upon the electors and the representatives. The one can't be injured, and the other indemnified. Further, if the non-electors should not be taxed by the British parliament, they would not be taxed at all; and it would be iniquitous, as well as a solecism in the political system, that they should partake of all the benefits resulting from the imposition and application of taxes, and derive an immunity from the circumstance of not being qualified to vote. Under this constitution, then, a double or virtual representation may be reasonably supposed. The electors, who are inseparably connected in their interests with the non-electors, may be justly deemed to be the representatives of the non-electors, at the same time they exercise their personal privilege in their right of election, and the members chosen, therefore, the representatives of both." On the other hand, "the inhabitants of the colonies are, as such, incapable of being electors, the privilege of election being exercisable only in person; and, therefore, if every inhabitant of America had the requisite freehold, not one could vote, but upon the supposition of his ceasing to be an inhabitant of America and becoming a resident in Great Britain,—a supposition which would be impertinent, because it shifts the question." Furthermore, "should the colonies not be taxed by parliamentary impositions, their respective legislatures have a regular, adequate, and constitutional authority to tax them;

and, therefore, there would not necessarily be an iniquitous and absurd exemption, from their not being represented by the house of commons." Finally, "there is not that intimate and inseparable relation between the electors of Great Britain and the inhabitants of the colonies, which must inevitably involve both in the same taxation. On the contrary, not a single actual elector in England might be immediately affected by a taxation in America, imposed by a statute which would have a general operation and effect upon the properties of the inhabitants of the colonies. The latter might be oppressed in a thousand shapes, without any sympathy, or exciting any alarm in the former. Moreover, even acts oppressive and injurious to the colonies in an extreme degree, might become popular in England, from the promise or expectation that the very measures which depress the colonies, would give ease to the inhabitants of Great Britain. It is, indeed, true that the interests of England and the colonies are allied, and an injury to the colonies, produced into all its consequences, will eventually affect the mother country. Yet, these consequences, being generally remote, are not at once foreseen; they do not immediately alarm the fears and engage the passions of the English electors,—the connection between a freeholder of Great Britain and a British American being deducible only through a train of reasoning which few will take the trouble, or can have an opportunity, if they have capacity, to investigate. Wherefore, the relation between the British Americans and the English electors is a knot too infirm to be relied on as a competent security, especially against the force of a present, counteracting expectation of relief." In conclusion, then, "if the commons of Great Britain have no right by the constitution to 'give and grant' property not belonging to themselves but to others, without their consent actually or virtually given; . . . if it appears that the colonies are not actually represented by the commons of Great Britain, and that the notion of a double or virtual representation doth not with any propriety apply to the people of America; then the principle of the Stamp Act must be given up as indefensible on the point of representation, and the validity of it rested upon the power which they who framed it, have to carry it into execution."

Having, by this brilliant stroke of debating ability, broken the very centre of the enemy's line—their famous doctrine of virtual representation—Dulany finds himself for a moment embarrassed by the very extent of his own success. Has he not proved too much? For, if the colonies may not be taxed without being either actually or virtually represented, and if, indeed, they are represented neither actually nor virtually, then the alarming inference seems to follow, that "the subordination or dependence of the colonies, and the superintendence of the British parliament, cannot be consistently established." If, indeed, he has proved all that, he has proved far more than either he or his fellow colonists had then desired to prove, and far more, of course, than their fellow subjects in Great Britain can hear of without abhorrence and dismay. To meet this embarrassment, is his next important step. Does, then, the denial of the right of parliament to tax unrepresented colonies, involve the denial of the general authority of parliament over them? By no means. The real question at issue is not one of all power or none, but merely of power sufficient for the unity and welfare of the whole empire. Surely, the general authority of parliament may be exerted to every useful purpose required for the due subordination of the unrepresented colonies, without proceeding to the extent of laying taxes upon them. Who does not see that parliament may leave to the colonies their ancient privilege of taxing themselves for the general support of the empire, without by that act dissolving the connection of those colonies with the empire, or their due allegiance to the empire? "May not, then, the line be distinctly and justly drawn between such acts as are necessary or proper for preserving or securing the dependence of the colonies, and such as are not necessary or proper for that very important purpose?" "Because the parliament may, when the relation between Great Britain and her colonies calls for an exertion of her superintendence, bind the colonies by statute, therefore a parliamentary interposition in every other instance is justifiable,—is an inference that may be denied." "If, moreover, Great Britain hath an equitable claim to the contribution of the colonies, it ought to be proportioned to their circumstances; and they might, surely, be indulged with discharging it in the most easy and satisfactory manner to themselves. If ways and means convenient and conciliating would produce their contribution, as well as oppressive and disgusting exactions, it is neither consistent with humanity nor policy to pursue the latter. A power may even exist without an actual exercise of it; and it indicates as little good sense as good nature to exercise it, only that the subjects of it may feel the rod that rules them."

But what, finally, is the practical use which this powerful debater would make of his apparent victory over the advocates of parliamentary taxation? He seems to have shown that the theory of virtual representation of the colonies is untenable. What then? In case parliament should still persist in taxing those colonies, what course of action does Daniel Dulany recommend to them? A nullification of such acts of parliament? A total rejection of the authority of parliament? Armed resistance? Revolution? Independence? Heaven forbid! "I would be understood. I am upon a question of propriety, not of power; and though some may be inclined to think it is to little purpose to discuss the one, when the other is irresistible, yet are they different considerations; and, at the same time that I invalidate the claim upon which it is founded, I may very consistently recommend a submission to the law—whilst it endures."

And is this all? Nay, but while we make no unlawful resistance to the authority of parliament, we should so shape our affairs as to render such an exertion of its authority quite unprofitable to those who have advised it. "If in consequence of . . . the imposition of taxes upon their properties, the colonies should only be driven to observe the strictest maxims of frugality, . . . to use new methods of industry, and to have recourse to arts for a supply of necessaries, the difficulty in succeeding would prove less than the apprehension of miscarrying, and the benefit greater than the hope of it." "For food, thank God, they do not, and for raiment they need not, depend upon Great Britain." "Let the manufacture of America be the symbol of dignity, the badge of virtue, and it will soon break the fetters of distress. A garment of linsey-woolsey, when made the distinction of real patriotism, is more honorable and attractive of respect and veneration, than all the pageantry, and the robes, and the plumes, and the diadem of an emperor without it. Let the emulation be not in the richness and variety of foreign productions, but in the improvement and perfection of our own. Let it be demonstrated that the subjects of the British empire in Europe and America are the same—that the hardships of the latter will ever recoil upon the former.

"In theory it is supposed that each is equally important to the other,—that all partake of the adversity and depression of any. The theory is just, and time will certainly establish it. But if another principle should be ever hereafter adopted in practice, and a violation, deliberate, cruel, ungrateful, and attended with every circumstance of provocation, be offered to our fundamental rights, why should we leave it to the slow advances of time . . . to prove what might be demonstrated immediately? Instead of moping, and puling, and whining, to excite compassion, in such a situation we ought with spirit, and vigor, and alacrity, to bid defiance to tryanny, by exposing its impotence, by making it as contemptible as it would be detestable. By a vigorous application to manufactures, the consequence of oppression in the colonies, to the inhabitants of Great Britain, would strike home, and immediately, and none would mistake it. Craft and subtlety would not be able to impose on the most ignorant and credulous; for, if any should be so weak of sight as not to see, they would not be so callous as not to feel it. Such conduct would be the most dutiful and beneficial to the mother country. It would point out the distemper when the remedy might be easy, and a cure at once effected by a simple alteration

of regimen." "In common life, a tameness in bearing a depriva-
tion of part of a man's property, encourages rapacity to seize
the rest." "Any oppression of the colonies would intimate an
opinion of them I am persuaded they do not deserve, and their
security, as well as honor, ought to engage them to confute."
"If the case supposed should really happen, the resentment I
should recommend would be a legal, orderly, and prudent resentment, to be expressed in a zealous and vigorous industry,
in an immediate use and unabating application of the advantages we derive from our situation."

To the plan of American opposition thus outlined by Daniel
Dulany—that of denying the propriety of parliamentary taxation, while resorting to all manly and lawful measures for convincing parliament of the impolicy of such taxation—to this
plan, he himself remained faithful through the remainder of
the conflict. When, however, his fellow colonists passed the
bounds of constitutional opposition and resorted to measures
which were seditious and revolutionary, he declined, with perfect consistency, to take any further part in the movement; and
for this he was bitterly denounced as a Tory, his property was
confiscated, and the safety of his person imperilled. Though
he could not join with those of his fellow colonists who had resolved upon measures which seemed to him to be unwise and
unjustifiable, neither could he bring himself to take up arms
against them. He therefore went into complete seclusion, from
which he never afterward emerged.

There can be no doubt that the line of colonial policy thus
advocated by Daniel Dulany, with so much legal ability and
with so much literary skill, made a deep impression upon a vast
number of his fellow colonists, whom it convinced of the duty
and the wisdom of making a fearless stand against the measures
of the ministry, but without any rupture of allegiance. It is
apparent, also, that the learning, the logical force, the boldness, and the fair-mindedness of Dulany's pamphlet had no
small effect upon the leaders of liberal politics in England, and

especially upon William Pitt, all of whom it seems to have aided in defining and justifying the policy which they themselves should advocate in parliament with respect to the American colonies. For example, on the fourteenth of January, 1766, just three months after the publication of Dulany's pamphlet, Pitt appeared in the house of commons for the first time after a long absence, and spoke with tremendous power in favor both of an immediate repeal of the Stamp Act, and of the final abandonment of all measures looking towards the taxation of the colonies by parliament. In one of the speeches which he made in the course of that debate, he held up Dulany's pamphlet to the approval and the admiration of the imperial legislature; and though but a meagre outline of his speech is now in existence, even from such outline it is made clear that in all but one of the great features of his argument as to the constitutional relations of Great Britain to her colonies, he followed the very line of reasoning set forth by Daniel Dulany—an old Eton boy like himself.

No other American writings, in immediate response to the passage of the Stamp Act, are stronger in thought, or nobler in form, or more precious to us now as authentic utterances of the very mind and conscience and heart of the American people in that awful crisis of their affairs, than are the several papers put forth by the Stamp Act Congress—a renowned assemblage, which was convened in the city of New York, and which transacted its entire work within the space of seventeen days of the month of October, 1765. Its public papers consist, in the first place, of fourteen formal declarations of rights and grievances; and, in the second place, of three elaborate addresses, one to the king, one to the house of lords, and one to the house of commons.

He who would truly estimate the moral as well as the intellectual quality of American resistance to the claims of the British parliament, at the moment when the issue was first squarely made and met, will find it needful to read these official announcements of political faith touching imperial problems, the first ever issued by an inter-colonial body of American-Englishmen, then for the first time united against a common danger, and standing up, as their ancestors in the old home had often done before them, against dangerous encroachments upon their rights. Expressed in legal and constitutional language, and employing many of those aphorisms of justice and of civic courage which had been freely used by Englishmen ever since Magna Charta—exactly five hundred and fifty years before—they constitute the first group in that wonderful series of state-papers which the American colonists, speaking through their official representatives, sent forth to the world during the period of their Revolution. In whatever light we may view them, these papers of the Stamp Act Congress are masterly and impressive pieces of political statement—learned, wise, firm, temperate, conservative, even reverent—as far removed from truculence as from fear. As mere indices of personal character, as materials on which to frame a wise and safe imperial policy, they should have been invaluable to the leaders of English statesmanship at that time. Obviously, a people capable of such political statements were of stuff unfit to make slaves of. Had the king of England been equal to his great opportunity, he would have recognized these men as politicians too clear-headed to be caught by any sophisms of prerogative, as subjects too self-respecting to lie down in quiet under the violation of their ancient rights; and, instead of trying to trample them into any sort of political subordination, he would have made haste to welcome them, for the loftiness and efficiency of their characters, to the fullest privileges of the empire.

In December, 1765, in the midst of the ferment occasioned by the fact that the Stamp Act, which was then nominally in force in all the American colonies, was practically nullified in thirteen of them, there appeared in Philadelphia, in opposition to the policy out of which that Act had sprung, a notable pamphlet, the peculiar strength of which lay in its good sense united with good humor and expressed in good English. It was entitled "The Late Regulations respecting the British Colonies on the Continent of America, Considered in a Letter from a Gentleman in Philadelphia to his Friend in London." It was immediately republished in London; and "though," as a contemporary observer wrote, "the town has been in a manner glutted with pamphlets on America, yet its sale has been rapid. It . . . has gained the author much reputation." The author, whose reputation as a political writer was thus breaking upon the world, was John Dickinson, who, as a member of the Stamp Act Congress, had drafted at least two of its public papers, and whose later literary services on behalf of the Revolution were so brilliant as to win for him the title of its "Penman."

Early in the year 1766, and before the hope of a speedy repeal of the offensive Stamp Act had reached these shores, there was published in New York another striking pamphlet on the same side of the question, bearing some of the earmarks of John Dickinson, though perhaps bolder in thought and more trenchant in phrase: "Considerations upon the Rights of the Colonists to the Privileges of British Subjects, introduced by a Brief Review of the Rise and Progress of English Liberty, and concluded with some Remarks upon our Present Alarming Situation." The real aim of this writer comes out in his open avowal of that doctrine of Nullification which was already going into practice there amid multitudinous curses and groans: "Let us at once boldly plead to the jurisdiction of parliament. Let us totally disallow the force of that Act so evidently calculated to enslave us."

While the Americans in America were thus pondering the anxious problems thrust upon them by the new taxing-policy of the mother country, it happened that an American man of letters, just then in London, was moved by the same cause to give utterance to his own indignant emotion, in the form of a somewhat pugnacious satire in verse, entitled "Oppression." This poem, which bears on every page the note of Charles

Churchill, was probably written in the latter part of 1764. It made its first appearance in London in 1765. The author, not revealing his name, but describing himself as

> An uncouth genius from a western wood,
> Who 've neither wealth, election votes to bribe,
> Nor will to hackney falsehood for a tribe,

has been watching with alarm and indignation the arbitrary measures and the corrupt methods of the court and parliament, all under the malefic leadership of Lord Bute. As a British subject, he feels the disaster which all this threatens to public and private life in the motherland—to the very integrity and benignity of the imperial constitution itself; but as a British subject of American birth and connections, he is simply enraged to see with what frivolity, in what a riot of wantonness and scorn, the most sacred rights, the dearest interests, of his far-off and unvoiced fellow colonists are here bartered away. This, then, is the broad ground and justification of his satiric wrath:—

> When gathering murmurs spread throughout the realm,
> And favorite pilots bungle at the helm;
> When tyrants skulk behind a gracious throne,
> And practice—what their courage dare not own;
> When ministers like screening Grenville rule,—
> A pendant talker and a Butean tool;
> When law is chained, when Mansfield holds the rod,
> And justice trembles at his partial nod;
> When naught but fawning, flattery and lies
> Are the just emblems of our brave and wise;
>
> .   .   .   .
>
> When countries groan beneath Oppression's hand,
> And pensioned blockheads riot through the land;
> When colonies a savage excise pay,
> To feed the creatures of a motley day;
>
> .   .   .   .
>
> When dunce on dunce successive rules our state,
> Who can't love Pitt, and who a Grenville hate?
> When all these ills, and thousands yet untold,

Destroy our liberty, and rob our gold,
Should not then Satire bite with all its rage,
And just resentment glow through every page?
Who can indignant bear to hear such crimes,
And not commence an author of the times?

But, in the very sordidness and hypocrisy of politics about
the court, and in the facility with which the claims of America
have been betrayed there even by her own sons, there seems
to him to be the added and most impressive reason why he, an
American in England, should not succumb to influences that
would either keep him silent, or make him false:

And shall I mingle with the courtly throng,
When truth and reason tell me they are wrong?
Or, if poetic madness seize my brain,
Shall I not rhyme, when conscience guides my strain?
Shall I subscribe to every dunce's nod,
Call Pitt a villain, or Lord Bute a god?

.   .   .   .

Shall I extol the late severe excise,
Call it mere naught, and damn myself by lies?
Shall I my country, at thy distant call,
Not mark vile H . . . that first proposed thy fall?
Or shall I turn a traitor to my clime,
And be, like him, accursed to latest time?

.   .   .   .

I want no places at a servile court,
To be the dupe of ministerial sport;
Where honesty sincere but seldom dwells;
Where every tongue with adulation swells;
Where great fools smile, though greater fools may laugh;
Where fawns our H . . . at best a mere state calf;
Where miscreants in every scene of strife,
Get bread, for bastards and themselves, for life;
Where favorite falsehood only seems to charm,
And statesmen promise never to perform;

.   .   .   .

Where public virtue meets with abject hate,
Gives way to pleasure and intrigues of state;
Where men devoid of decency as grace,

Get titles, pensions, perquisites, and place;
Where every ill that now annoys our state,
Have their fell source—from thence their baleful date.

Following the precedent then abundantly established among English writers in opposition, this American satirist proceeds to single out and to imprecate Lord Bute as the author and the arch manipulator of all these political woes, particularly of the vexations and calamities now brought upon America:

Do not our shores now swarm by your command,
With licensed officers by sea and land?—
A crew more dreadful than our savage foes,
A locust tribe that feed on others' woes?

And this execrable colonial policy that

half the Western World annoys,
That mars their trade, their liberty destroys,
That makes them slaves, or mere mechanic tools
To work for nought, as fools do work for fools,

is in no way redeemed by the method of its administration in America at the hands of Lord Bute's hirelings, who, indeed, contrive by their insolence to crown the whole system with the last refinements of vexation:

Must it not fill all men of sense with scorn,
To see a muckworm of the earth low born,—
A creature but at best a custom clerk,
The chance production of some amorous spark,
In ignorance supreme, profoundly dark,—
To see him seat his mighty self in state,
With arms akimbo deal to each his fate;
To see the hornèd scribbler force along
And elbow here and there the busy throng?
What awful consequence transforms his face,
To show the importance of his mighty place,
As if in him all excise solely hung,
And fates of kingdoms balanced on his tongue!

But, now, these wrongs, great or petty, inflicted upon the colonies by the hard policy of Lord Bute—all these stings and stabs of oppression—how long can America be expected to

endure them? The poet's answer to that question takes the
form of a prophecy which to us may seem almost droll in its
moderation, but which may also have an interest for us as being
a very early example of those numerous hypothetical Declarations of Independence which were pronounced during the ten
or twelve years preceding the real one, and which uncon-
sciously heralded its advent:

> Ere five score years have run their tedious rounds,—
> If yet Oppression breaks o'er human bounds,
> As it has done the last sad passing year,
> Made the New World in anger shed the tear,—
> Unmindful of their native, once-loved isle,
> They 'll bid Allegiance cease her peaceful smile,
> While from their arms they tear Oppression's chain,
> And make lost Liberty once more to reign.

Yet not with such a menace could even this fierce lover of
liberty permit his satire to close; and in a relenting strain
which has in it the very pathos of filial supplication, he affirms
the affectionate fidelity of the colonies to the empire of which
they would gladly remain a part:

> But let them live, as they would choose to be,
> Loyal to king, and as true Britons free,
> They 'll ne'er by fell revolt oppose that crown
> Which first has raised them, though now pulls them down;
> If but the rights of subjects they receive,
> 'T is all they ask—or all a crown can give.*

* Excepting the citation of the title of this notable poem, as given by
Sabin and by Hildeburn, I do not remember to have seen any allusion to it
by any writer. I first stumbled upon it at the Harvard library, and could
not fail to observe its political and literary significance in relation to the
subject of this book. Neither Hildeburn nor Sabin has anything to suggest
as to its author. I am inclined, from internal evidence, to attribute it to the
once celebrated Arthur Lee, who was born in Virginia in 1740, was educated at Eton College and at the University of Edinburgh, and having settled as a physician in his native colony, went back to England at the outbreak of the great dispute intending to become a lawyer and a politician.
His biographer writes very loosely as to dates, and mentions this event as
occurring "about the year 1766." *Life of Arthur Lee*, by Richard Henry
Lee, i. 15. He had a knack both for rhyme and for vituperation; and may
have tried, in 1765, to imitate the satire of Churchill, as, a few years later,
he tried to imitate the invective of Junius.

IN *March of 1766 the Stamp Act was repealed, but Parliament refused to admit that it did not have the power to tax the colonies. There followed in rapid succession the passage of the Townshend Acts, the dispatch of British troops to Boston, the Boston Massacre, the establishment of the colonial Committees of Correspondence, and the closing of the port at Boston. Finally, the colonies answered the call of the Virginia House of Burgesses, and the First Continental Congress assembled in Philadelphia on September 5, 1774.*

Despite this evidence of widespread resistance, by no means all of the colonists could agree with the poet that the "Oppression breaks o'er human bounds . . ." There was a substantial group of men who could say with Joseph Galloway, "We want the aid and assistance and protection of the arm of our mother country. . . . Can we wish to become aliens to the mother state?"

The Loyalists and Their Literature

THERE cannot be a more authentic introduction to the Loyalists of our Revolution, than is to be had through an acquaintance with their literature. As we turn over the pages of that literature—political essays, pamphlets, sermons, songs, satires, epigrams, burlesques, lampoons—a literature now having an almost pathetic insignificance as it slumbers under a hundred years of dust and contempt—perhaps the first notable fact that calls for attention is, that, in point of time, its development lags somewhat behind that of the Revolutionist party, and does not become of much value until within the twelvemonth preceding the Lexington and Concord skirmishes—that is, until about the time of the Congress of 1774.

Of course, from the very beginning of the dispute there had been American writers who, while doubting the wisdom of the colonial policy of the English ministry, likewise doubted the soundness of the constitutional claim set up in opposition to it by many of their American brethren; and, at any rate, deprecated all violent or extreme measures in the assertion of that claim. Nevertheless, during the eight or ten years prior to 1774, it might fairly have been assumed that this Anglo-American dispute was but one of a long series of political disagreements that had broken out, at various times, in John Bull's large and vivacious family, and that this particular dispute would probably run its natural course and come to an end, just as its predecessors had done, without any permanent rupture of the interior relations of the family, and, indeed, to the great advantage of all its members through a clearer definition of those constitutional principles which had enabled them all to live together so long under the same enormous and kindly roof. Not until after the failure of Lord North's clever device for inducing the Americans to take the taxation which they liked so little, along with that cheering beverage which they liked so much, was it necessary for any person to regard the dispute as one of peculiarly deep and tragical import. It was, perhaps, on account of this confidence of theirs in the natural limitations of the problem then vexing the colonies and the mother country, that so many of the ablest conservative writers in America refrained, in that stage of affairs, from engaging very actively in the discussion. Thus it is that we may in a measure explain why, in this controversy, so little part was taken prior to 1774 by the most powerful of all the Loyalist writers— Daniel Leonard, Joseph Galloway, Samuel Seabury, Jonathan Boucher, and Jonathan Odell.

But with the events of the years 1773 and 1774 came a total change in the situation, and in the attitude of all parties toward it: first, the repulsion of the gentle tea ships by several American communities, and the destruction of valuable property belonging to liegemen of the king; then the series of stern retaliatory measures to which parliament was thereby drawn; finally, by a large portion of the colonists, the fearless summons for a great council of their own delegates, solemnly to determine and to proclaim some common plan of action. With the gathering of this celebrated council—the first Continental Congress—the wayfaring American though a fool could not err in reading, in very crimson letters painted on the air in front of him, the tidings of the arrival of a race-crisis altogether transcending those ordinary political altercations which had from time to time disturbed, and likewise quickened and clarified, the minds of his English ancestors.

Naturally, therefore, from about this time the process of political crystallization among the colonists went on with extraordinary rapidity. Then, every man had to define both to himself and to his neighbor, what he thought, how he felt, what he meant to do. Then, too, the party of insubordination in these thirteen agitated communities had, for the first time, a common and a permanent organ for the formulation of the political doctrine and purpose which should sway them all. Finally, around this official and authoritative statement of doctrine and purpose, the opposing tendencies of thought could clash and do intelligent battle—having a set of precise propositions to fight for or to fight against, and having, likewise, the grim consciousness that such fight was no longer a merely academic one.

In a valid sense, therefore, it may be said that the formation of the great Loyalist party of the American Revolution dates from about the time of the Congress of 1774. Moreover, its period of greatest activity in argumentative literature is from that time until the early summer of 1776, when nearly all further use for argumentative literature on that particular subject was brought to an end by the Declaration of Independence. The writings of the Loyalists, from the middle of 1776 down to 1783, form no longer a literature of argumentative discussion, but rather a literature of emotional appeal, exultant, hortatory, derisive, denunciatory—a literature chiefly lyrical and satirical.

Even yet, in this last decade of the nineteenth century, it is by no means easy for Americans—especially if, as is the case with the present writer, they be descended from men who thought and fought on behalf of the Revolution—to take a disinterested attitude, that is, an historical one, toward those Americans who thought and fought against the Revolution. Both as to the men and as to the questions involved in that controversy, the rehearsal of the claims of the victorious side has been going on among us, now for a hundred years or more, in tradition, in history, in oration, in song, in ceremony. Hardly have we known, seldom have we been reminded, that the side of the Loyalists, as they called themselves, of the Tories, as they were scornfully nicknamed by their opponents, was even in argument not a weak one, and in motive and sentiment not a base one, and in devotion and self-sacrifice not an unheroic one. While the war was going forward, of course the animosities aroused by it were too hot and too fierce, especially between the two opposing groups of Americans, to permit either party in the controversy to do justice to the logical or to the personal merit of the other. When at last the war came to an end, and the champions of the Revolution were in absolute triumph, then the more prominent Tories had to flee for their lives; they had to flee from the wrath that had come, and to bury themselves, either in other lands or in obscure places of this land. Then, of course, they and all their detested notions and emotions and deeds, whether grand or petty or base, went down out of sight, submerged beneath the abhorrence of the victorious Revolutionists, and doomed, as it appears, to at least one solid century of oratorical and poetical infamy, which has found its natural and organized expression in each recurring Fourth of July, and in each reappearance of the birthday of Washington. May it not, however, at last be assumed that a solid century should be, even under such conditions, a sufficient refrigerator for overheated political emotion? May we not now hope that it will not any longer cost us too great an effort to look calmly, even considerately, at least fairly, upon what, in the words and acts of the Tories, our fathers and grandfathers could hardly endure to look at all? And, surely, our willingness to do all this can hardly be lessened by the consideration that, "in dealing with an enemy, not only dead, but dead in exile and in defeat, candor prescribes the fullest measure of generous treatment." At any rate, the American Revolution affords no exemption from the general law of historic investigation—that the truth is to be found only by him who searches for it with an unbiased mind. Until we shall be able to take, respecting the problems and the parties of our own Revolution, the same attitude which we freely and easily take respecting the problems and parties of other revolutions—that is, the attitude, not of hereditary partisans, but of scientific investigators —will it be forbidden us to acquire a thoroughly discriminating and just acquaintance with that prodigious epoch in our history.

As preliminary to some examination of the argumentative value of the position taken by the Loyalist party, let us inquire, for a moment, what recognition may be due to them simply as persons. Who and what were the Tories of the American Revolution? As to their actual number, there is some difficulty in framing even a rough estimate. No attempt at a census of political opinions was ever made during that period; and no popular vote was ever taken of a nature to indicate, even approximately, the numerical strength of the two opposing schools of political thought. Of course, in every community there were Tories who were Tories in secret. These could not be counted, for the good reason that they could not be known. Then, again, the number of openly avowed Tories varied somewhat with variations in the prosperity of the Revolution. Still further, their number varied with variations of locality. Throughout the entire struggle, by far the largest number of Tories was to be found in the colony of New York, particularly in the neighborhood of its chief city. Of the other middle colonies, while there were many Tories in New Jersey, in Delaware, and in Maryland, probably the largest number lived in Pennsylvania —a number so great that a prominent officer in the Revolutionary army described it as the "enemies' country." Indeed, respecting the actual preponderance of the Tory party in these two central colonies, an eminent champion of the Revolution bore this startling testimony: "New York and Pennsylvania were so nearly divided—if their propensity was not against us—that if New England on one side and Virginia on the other had not kept them in awe, they would have joined the British." Of the New England colonies, Connecticut had the greatest number of Tories; and next, in proportion to population, was the district which was afterwards known as the State of Vermont. Proceeding to the colonies south of the Potomac, we find that in Virginia, especially after hostilities began, the Tories were decidedly less in number than the Whigs. In North Carolina, the two parties were about evenly divided. In South Carolina, the Tories were the more numerous party; while in Georgia their majority was so great that, in 1781, they were preparing to detach that colony from the general movement of the rebellion, and probably would have done so, had it not been for the embarrassing accident which happened to Cornwallis at Yorktown in the latter part of that year.

If we may accept these results as giving us a fair, even though crude, estimate concerning the local distribution of the Tories, we have still to come back to the question which deals with their probable number in the aggregate. Naturally, on such a problem, the conclusions reached by the opposing parties would greatly differ. Thus, the Tories themselves always affirmed that could there have been a true and an unterrified vote, they would have had a great majority; and that the several measures of the Revolution had not only never been submitted to such a test, but had been resolved upon and forced into effect by a few resolute leaders who, under the names of committees of correspondence, committees of observation, committees of safety, conventions, and congresses, had assumed unconstitutional authority, and had pretended, without valid credentials, to speak and to act for the whole population of their towns, or counties, or provinces. To translate the Tory explanation into the language of the present day, it may be said that, in their belief, the several measures of the Revolution were the work of a well-constructed and powerful political machine, set up in each colony, in each county, in each town, and operated with as much skill and will and unscrupulousness as go into the operation of such machines in our time. This opinion, which, in its substance, was most ably presented in those days by the Tory writers, has been adopted by a very candid English historian now living, who says of the American Revolution that, like most other revolutions, it "was the work of an energetic minority, who succeeded in committing an undecided and fluctuating majority to courses for which they had little love, and leading them step by step to a position from which it was impossible to recede."*

Certainly, with such an estimate as to the superior numbers of the Tories, their own opponents did not agree; but they did admit that the Tory party was at any rate a very large one. Perhaps no statesman on the Whig side was better informed on such a subject that John Adams, or was less inclined to make an undue concession to the enemy; and he gave it as his opinion that about one-third of the people of the thirteen States had been opposed to the measures of the Revolution in all its stages. This opinion of John Adams, which he affirmed more than once in the latter part of his life, was on one occasion mentioned by him in a letter to his old compatriot, Thomas McKean, chief-justice of Pennsylvania, a signer of the Declaration of Independence, and a member of every American Congress from that of 1765 to the close of the Revolution. "You say," wrote McKean in reply, "that . . . about a third of the people of the colonies were against the Revolution. It required much reflection before I could fix my opinion on this subject; but on mature deliberation I conclude you are right, and that more than a third of influential characters were against it."

Out of three millions of people, then, at least one million did not approve of the policy of carrying their political op-

* Lecky, *A History of England in the Eighteenth Century*, new ed., iv. 224.

position to the point of rebellion and separation. According to John Adams and Thomas McKean, every third American whom we could have encountered in this part of the world between 1765 and 1783 was a Loyalist. Surely, an idea—a cause—that was cherished and clung to, amid almost every form of obloquy and disaster, by so vast a section of American society, can hardly deserve any longer to be turned out of court in so summary and contemptuous a fashion as that with which it has been commonly disposed of by American writers.

After the question of number, very properly comes that of quality. What kind of people were these Tories, as regards intelligence, character, and standing in their several communities?

And here, brushing aside, as unworthy of historical investigators, the partisan and vindictive epithets of the controversy—many of which, however, still survive even in the historical writings of our own time—we shall find that the Loyalists were, as might be expected, of all grades of personal worth and worthlessness; and that, while there was among them, no doubt, the usual proportion of human selfishness, malice, and rascality, as a class they were not bad people, much less were they execrable people—as their opponents at the time commonly declared them to be.

In the first place, there was, prior to 1776, the official class; that is, the men holding various positions in the civil and military and naval services of the government, their immediate families, and their social connections. All such persons may be described as inclining to the Loyalist view in consequence of official bias.

Next were certain colonial politicians who, it may be admitted, took a rather selfish and an unprincipled view of the whole dispute, and who, counting on the probable, if not inevitable, success of the British arms in such a conflict, adopted the Loyalist side, not for conscience's sake but for profit's sake, and in the expectation of being rewarded for their fidelity by offices and titles, and especially by the confiscated estates of the rebels, after the rebels themselves should have been defeated, and their leaders hanged or sent into exile.

As composing still another class of Tories, may be mentioned probably a vast majority of those who stood for the commercial interests, for the capital and the tangible property of the country, and who, with the instincts natural to persons who have something considerable to lose, disapproved of all measures for pushing the dispute to the point of disorder, riot, and civil war.

Still another class of Loyalists was made up of people of professional training and occupation—clergymen, physicians, lawyers, teachers—a clear majority of whom seem to have been set against the ultimate measures of the Revolution.

Finally, and in general, it may be said that a majority of those who, of whatever occupation, of whatever grade of culture or of wealth, would now be described as conservative people, were Loyalists during the American Revolution. And by way of concession to the authority and force of truth, what has to be said respecting the personal quality commonly attaching to those who, in any age or country, are liable to be classed as conservative people? Will it be denied that within that order of persons, one may usually find at least a fair portion of the cultivation, of the moral thoughtfulness, of the personal purity and honor, existing in the entire community to which they happen to belong?

Precisely this description, at any rate, applies to the conservative class in the American colonies during that epoch— a majority of whom dissented from those extreme measures which at last transformed into a revolution a political movement which began with the avowed purpose of confining itself to a struggle for redress of grievances, and within the limits of constitutional opposition. If, for example, we consider the point with reference to cultivation and moral refinement, it may seem to us a significant fact that among the members of the Loyalist party are to be found the names of a great multitude of the graduates of our colonial colleges—especially of Harvard, William and Mary, Yale, Princeton, and Pennsylvania. Thus, in an act of banishment passed by Massachusetts, in September, 1778, against the most prominent of the Tory leaders in that State, one may now read the names of three hundred and ten of her citizens. And who were they? Let us go over their names. Are these the names of profligates and desperadoes, or even of men of slight and equivocal consideration? To any one at all familiar with the history of colonial New England, that list of men, denounced to exile and loss of property on account of their opinions, will read almost like the beadroll of the oldest and noblest families concerned in the founding and upbuilding of New England civilization. Moreover, of that catalogue of three hundred and ten men of Massachusetts, banished for an offence to which the most of them appear to have been driven by conscientious convictions, more than sixty were graduates of Harvard. This fact is probably a typical one; and of the whole body of the Loyalists throughout the thirteen colonies, it must be said that it contained, as one of its ablest antagonists long after admitted, "more than a third of influential characters"—that is, a very considerable portion of the customary chiefs and representatives of conservatism in each community.

By any standard of judgment, therefore, according to which we usually determine the personal quality of any party of men and women in this world—whether the standard be intellectual, or moral, or social, or merely conventional—the Tories of the Revolution seem to have been not a profligate party, nor an unprincipled one, nor a reckless or even a light-minded one, but, on the contrary, to have had among them a very considerable portion of the most refined, thoughtful, and conscientious people in the colonies. So true is this, that in 1807 a noble-minded Scottish woman, Mistress Anne Grant of Laggan, who in her early life had been familiar with American colonial society, compared the loss which America suffered in consequence of the expatriation of the Loyalists by the Revolution, to the loss which France suffered in consequence of the expatriation of so many of her Protestants by the revocation of the Edict of Nantes.

So much, then must be said on behalf of the Tories of the Revolution—in point of numbers, they were far from inconsiderable, and in point of character, they were far from despicable. On the one hand, they formed no mere rump party. If they were not actually a majority of the American people— as they themselves always claimed to be, and as some careful scholars now think they were—they did at least constitute a huge minority of the American people: they formed a section of colonial society too important on the score of mere numbers to be set down as a paltry handful of obstructives; while in any rightful estimate of personal value, quite aside from mere numbers, they seem to deserve the consideration which conscientious and cultivated people of one party never ask in vain of conscientious and cultivated people of the opposite party— at least after the issues of the controversy are closed.

Pressing forward, then, with our investigation, we proceed to apply to the American Loyalist that test by which we must judge any party of men who have taken one side, and have borne an important share in any great historical controversy. This is the test of argumentative value. It asks whether the logical position of the party was or was not a strong one.

Even yet it is not quite needless to remind ourselves that the American Revolution was a war of argument long before it became a war of physical force; and that, in this war of argument, were involved a multitude of difficult questions—constitutional, legal, political, ethical—with respect to which honest and thoughtful people were compelled to differ. All these questions, however, may, for our purposes, be reduced to just two: first, the question of what was lawful under the existing constitution of the British empire; and secondly, the question of what was expedient under the existing circumstances of the colonies. Now, paradoxical as it may seem to many of the American descendants of the victorious party, each of those questions had two very real and quite opposite sides; much was to be said for each side; and for the Tory side so much was to be said in the way of solid fact and of valid reasoning, that an intelligent and a noble-minded American might have taken that side, and might have stuck to it, and might have gone into battle for it, and might have imperiled all the interests of his life in defense of it, without any just impeachment of his reason or of his integrity—without deserving to be called, then or since then, either a weak man or a bad one.

That we may develop before our eyes something of the argumentative strength of the Loyalist position, in the appeal which it actually made to honest men at that time, let us take up for a moment the first of the two questions to which, as has just been said, the whole dispute may be reduced—the question of what was lawful under the existing constitution of the British empire. Let us strike into the very heart of that question. It was the contention of the American Whigs that the British parliament could not lawfully tax us, because by so doing it would be violating an ancient maxim of the British constitution: "No taxation without representation." Have we not all been taught from our childhood that the citation of that old maxim simply settled the constitutional merits of the whole controversy, and settled it absolutely in favor of the Whigs? But did it so settle it? Have we not been accustomed to think that the refusal of the American Tories to give way before the citation of that maxim was merely a case of criminal stupidity or of criminal perversity on their part? But was it so?

On the contrary, many of the profoundest constitutional lawyers in America, as well as in England, both rejected the foregoing Whig contention, and at the same time admitted the soundness and the force of the venerable maxim upon which that contention was alleged to rest. Thus the leading English jurists, who supported the parliamentary taxation of the colonies, did not dispute that maxim. Even George Grenville, the author and champion of the Stamp Act, did not dispute it. "The colonies claim, it is true," said he, "the privilege which is common to all British subjects, of being taxed only with their own consent, given by their representatives. And may they ever enjoy the privilege in all its extent; may this sacred pledge of liberty be preserved inviolate to the utmost verge of our dominions, and to the latest pages of our history! I would never lend my hand toward forging chains for America, lest, in so doing, I should forge them for myself. But the remonstrances of the Americans fail in the great point of the colonies not being represented in parliament, which is the common council of the whole empire, and as such is as capable of imposing internal taxes as impost duties, or taxes on inter-colonial trade, or laws of navigation."

These words of Grenville may help us to understand the position of the American Loyalists. They frankly admitted the maxim of "No taxation without representation"; but the most of them denied that the maxim was violated by the acts of parliament laying taxation upon the colonies. Here everything depends, they argued, on the meaning to be attached to the word representation; and that meaning is to be ascertained by ascertaining what was understood by the word in England at the time when this old maxim originated, and in the subsequent ages during which it had been quoted and applied. Now, the meaning then attached to the word in actual constitutional experience in England is one which shows that the commons of America, like the commons of England, are alike represented in that great branch of the British parliament which proclaims its representative character in its very name—the house of commons. During the whole period in which the maxim under consideration had been acquiring authority, the idea was that representation in parliament was constituted, not through any uniform distribution, among individual persons, of the privilege of voting for members, but rather through a distribution of such privilege among certain organized communities, as counties, cities, boroughs, and universities, to which at an early day this function had been assigned according to a method then deemed equable and just. Furthermore, as it has been from the

beginning, so is it still a principle of parliamentary representation, that from the moment a member is thus chosen to sit in
parliament, he is the representative of the whole empire and not
of his particular constituency. He "is under no obligation, therefore, to follow instructions from the voters or the inhabitants of
the district from which he is chosen. They have no legal means
of enforcing any instructions. They cannot demand his resignation. In fact, a member cannot resign." Moreover, the members
of the house of lords "represent, in principle, the interests of
the whole empire, and of all classes, as truly as the commons."
Therefore, the historic meaning of the word representation, as
the word has always been used in English constitutional experience, seemed fairly to justify the Loyalist contention, that
the several organized British communities in America, as an
integral part of the British empire, were to all intents and purposes represented in the British parliament, which sat at the
capital as the supreme council of the whole empire, and exercised legislative authority coextensive with the boundaries
of that empire.

It was no sufficient reply to this statement to say, as some
did say, that such representation as has just been described
was a very imperfect kind of representation. Of course it was an
imperfect kind of representation; but, whatever it was, it was
exactly the kind of representation that was meant by the old
constitutional maxim thus cited; for it was the only kind of
representation practiced, or known, or perhaps even conceived
of in England during all those ages which had witnessed the
birth and the growth of this old formula. The truth is that representation, as a political fact in this world, has thus far been
a thing of degrees—a thing of less and of more; that perfect
representation has even yet not been anywhere attained in this
world; that in the last century representation in England was
very much less perfect than it has since become; and, finally,
that, in the period now dealt with, what had always been meant
by the word representation in the British empire was satisfied
by such a composition of the house of commons as that, while

its members were voted for by very few even of the common people in England, yet, the moment that its members were elected, they became, in the eye of the constitution and in the spirit of this old formula, the actual representatives of all the commoners of the whole empire, in all its extent, in all its dominions and dependencies.

Accordingly, when certain English commoners in America at last rose up and put forward the claim that, merely because they had no votes for members of the house of commons, therefore that house did not represent them, and therefore they could not lawfully be taxed by parliament, it was very naturally said, in reply, that these English commoners in America were demanding for themselves a new and peculiar definition of the word representation; a definition never up to that time given to it in England, and never of course up to that time claimed or enjoyed by English commoners in England. For, how was it at that time in England with respect to the electoral privilege? Indeed, very few people in England then had votes for members of the house of commons—only one-tenth of the entire population of the realm. How about the other nine-tenths of the population of the realm? Had not those British subjects in England as good a right as these British subjects in America to deny that they were represented in parliament, and that they could be lawfully taxed by parliament? Nay, such was the state of the electoral system that entire communities of British subjects in England, composing such cities as Leeds, Halifax, Birmingham, Manchester, and Liverpool—communities as populous and as rich as entire provinces in America—had no votes whatever for members of parliament. Yet, did the people of these several communities in England refuse to pay taxes levied by act of parliament—that is, did they, for that reason, proclaim the nullification of a law of the general government? "We admit," continued the American Loyalists, "that for all these communities of British subjects—for those in England, as well as for these in America—the existing representation is very imperfect; that it should be reformed and made larger and more uniform than it now is; and we are ready and anxious to join in all forms of constitutional agitation, under the leadership of such men as Chatham, and Camden, and Burke, and Barré, and Fox, and Pownall, to secure such reform; and yet it remains true that the present state of representation throughout the British empire, imperfect as it is, is representation in the very sense understood and practiced by the English race whenever hitherto they have alleged the maxim,—'No taxation without representation.' That old maxim, therefore, can hardly be said to be violated by the present imperfect state of our representative system. The true remedy for the defects of which we complain is reform—reform of the entire representative system both in England and in America—reform by means of vigorous political agitation—reform, then, and not a rejection of the authority of the general government; reform, and not nullification; reform, and not a disruption of the empire."

Such is a rough statement, and, as I think, a fair one, of the leading argument of the American Loyalists with respect to the first of the two great questions then dividing the American people, namely, the question of what was lawful under the existing constitution of the British empire. Certainly, the position thus taken by the Loyalists was a very strong one—so strong, in fact, that honest and reasonable Americans could take it, and stand upon it, and even offer up their lives in defense of it, without being justly liable to the charge that they were either peculiarly base, or peculiarly stupid.

Indeed, under this aspect of legality, the concession just made by us does scant justice to the Tories—or to the truth. The dispute, it must be remembered, had risen among a people who were then subjects of the British empire, and were proud of the fact; who exulted in the blessings of the British constitution; and who, upon the matter at issue, began by confidently appealing to that constitution for support. The contention of the Tories was that, under the constitution, the authority of the imperial parliament was, even for purposes of revenue legislation, binding in America, as in all other parts of the empire, and even though America should have no members in the house of commons. This the Whigs denied. It was, then, a question of British constitutional law. Upon that question, which of the two parties was in the right? Is it now possible to doubt that it was the Tories? A learned American writer upon the law, now one of the justices of the Supreme Court of the United States, in referring to the decision of Mr. Chief-Justice Hutchinson sustaining the legality of writs of assistance, has given this opinion: "A careful examination of the question compels the conclusion . . . that there was at least reasonable ground for holding, as a matter of mere law, that the British parliament had power to bind the colonies." This view, of course, has been sustained by the highest English authorities upon British constitutional law, from the time of Lord Mansfield to the present. "As a matter of abstract right," says Sir Vernon Harcourt, "the mother country has never parted with the claim of ultimate supreme authority for the imperial legislature. If it did so, it would dissolve the imperial tie, and convert the colonies into foreign and independent states." "The constitutional supremacy of the imperial parliament over all the colonial possessions of the crown," says another eminent English writer, "was formally reasserted in 1865, by an act passed to remove certain doubts respecting the powers of colonial legislatures. . . . It is clear that imperial acts are binding upon the colonial subjects of the crown, as much as upon all other British subjects, whenever, by express provision or by necessary intendment, they relate to or concern the colonies."

But after the question as to what was lawful under the existing constitution of the British empire, came the question as to what was expedient under the existing circumstances of the American colonies. Now, as it happened, this latter question had two aspects, one of which pointed toward the expediency of rejecting the taxing power of parliament, even though such power did exist under the constitution; the other pointed toward the expediency of separation from the empire.

Having in view, at present, the former aspect of this question, the American Whigs went forward and took the ground that, if the claim of parliament to tax them was indeed justified by the constitution, then so much the worse for the constitution—since it was a claim too full of political danger to be any longer submitted to: "If parliament, to which we send no members, may tax us three pence on a pound of tea, it may, if it pleases, tax us a shilling, or a guinea. Once concede to it this right to tax us at all, and what security have we against its taxing us excessively?—what security have we for our freedom or our property against any enormity of oppression?" And what was the answer of the American Tories to this argument? "Yes," said the Tories, "you allege a grave political danger. But does it really exist? Is it likely ever to exist? Are you not guilty of the fallacy of arguing against the use of a power, simply from the possibility of its abuse? In this world every alleged danger must be estimated in the light of common sense and of reasonable probability. In that light, what ground have we for alarm? The line drawn by the supreme legislature itself for the exercise of its own power, is a perfectly distinct one,— that it should tax no part of the empire to a greater amount than its just and equitable proportion. As respects America, the supreme legislature has not yet overstepped that line; it has shown no disposition to overstep that line; we have not the slightest reason to suppose that it ever will overstep that line. Moreover, all the instincts of the English race are for fair play, and would be overwhelmingly against such an injustice, were parliament to attempt it. It is thought in England that as we, British subjects in America, receive our share of the benefits of membership of the empire, so we ought to pay our share toward the cost of those benefits. In apportioning our share of the cost, they have not fixed upon an amount which anybody, even here, calls excessive; indeed, it is rather below than above the amount that might justly be named. Now, in this world, affairs cannot be conducted—civilization cannot go on—without confidence in somebody. And in this matter, we deem it reasonable and prudent to have confidence in the good sense and in the justice of the English race, and especially of the house of commons, which is the great council of the commoners of the English race. True, we do not at present send members to that great council, any more than do certain great taxpaying communities in England; but, then, no community even in England has, in reality, so many representatives in parliament —so many powerful friends and champions in both houses of parliament—as we American communities have: not only a great minority of silent voters, but many of the ablest debaters and party leaders there,—Barré, and Pownall, and Conway, and Fox, and Edmund Burke in the lower house, and in the upper house Lord Camden, and, above all, the great Earl of Chatham himself. Surely, with such men as these to speak for us, and to represent our interests in parliament and before the English people, no ministry could long stand, which should propose any measure liable to be condemned as grossly beyond the line of equity and fair play."

The Americans who took this line of reasoning in those days were called Tories. And what is to be thought of this line of reasoning today? Is it not at least rational and fair? Even though not irresistible, has it not a great deal of strength in it? Even though we, perhaps, should have declined to adopt it, are we not obliged to say that it might have been adopted by Americans who were both clear-headed and honest-minded?

And thus we are brought to the second aspect of the question of expediency—the great and ultimate issue of the whole controversy—that of Independence, which, however, need not be dealt with by us till, in the course of this history, we reach the year wherein that doctrine suddenly leaped into the arena and demanded recognition. In the meantime, for a clearer understanding of the Loyalist attitude toward all matters in dispute prior to that of Independence, it will be profitable for us here to note three grave errors closely connected with the whole subject, and still prevalent in popular American expositions of it.

First, it is an error to represent the Tories of the American Revolution as a party of mere negation and obstruction. They did deny, they did attempt to obstruct; but they also had positive political ideas, as well as precise measures in creative statesmanship to offer in the place of those ideas and measures to which they made objection, and which they would have kept from prevailing if they could.

Secondly, it is an error to represent the Tories of the American Revolution as a party opposed either to any reform in the relations of the colonists with the mother country, or to the extension of human rights and liberties here or elsewhere. From the beginning of the agitation, they clearly saw, they strongly felt, they frankly declared, that the constitutional relations of the colonies with the mother country were in a crude state, were unsatisfactory, were in need of being carefully revised and reconstructed. This admission of theirs, they never recalled. Quite aside from the question of its legality, they doubted the expediency, under modern conditions, of such an exertion of parliamentary authority as the ministry had forced into life. Upon these points, there was substantial agreement between all Americans; namely, that there was a wrong, that there was a danger, that there should be a reform. It was chiefly as to the method and the process and the scope of this needed reform, that Americans broke asunder into two great opposing parties. The exact line of cleavage between these two parties, together with the tone and the spirit characteristic of each party, may now be traced with precision in the history of the Congress of 1774. Within that body, the Tory party, both as regards its political ideas and its conscientiousness, was represented by Joseph Galloway, who then and there tried, but tried in vain, to induce the Congress to adopt such measures as would commit the American people to reform through reconciliation, rather than to reform through separation.

Thirdly, it is an error to represent the Tories of our Revolution as composed of Americans lacking in love for their native country, or in zeal for its liberty, or in willingness to labor, or fight, or even to die, for what they conceived to be its interests. As was most natural, the party which succeeded in carrying through the Congress of 1774 such measures and methods of political reform as, in fact, led to civil war, and, finally, to American Independence, took for itself the name of the patriotic party, its members being commonly called patriots. Beyond question, the Whig party was a patriotic party; but it is not now apparent that those Americans who failed in their honest and sacrificial championship of measures which would have given us political reform and political safety, but without civil war and without an angry disruption of the English-speaking race, can justly be regarded as having been, either in doctrine, or in purpose, or in act, an unpatriotic party.

ALTHOUGH the Loyalist arguments were answered by Alexander Hamilton, John Adams, and others, the issue was not to be settled by theoretical hairsplitting. During the night of April 18, 1775, Major Pitcairn led a detachment of British troops out of Boston bound for Concord to confiscate colonial powder and military stores. Blood was spilled on Lexington common the morning of the nineteenth; by the end of the year the debate had become a war.

But literary production did not cease; it changed character. From pamphlets and essays on constitutional law the colonists turned to more partisan forms of literature.

Satire and the Revolutionary Controversy

AFTER a variety of commotions, all of which portended bloodshed, a rebellious war broke out on the nineteenth of this month. On that day, our troops were attacked at Lexington and Concord, the whole country rising upon them; and a straggling encounter ensued from these towns to this place." Such is the euphemistic version of the leading events of an unforgettable day, as given by a British officer in a letter written from Boston on the 25th of April, 1775. "From Concord back to Lexington," wrote another British officer, with less disposition to smooth the rough edges of history, "we sustained a constant fire from every fence, house, hollow way, and height, as we passed along. Here Lord Percy joined us with the first brigade: he had left Boston at nine o'clock that morning. It was a necessary reinforcement, for the whole country were in arms, and all the picked men for forty miles around. We got back to Boston with the loss of upwards of fifty men, and many more wounded. This finished our excursions against rebel magazines. I cannot tell the rebel loss."

Perhaps the first visible result of this "straggling encounter" was that, on the following morning, the British army awoke to find itself closely shut up within the town of Boston, and its curiosity to become better acquainted with the interior of New England thereafter effectually restrained by a motley rabble of armed peasants encamped in its neighborhood. Moreover, it should be here noted that, for the remainder of this year 1775, among the direct consequences of what happened on the nineteenth of April, were the American capture of Ticonderoga and Crown Point, on the 10th of May; the battle of Bunker Hill, on the 17th of June; the appointment of Washington as commander-in-chief, on the 19th of June; the capture of Montreal by an American force under Montgomery, on the 12th of November; and, finally, the disastrous failure of the American attack on Quebec, on the 31st of December.

So ended the year in which the physical conflict of the Revolution began. And, thus, all tokens point to that day of evil, April the nineteenth, 1775, as the one by which the entire period of the Revolution is cut into two nearly equal but sharply contrasted sections. After ten years of words, the disputants come at last to blows. Prior to this day, the Revolutionary controversy was a political debate: after that, it was a civil war. Of the immense transformation then and there made in the very character and atmosphere of the struggle—in its ideas, its purposes, its spirit, its tone—no modern person can in any other way procure for himself so just and so vivid a picture as by studying the writings produced among us immediately before and immediately after that fatal day. Of the former, we have just inspected the most characteristic examples. It remains for us now to look at the chief representatives of the latter.

There was then at Philadelphia, watching all these dreadful developments, a very wise old man, who loathed war, not merely as a brutal way of solving practical difficulties among men, but as a singularly inapt, clumsy, and inconclusive way; a man who, having been resident in England during the previous ten years, had there put all his genius, all the energy of his heart and will, all his tact and shrewdness, all his powers of fascination, into the effort to keep the peace between these two kindred peoples, to save from disruption their glorious and already planetary empire, and especially to avert the very appeal to force which had at last been made. By a glance at the comments upon the new situation, which Benjamin Franklin then made from day to day, chiefly in the form of letters to a few distinguished friends in England, as Joseph Priestley and William Strahan, we may now most surely introduce ourselves to the very thoughts and passions of the noblest Americans in that sorrowful time, and may perceive both the prodigious transformation in the nature of the controversy wrought through this change in its method, and also by how impassable a gulf the America subsequent to April nineteenth, 1775, is separated from the America prior to that fatal day.

Thus, on the sixteenth of May, Franklin writes to Priestley: "You will have heard, before this reaches you, of a march stolen by the regulars into the country by night, and of their expedition back again. They retreated twenty miles in six hours. The governor had called the assembly to propose Lord North's pacific plan, but, before the time of their meeting, began cutting their throats. You know it was said he carried the sword in one hand and the olive branch in the other; and it seems he chose to give them a taste of the sword first. . . . All America is exasperated by his conduct, and more firmly united than ever. The breach between the two countries is grown wider and in danger of becoming irreparable." On the fifth of July, he writes to Strahan: "You have begun to burn our towns, and murder our people. Look upon your hands—they are stained with the blood of your relations! You and I were long friends; you are now my enemy, and I am, Yours, B. Franklin." On the seventh of July, to Priestley he writes: "The Congress met at a time when all minds were so exasperated by the perfidy of General Gage, and his attack on the country people, that propositions for attempting an accommodation were not much relished; and it has been with difficulty that we have carried another humble petition to the crown, to give Britain one more chance, one opportunity more, of recovering the friendship of the colonies; which, however, I think she has not sense enough to embrace, and so I conclude she has lost them forever. She has begun to burn our seaport towns. . . . She may doubtless destroy them; but, if she wishes to recover our commerce, are these the probable means? . . . If she wishes to have us subjects, and that we should submit to her as our compound sovereign, she is now giving us such miserable specimens of her government, that we shall detest and avoid it, as a complication of robbery, murder, famine, fire, and pestilence."

On the third of October, Franklin again writes to Priestley: "Tell our dear good friend, Dr. Price, who sometimes has his doubts and despondencies about our firmness, that America is determined and unanimous,—a very few Tories and placemen excepted, who will probably soon export themselves. Britain, at the expense of three millions, has killed one hundred and fifty Yankees this campaign—which is twenty thousand pounds a head; and at Bunker's Hill she gained a mile of ground, half of which she lost again by our taking post on Ploughed Hill. During the same time sixty thousand children have been born in America. From these data, his mathematical head will easily calculate the time and expense necessary to kill us all, and conquer our whole territory."

On the same date, to another friend in England, he writes: "I wish as ardently as you can do for peace, and should rejoice exceedingly in coöperating with you to that end. But every ship from Britain brings some intelligence of new measures that tend more and more to exasperate; and it seems to me that until you have found by dear experience the reducing us by force impracticable, you will think of nothing fair and reasonable. . . . If you would recall your forces and stay at home, we should meditate nothing to injure you. A little time so given for cooling on both sides, would have excellent effects. But you will goad and provoke us. You despise us too much; and you are insensible of the Italian adage, that 'there is no little enemy.' I am persuaded that the body of the British people are our friends; but they are changeable, and by your lying gazettes may soon be made our enemies. Our respect for them will proportionably diminish, and I see clearly we are on the high road to mutual enmity, hatred, and detestation. A separation of course will be inevitable. It is a million of pities, so fair a plan as we have hitherto been engaged in for increasing strength and empire with public felicity, should be destroyed by the mangling hands of a few blundering ministers. . . . We hear that more ships and troops are coming out. We know that you may do us a great deal of mischief; . . . but if you flatter yourselves with beating us into submission, you know neither the people nor the country."

Of course, a swift change in the literary expression of the controversy resulted from this change in its sphere and its weapons—this transition from reason to force, this abandonment of arguments for arms.

The deep, true love of Americans for the mother country, their pride in the British empire, their sincerity in the belief that all their political demands were compatible with their own loyalty and with the honor of England, their desire that the solution of every vexing problem should be reached in peace—all these were realities, realities as genuine as they were pathetic. In the transactions of the nineteenth of April, 1775, at the hands of official representatives of the mother country, all these sacred realities were foully dealt with—they were stamped upon, were spit upon, they were stabbed and shot at and covered with blood and cast into the mire. Accordingly, reaching this fatal point in his journey across the period of the Revolution, the student of its literature becomes then and there conscious of crossing a great spiritual chasm—of moving from one world of ideas and sentiments to a world of ideas and sentiments quite other and very different. As the news of the transactions of that day travels from man to man, upon white lips, up and down the country, all at once with each group of listeners there seems to come a spiritual revolution: in place of what was before in their hearts, are now mute astonishment as of persons stunned, a shock of horror and pain, the anguish born of affection spurned with insult and of patriotic devotion crushed under outrage; next, a consciousness of the futility of all further appeals to reason, to tradition, to law, to right; then, the conviction that henceforward all these wonderful questions about stamps and paints and glass and tea, about the right of representation and the right of petition, about the British parliament and the British crown, are simply things of a very dead past, mere antiquarian trinkets and gew-gaws, themes for human discourse as obsolete as the gossip of that polite society that went down under the Deluge. Moreover, instead of all these politico-metaphysical conundrums, Americans find staring them in the face this altogether serious and not at all metaphysical question—whether their homes are to be forcibly entered by red-coated ruffians, their property to be seized, their wives and daughters to be outraged, and themselves to be shot down on their own doorsills for making objection. Certainly, the thing next to be done by them, is to fight; but for what? For the privilege of resuming, on better terms, their old place in the British empire? Away with the British empire on any terms! For the red flag of their king? What care they any more for the red flag of a king who has made that flag redder yet in the blood of subjects who loved him and who never meant to be disloyal to him?

As to American literature, from this day forward it can only be in the moods and forms of the new situation: for the enemy, words of loathing, of scorn, of defiance, gibes, scoffings, mockings, taunts; for friends, words of faith, words of deathless resolution, words of indomitable cheer, with songs that may move men to fight in the cause of the new fatherland and gaily to die for it. As it proved, the most prominent and the most characteristic form of literature developed under the conditions of American society after the nineteenth of April, 1775, was Satire.

A most enticing opportunity for satire was furnished, during the year 1775, by the character and results of these first collisions between the British troops and the poor, ill-equipped, and ill-disciplined provincials, who, as had been frankly promised, were to be scared or beaten into submission at a single display of imperial force.

If we would now perceive the point and edge of this earliest development of regular satire during the Revolutionary controversy, we must remember that, as was not at all strange, the British entered upon the war with no expectation that it was to be a long and a desperate one, and especially with extreme contempt for the military resources and for the military qualities of their insubordinate colonists, basing their judgment, apparently, upon two supposed facts: first, that the Americans were a people lacking in warlike courage, and, secondly, that being quite without military discipline, and quite without the willingness to submit themselves to it, their volunteer troops could never stand up against British regulars. Moreover, as it happened, in the months immediately before the opening of hostilities, this strong Britannic contempt was again and again flung into speech by indiscreet representatives of it, and in a way admirably calculated to give it the widest celebrity and the sharpest sting. Thus, in the house of lords, the Earl of Sandwich, a member of the ministry, had declared that as soldiers the Americans were "raw, undisciplined, and cowardly"; that they could never "look British regulars in the face"; that "the very sound of a cannon would send them off as fast as their feet could carry them." So, also, Major Pitcairn, who was shot dead while gallantly entering the American redoubt at Bunker Hill, had boasted, on embarking at Portsmouth for America, that "if he drew his sword but half out of the scabbard, the whole banditti of Massachusetts Bay would flee from him." Sir Jeffrey

Amherst, likewise, was reported to have said that "with five thousand English regulars he would engage to march from one end to the other of the continent of North America."

When, accordingly, early one morning in the spring of 1775, on Lexington common, a considerable force of these invincible British regulars first saw in front of them a little group of undisciplined and cowardly yeomen, they very promptly fired upon them; and having thus killed eight, and wounded nine, they burst into a laugh, and with a few good round British oaths they swore that, of course, the Yankees could never bear the smell of gunpowder. Nevertheless, on that same day, and even before many hours had passed by, these same British regulars, having ceased to laugh, and having found rather urgent occasion to return speedily to Boston, were so chased, and fired upon, and otherwise harassed, by the cowardly provincials, that they themselves were thought to have manifested some antipathy to gunpowder, and even to have illustrated their martial prowess chiefly by the quality of speed in making a retreat. Certainly, the despicable Yankees must have been superhuman beings to have foreborne from the uproar of loud derision in the presence of this grotesque example of the military anti-climax, in which, indeed, were materials for satire too choice to be disregarded by our young brood of American versifiers then and there looking on.

A rough specimen of such satirical work as they then did, may be seen in an anonymous ballad soon afterward scattered broadside over the land, and entitled "The King's Own Regulars, and their Triumph over the Irregulars; a New Song, to the Tune of 'An Old Courtier of the Queen's, and the Queen's Old Courtier.'" Thus adopting for his ballad the long, rambling, ludicrous verse then familiar to all in the famous English ballad bearing the first part of the same title, the poet represents one of these British regulars in America as giving a blunt, soldierly account of the achievements of the force to which he belonged, and especially to the little incident of their retreat from Concord, palliating the disgrace of it by ironical ex-

cuses which really cut the other way and made the disgrace
more obvious:

> Since you all will have singing, and won't be said nay,
> I cannot refuse, when you so beg and pray;
> So I 'll sing you a song, as a body may say,—
> 'T is of the King's Regulars, who ne'er ran away.
> O! the Old Soldiers of the King, and the King's Own
>   Regulars.
>
> .   .   .   .
>
> No troops perform better than we at reviews,—
> We march, and we wheel, and whatever you choose;
> George would see how we fight, and we never refuse;
> There we all fight with courage—you may see 't in the news.
>
> .   .   .   .
>
> Grown proud at reviews, great George had no rest;
> Each grandsire, he had heard, a rebellion suppressed;
> He wished a rebellion—looked round, and saw none—
> So resolved a rebellion to make—of his own.
>
> The Yankees he bravely pitched on, because he thought they
>   would n't fight,
> And so he sent us over to take away their right;
> But lest they should spoil our review clothes, he cried braver
>   and louder,
> For God's sake, brother kings, don't sell the cowards any
>   powder.
>
> Our General with his council of war did advise,
> How at Lexington we might the Yankees surprise;
> We marched—and re-marched—all surprise at being beat,
> And so our wise General's plan of surprise was complete.
>
> For fifteen miles, they follow'd and pelted us—we scarce had
>   time to draw a trigger;
> But did you ever know a retreat performed with more vigor?
> For we did it in two hours, which saved us from perdition;
> 'T was not in going out, but in returning, consisted our ex-
>   pedition.
>
> .   .   .   .
>
> Of their firing from behind fences, he makes a great pother:
> Every fence has two sides, they made use of one, and we only
>   forgot to use the other;

That we turned our backs and ran away so fast,—don't let
　　that disgrace us,—
'T was only to make good what Sandwich said, that the
　　Yankees could not face us!

As they could not get before us, how could they look us in the
　　face?
We took good care they should n't—by scampering away
　　apace;
That they had not much to brag of, is a very plain case—
For if they beat us in the fight, we beat them in the race!
O! the Old Soldiers of the King, and the King's Own
　　Regulars.

Another satirical versifier, dwelling upon the comic aspects
of the retreat of the British regulars from Concord, conceived
the idea of adding to the general mirth and of still further
making light of these light-footed gentlemen, by means of a
pretended epistle, as from the pen of a shrewd and grinning
Irishman on the Yankee side of the line, and addressed

To the Troops in Boston

By me faith, but I think ye 're all makers of bulls,
Wid your brains in your breeches, your guts in your skulls!
Get home wid your muskets, and put up your swords,
And look in your books for the maneing of words:
Ye see now, me honeys, how much ye 're mistaken,—
For Concord by discord can never be baten!

How brave ye wint out wid your muskets all bright,
And thought to befrighten the folks wid the sight;
But whin ye got there, how they powder'd your pums,
And all the way home how they pepper'd your ——;
And is it not, honeys, a comical crack,
To be proud in the face, and be shot in the back!

How came ye to think, now, they did not know how
To be afther their firelocks as smartly as you?
Why, ye see now, me honeys, 't is nothing at all—
But to pull at the trigger—and pop goes the ball.

And what have ye got now, wid all your designin',
But a town widout victuals to sit down and dine in;

> And to look on the ground like a parcel of noodles,
> And sing how the Yankees have conquer'd the Doodles?
> I'm sure if ye 're wise, ye 'll make peace for a dinner,—
> For fightin' and fastin' will soon make ye thinner.

From mere irony, from playful ridicule to stern derision, to proud and scoffing defiance, was for the American satirists in 1775 an easy transition, as the spring of that year advanced into the summer and the autumn, and as the incompetence of British generalship in America continued to develop its almost incredible score of blunders and disasters:

> Your dark, unfathomed councils, our weakest heads defeat,
> Our children rout your armies, our boats destroy your fleet;
> And to complete the dire disgrace, coop'd up within a town,
> You live the scorn of all our host, the slaves of Washington!

> "Great heaven!—is this the nation, whose thundering arms
>   were hurled
> Through Europe, Afric, India?—whose navy ruled the world?
> The lustre of whose former deeds, whose ages of renown,
> Lost in a moment, are transferred to us and Washington?

These examples of spontaneous and artless satire, from American verse-writers whose names are lost perhaps beyond recovery, may suffice to show us how the new ideas, the new hatreds, the new hopes, begotten of the first clash of arms, of the first blood and anguish of defeat or victory, found their prompt and almost unstudied utterance among us in a vast miscellany of humorous and sarcastic rhymes. It is now our pleasant duty to extend and deepen our studies in this field, and to note how the copious materials for satire furnished by this earliest chapter of military experience in the Revolution, called [Philip Freneau] into the American service. . . .

In a former part of this work, the attempt has already been made to trace the poetic career of Freneau down to a time just prior to the events now reached by us. Though he had already given ample proof of his capacity for higher and sweeter work than that of satire,* he then turned away from such work with full deliberation, as from something for which his own age and country did not care, and devoted his whole strength as a poet to the service of satire—of satire upon the political and military enemies of the Revolution. Whether it was by nature, whether it was by culture, Freneau succeeded in confronting the enemy, both foreign and domestic, with a visage as stern, with a scorn as bitter, with a loathing as ruthless as that required by the unamiable muse whom he had chosen for his mistress. It will scarcely be doubted by any reader of Freneau's verse, that, in the development of that awful tempest of partisan rancor and race hatred which we call the American Revolution, this man was faithful to his vocation of stimulating its violence to the utmost; or that, at its close, the thought could ever have rested as a burden upon his conscience, that any lull or pause in the ferocity of the great conflict had been due to the least self-restraint on his part in the expression of political and personal acrimony towards the armed or the unarmed foes of the Revolution. Indeed, in one of his earliest satires he acknowledges the pitiless nature of his purpose, the implacable fierceness of his method:

> Rage gives me wings, and, fearless, prompts me on
> To conquer brutes the world should blush to own;
> No peace, no quarter, to such imps I lend—
> Death and perdition on each line I send.

In one of his latest satires, also, he causes the party-shifting printer, Hugh Gaine, in confessing the publication of some of Freneau's verses, to give a powerful and a really just description of the poet's relentless asperity in satire:

> To gain a mere trifle, a shilling or so,
> I printed some treason for Philip Freneau,—
> Some damnable poems reflecting on Gage,

* Philip Freneau was born on January 2, 1752, and graduated from the College of New Jersey (now Princeton University) in 1771. Professor Tyler thought his early poetry anticipated "the poetic and spiritual traits" of Wordsworth. [Ed.]

The king, and his council, and writ with such rage,
So full of invective and loaded with spleen,
So pointedly sharp, and so hellishly keen,
That, at least in the judgment of half our wise men,
Alecto herself made the nib to his pen.

Freneau's training for the business of a satirist was thorough.
From his youth up, he had been a particular student of Latin
literature—that literature, the only original and supremely
powerful element in which is satire. As could be said of but few
of his American contemporaries, he had found his way, also, to
the French poets and satirists. If the minor English poets of his
own early manhood, feeble and even bastard as was their art—
Shenstone, Macpherson, Mason, Akenside, Warton—seem to
have had for him as a contemporary a charm which they can
never have, it may be hoped, for any later member of the human
family, it still remains to be told that his true masters in English verse were Churchill, Pope, and Dryden, and in their special work as satirists.

Moreover, Freneau began his career as a satirist at a fortunate moment—at a moment when just such a satirist was in
demand, and when the materials for just such satire—sincere,
infuriate, savage, remorseless satire—were furnished to his
hand in profuse abundance by the political and the military
incidents that were transacting all around him. The first un-
mistakable flashes of his satiric power which can now be recognized on themes connected with the Revolution, belong to that
pathetic and heroic year, 1775, when, at last, after more than a
decade of intellectual controversy, the crash of the physical
controversy began to be heard, reverberating all along the continent from Lexington common and from the grim hill by the
side of Charlestown. As many as four or five poems, all elastic
with vigor, and all steeped in satiric passion and acerbity,
leaped from his pen that year: "On the Conqueror of America
Shut up in Boston," and "General Gage's Soliloquy," both published in August; "The Midnight Consultations, or, A Trip to
Boston," and "Libera Nos, Domine," both published in Sep-

tember; and, finally, "MacSwiggen," published probably in November or December.

Thus, the first four of these poems appeared within the two months of August and September; and the American situation at that very time both illustrates, and is illustrated by, them. In the last of the four the vision sweeps over the entire scene, up and down the continent, and takes account of all our chief assailants there. In the first three, the scene is confined to the neighborhood of Boston, the conspicuous person in it being General Thomas Gage, who, after two futile and disastrous attempts at penetrating the interior of the country, is with his half-fed army shut up in Boston and there beleaguered by a despicable mob composed of those American peasants whom he had just before, with great bluster and pomp of words, denounced as rebels, and doomed to the halter. These are the salient facts upon which the eye of the American satirist fastens; and first catching up the damning name which the British general had sought to fix upon two millions of people, their poet flings back the sombre compliment with ample reparation:

> 'Rebels you are'—the British champion cries.
> Truth, stand thou forth, and tell Tom Gage he lies!
> 'Rebels!'—and see, this mock imperial Lord
> Already threats those 'rebels' with the cord!
>
> The hour draws nigh, the glass is almost run,
> When truth must shine, and scoundrels be undone,
> When this base miscreant shall forbear to sneer—
> And curse his taunts and bitter insults here."

Of course, never has any man of Anglo-Saxon blood delighted, at first, in the name of rebel: the taste for it among us is an acquisition attainable only through culture. In the bestowment of that sort of culture, Freneau was quite ready to be of use to his countrymen:

> If to control the cunning of a knave,
> Freedom adore, and scorn the name of slave,
> If to protest against a tyrant's laws,

And arm for vengeance in a righteous cause,
Be deemed rebellion—'t is a harmless thing,
This bug-bear name, like death, has lost its sting.

At the same time he warns them not to forget that the mighty
Power which, through its representative, now applies to Americans the word rebels, has an awful record for unshrinking
thoroughness in dealing with such offenders:

If Britain conquers, help us, Heaven, to fly!
Lend me your wings, ye ravens of the sky.
If Britain conquers,—we exist no more:
These lands shall redden with their children's gore,
Who turned to slaves, their fruitless toils shall moan—
Toils in these fields that once they called their own!

To arms! to arms!—and let the trusty sword
Decide who best deserves the hangman's cord;
Nor think the hills of Canada too bleak,
When desperate freedom is the prize you seek.
          .   .   .   .

Haste! to your tents in fetters bring
These slaves that serve their tyrant of a king.
So just, so virtuous, is your cause, I say
Hell must prevail—if Britain wins the day!

The longest and perhaps also the most powerful of these
satires for the year 1775, is the one entitled "The Midnight
Consultations, or, A Trip to Boston." Though not published
until September, its time is a midnight in June—the midnight
following the Bunker Hill fight; and the British chiefs, again
baffled by the rebels as they had been two months before, and
now disheartened by the amazing power of resistance, and even
of aggression, displayed by these ill-armed rustics, are represented as having come together for consultation at the house
of General Gage. The poet, guided by what he calls the "glim-
mering beam" of the polestar, has in a vision made his journey
thither at that very time, in order, as he says,

To view the peevish, half-starved spectres there,

and to see for himself just how these, our lately confident assailants,

> sicken in these hostile climes,
> Themes for the stage, and subjects for our rhymes.

As he comes upon the scene, and remembers the sufferings which these brutal invaders have already brought, and the still greater sufferings which they are destined to bring—unless driven back—his anger breaks out in the form of an impassioned apostrophe to his imperiled country, imploring her, at last, to call forth and to use the enormous resources for destruction which nature has deposited in her forests and her mines:

> Know your own strength—in rocky deserts bred,
> Shall the fierce tiger by the dog be led,
> And bear all insults from that snarling race
> Whose courage lies in impudence of face?

After this gust of wrath, the poet comes into the beleaguered city, and soon finds his way

> to the dome of state
> Where Gage resides—our western potentate,
> Chief of ten-thousand, all a race of Huns,
> Sent to be slaughtered by our rifle-guns;
> Sent by our angry Jove—sent sword in hand
> To murder, burn, and ravage through the land.

At Gage's house, he looks in upon the chiefs assembled there —seeing, of course, Gage himself; and Admiral Graves, commander of the British war-ships in the harbor; and General Burgoyne already known in America for his personal vanity and his windy rhetoric; and Lord Percy, who was accused of having shown rather too much agility in getting away from the scene of danger; and, finally, General Howe:

> Twelve was the hour—congenial darkness reigned,
> And no bright star a mimic daylight feigned.
> First, Gage we saw—a crimson chair of state
> Received the honor of his Honor's weight.

This man of straw the regal purple bound,
But dullness, deepest dullness, hovered round.
  Next Graves, who wields the trident of the brine,
The tall arch-captain of the embattled line,
All gloomy sate—mumbling of flame and fire,
Balls, cannons, ships, and all their damned attire;
Well pleased to live in never-ending hum,
But empty as the interior of his drum.
  Hard by, Burgoyne assumes an ample space,
And seemed to meditate with studious face,
As if again he wished our world to see
Long, dull, dry, letters writ to General Lee—
Huge scrawls of words through endless circuits drawn,
Unmeaning as the errand he 's upon.
Is he to conquer—he subdue our land—
This buckram hero, with his lady's hand?
By Caesars to be vanquished is a curse,
But by a scribbling fop—by heaven, is worse!

  Lord Percy seemed to snore—but may the muse
This ill-timed snoring to the peer excuse:
Tired was the long boy of his toilsome day—
Full fifteen miles he fled, a tedious way.
    .   .   .   .

  Howe, vext to see his starving army's doom,
Once more besought the skies for 'elbow room.'
    .   .   .   .

He cursed the brainless minister that planned
His bootless errand to this hostile land;
But awed by Gage, his bursting wrath recoiled,
And in his inmost bosom doubly boiled.

These, then are the British chiefs who, occupying the high places in the council room, are surrounded by a crowd of inferior officers—

                a pensioned clan,
A sample of the multitudes that wait,
Pale sons of famine at Perdition's gate;
    .   .   .   .

Knights, captains, squires—a wonder-working band!
Held at small wages till they gain the land.

The deliberations are opened by General Gage, who, humiliated and angry over the result of the war thus far, and especially over the battle of that day, gives vent to his spleen, and meanly trying to fasten the blame upon his subordinates, has only courage enough to fling a taunt at young Percy:

> Now Gage, rebounding from his cushioned seat,
> Swore thrice, and cried ' 'T is nonsense to be beat!
> Thus to be drubbed! Pray, warriors, let me know
> Which be in fault, myself, the fates, or you!
> Henceforth let Britain deem her men mere toys!
> Gods! to be frighted thus by country boys.
> Why, if our army had a mind to sup,
> They might have eat that schoolboy army up!
> Three thousand to twelve hundred thus to yield,
> And twice five hundred stretched upon the field!—
> O Shame to Britain, and the British name;
> Shame damps my heart, and I must die with shame,
> Thus to be worsted, thus disgraced and beat!—
> You have the knack, Lord Percy, to retreat;
> The death you 'scaped my warmest blood congeals,
> Heaven grant me, too, so swift a pair of heels!'
>
> .   .   .   .
>
> Thus spoke the great man in disdainful tone
> To the gay peer,—not meant for him alone.

By this taunt roused from his slumber, Lord Percy mildly defends himself—arguing that, since a well-aimed ball may hit a peer as well as a peasant, he is the wise peer who keeps aloof from danger as much as he may; and then he turns upon General Howe with the insinuation that, whatever may have been his own blame that day, the disaster on Bunker Hill was due chiefly to that officer. Of course, to this charge General Howe makes reply; and then, at the close of his speech, turning from their miserable past to their still more miserable future, he appeals to his comrades to unite in some plan to save themselves at least from starvation. Under this appeal, Gage solemnly announces to the council the great decision to which his mind has been brought in consequence of their deliberations:

> Gage smote upon his breast,
> And cried, 'What fate determines must be best.
>
> .   .   .   .
>
> Three weeks—ye gods! nay, three long years it seems,
> Since roast beef I have touched, except in dreams.
> In sleep, choice dishes to my view repair,—
> Waking, I gape and champ the empty air.
> Say, is it just that I, who rule these bands,
> Should live on husks, like rakes in foreign lands?—
> Come, let us plan some project ere we sleep,
> And drink destruction to the rebel sheep.
> On neighboring isles uncounted cattle stray,
> Fat beeves, and swine—an ill defended prey;
> These are fit victims for my noonday dish,
> These, if my soldiers act as I would wish,
> In one short week would glad your maws and mine—
> On mutton we will sup, on roast beef dine!'
>   Shouts of applause reechoed through the hall,
> And what pleased one as surely pleased them all;
> Wallace was named to execute the plan,
> And thus sheep-stealing pleased them to a man.

Certainly, the satire in all this is genuine. The comedy of such
a situation—the invincible troops of Great Britain discomfited
by provincial militia, and, pent up in a seaboard town, saving
themselves from actual starvation by a concerted resort to
sheep-stealing on the undefended islands in Boston harbor—
not only has in it something extremely grotesque, but has, likewise, a logical bearing on American hopes and fears touching
the issue of the contest that still lies before them; and all this
the poet fails not to make use of:

> What are these upstarts from a foreign isle,
> That we should fear their hate, or court their smile?
>
> .   .   .   .
>
> Laughs not the soul when an imprisoned crew
> Affect to pardon those they can't subdue;
> Though thrice repulsed, and hemmed up to their stations,
> Yet issue pardons, oaths, and proclamations?

And then it was—nearly a year before the project for Independence was to find official sanction—that this poet bitterly

and boldly proclaimed Independence as the only sensible and
adequate remedy for American wrongs:

> Too long our patient country wears their chains,
> Too long our wealth all-grasping Britain drains!
> Why still a handmaid to that distant land?
> Why still subservient to their proud command?
> Britain the bold, the generous, and the brave,
> Still treats our country like the meanest slave;
> Her haughty lords already share the prey,
> Live on our labors, and with scorn repay!
> Rise, sleeper, rise, while yet the power remains,
> And bind their nobles and their chiefs in chains.
> Fallen on disastrous times, they scorn our plea;—
> 'T is our own efforts that must make us free.
> Born to contend, our lives we place at stake,
> And grow immortal by the stand we make.

Nay, as upon their own unconquerable spirits, so upon the
face of nature itself, is written the promise of a great destiny
for the American people; and with the unhesitant tone and
gesture of a prophet, the poet proceeds to unroll the canvas on
which is painted the future of their nation, as one vast, united,
free, and peaceful empire of humanity, filling all the vast domain from the Atlantic to the Mississippi:

> The time shall come when strangers rule no more,
> Nor cruel mandates vex from Britain's shore;
> When commerce shall extend her shortened wing,
> And her rich freights from every climate bring;
> When mighty towns shall flourish free and great,—
> Vast their dominion, opulent their state;
> When one vast cultivated region teems
> From ocean's side to Mississippi's streams,
> While each enjoys his vine tree's peaceful shade,
> And even the meanest has no foe to dread.

It is a touching fact—it tells, indeed, of the deep reluctance
with which the American colonists accepted this robust remedy
of national Independence, and even of their early fluctuations
in mood after they had accepted it—that at the close of this
very satire, in which Freneau so early and so passionately demanded the rupture of every tie that bound us to the mother

land, even he relented—he, the impersonation of Revolutionary radicalism and fierceness—and yielding, for one brief moment, to the strong plea of filial affection, himself sent forth a
touching prayer for peace—for reconciliation—for a lasting
union between the colonies and the mother country, such as
they had enjoyed under the one English king who was ever
fondly loved in America:

> O heaven-born Peace, renew thy wonted charms;
> Far be this rancor, and this din of arms;
> To warring lands return, an honored guest,
> And bless our crimson shore among the rest.
> Long may Britannia rule our hearts again—
> Rule as she ruled in George the Second's reign;
> May ages hence her growing grandeur see,
> And she be glorious—but ourselves be free!

It must be told, however, that this sob of wounded affection—
this burst of natural grief over sacred ties that were breaking—
this naïve cry for an arrest of Revolutionary fury and hurly-
burly, and for a return to the subordination and the quietude of
the old colonial times—all this was, on Freneau's part, but a
momentary relapse into political soft-heartedness. As if to proclaim his remorse for such weakness, and his full recovery from
it, almost immediately afterward he sent forth his "Libera
Nos, Domine,"—a slashing, contemptuous, and fierce litany
for total and final deliverance from every shred of British rule
and contact:

> From a junto that labor for absolute power,
> Whose schemes disappointed have made them look sour;
> From the lords of the council, who fight against freedom,
> Who still follow on where the devil shall lead 'em;
>
> From the group at St. James's, that slight our petitions,
> And fools that are waiting for further submissions;
> From a nation whose manners are rough and abrupt,
> From scoundrels and rascals whom gold can corrupt;
>
> From pirates sent out by command of the king
> To murder and plunder, but never to swing,—

From Wallace, and Graves, and Vipers and Roses,
Whom, if heaven pleases, we 'll give bloody noses;

From the valiant Dunmore, with his crew of banditti,
Who plunder Virginians at Williamsburgh city;
From hot-headed Montague, mighty to swear,
The little fat man with his pretty white hair;

From bishops in Britain, who butchers are grown,
From slaves that would die for a smile from the throne;
From assemblies that vote against Congress proceedings—
(Who now see the fruit of their stupid misleadings);

From Tryon the mighty, who flies from our city,
And swelled with importance, disdains the committee,—
(But since he is pleased, to proclaim us his foes,
What the devil care we where the devil he goes);

From the scoundrel, Lord North, who would bind us in chains,
From a dunce of a king who was born without brains,
The utmost extent of whose sense is to see
That reigning and making of buttons agree;

From an island that bullies, and hectors, and swears,
I send up to heaven my wishes and prayers
That we, disunited, may freemen be still,
And Britain go on—to be damned, if she will!

FRENEAU'S *desire for independence was clear, yet as late as December of 1775 it was shared by only a handful of Americans. It remained for one who could speak the language of the common man to change the mood of the colonists—to translate the call for independence from poetry into prose, from a literary exercise into a popular demand.*

Thomas Paine and *Common Sense*

ON the last day of November, 1774, there arrived at Philadelphia a solitary English pilgrim, named Thomas Paine, nearly thirty-eight years of age, having with him neither scrip, nor bread, nor money in his purse, but having nevertheless an abundant willingness to make his way in the new world by his wits, particularly "as a clerk, or assistant tutor in a school, or assistant surveyor." For this rather forlorn adventurer, whose most imminent business in Philadelphia at that time was to "procure subsistence at least," the worst disadvantages of his condition were perhaps nearly balanced by a single item of good luck: he had brought with him from London a letter of introduction from Benjamin Franklin, testifying that the bearer was "an ingenious, worthy young man," and invoking on his behalf the primary and inexpensive charities of "advice and countenance."

Up to that time in his career, life had been upon the whole a somewhat baffling and unsatisfactory affair for this "ingenious, worthy young man"; and in spite of all energetic attempts on his part at climbing the steep hill, he had found himself, when well on toward middle life, still floundering and discomfited at the bottom of it.

The son of a staymaker at Thetford in Norfolk, where he was born in 1737, he had been taken from school at the age of thirteen and had been put to his father's trade. At one time, soon after the beginning of the Seven Years' War, wearied perhaps by the monotony of his too unhazardous occupation as a maker of stays, he had enlisted on board an English privateer.

Very soon exhausting the charm to be found in wielding the deadly cutlass, he had returned, though with evident reluctance, to the service of the innocuous needle, which he then for several years continued to ply for a livelihood at London, Dover, Sandwich, Margate, and perhaps elsewhere. When only twenty-two years old he had married; and when only twenty-three, he had become a widower. In 1762, after due solicitation, he had received an appointment in the excise, being set in the first instance "to gauge brewers' casks at Grantham," and afterward "to watch smugglers at Alford." In 1765, he had been dismissed from the excise for neglect of duty; his offense being that of writing out his official entries at home, without the trouble of an actual tour of his district, and of course without an actual inspection of the excisable articles on which he had occasion to pass—a most comfortable way of making specific assertions, making them, it will be observed, on purely speculative or unverified data—a method which might very likely stand this gentleman in good stead in later life when he should set up for a philosopher, but which could hardly be permitted to him so long as he was a mere exciseman. After the loss of his pittance from the government, he had returned once more to his trade, working for one Gudgeon, a staymaker at Diss; he had also for some time gained his daily bread as usher in an academy, first in Goodman's Fields, and then at Kensington; he had even earned an honest penny, at times, by ascending the pulpit in some chapel at Moorfields or elsewhere, and preaching the gospel to such saints and sinners as should have the grace to come and partake of his godly ministrations. In 1768, after humble petition on his part, he had been restored to the excise and given an appointment at Lewes, in Sussex. In 1771, being still an exciseman, he had taken unto himself, as his second wife, a young lady with whom he was already in partnership as grocer and tobacconist. In 1774, he had been once more and forever dismissed from the excise—this time for the offense of "having quitted his business without obtaining the board's leave for so doing, and being gone off on account of the debts which he hath contracted." Six days after this final dismissal from official service under the good king George the Third, Paine's household furniture, his stock in trade, and his other effects had been sold at auction at Lewes for the benefit of his creditors. Finally, two months later, he and his wife had subscribed their names to an amicable agreement for a separation —an incident which seems to have been viewed by them both not as an additional misfortune to either, but rather as a mitigation of such misfortune as either or both may have already had in this troublous world.

It was in this doleful plight that Thomas Paine went up to London, and laid before Franklin such credentials as induced the latter, on the thirtieth of September, 1774, to give him an honorable passport to recognition and friendly help in America.

Reaching Philadelphia late in the year 1774, Paine soon made his way to pleasant relations with some of the best people in that town. By the fourth of March, 1775, he was able to report to his illustrious benefactor in London, that he had already gained "many friends"; had received from "several gentlemen" offers of profitable employment as a tutor to their sons; and had begun to assist the bookseller, Robert Aitkin, in the conduct of a new magazine.

Not by tutorship, however, nor by surveyorship, nor even by editorship, but by authorship, was this man to achieve such success in America as then lay undreamed of before him; and very likely the peculiar and the marvelous aptitude he had in him for that particular function of authorship, was still hidden even from his own eyes—which, however, were never greatly lacking in vision of his own talents and virtues. Though in his thirty-eighth year, he had up to that time written nothing notable in all his life, and had never "published a syllable."*

* This is Paine's own assertion. *Political Writings*, i. 97. Did he forget his memorial on the "Case of the Officers of Excise," in 1772, of which he presented a copy to Goldsmith, with the explanation that four thousand copies had been printed? Goldsmith, *Works*, i. 320–321. Did he also forget his ode on "The Death of General Wolfe," written in 1759, which was published in the *Gentleman's Magazine*, and was also set to music and issued as a popular song?

We may picture him to ourselves, during his first year in Philadelphia—the year 1775—as an alert and eager stranger, gaining his livelihood chiefly by writing for Aitkin's magazine, haunting the bookshops, pushing his way to the acquaintance of leading citizens of the town, and after the assembling of Congress, on the tenth of May, pushing his way, likewise, to the acquaintance of leading citizens from all parts of the continent. Benjamin Rush describes him as at that time visiting familiarly "in the families of Dr. Franklin, Mr. Rittenhouse, and Mr. George Clymer, where he made himself acceptable by a turn he discovered for philosophical, as well as political, subjects." John Adams, who was then in Philadelphia as a member of Congress, and who at that period was accustomed to speak of Paine in a respectful and even in a complimentary way, long afterward said sneeringly, that Paine "got into such company as would converse with him, and ran about picking up what information he could concerning our affairs."

If, indeed, Paine so employed himself, it must be confessed that he was very well employed. He could hardly have done anything more to the point. Arriving in America in the midst of a great political revolution, and casting in his lot with a kindred people over whose political wrongs he was indignant, and with whose political aspirations he was in passionate sympathy, it is hard to see what worthier course he could have taken than to try to qualify himself for the best service he might render to the great cause by studying it in its origin, its history, its methods, its aims. And how could he better do this than by applying himself diligently to the very men who were the leaders in the great enterprise? On every hand, then, he gathered facts, opinions, impressions. He threw himself instantaneously into the American spirit; he became a naturalized American in body and soul; he caught at once the ideas that were in the air; with all his heart he responded to the immense, inarticulate impulse that was then moving a great people toward a great future. To the study, the acceptance, the advocacy of the American Revolution, Thomas Paine brought neither a wise, nor a profound, nor a cultivated mind—not even an accurate or a temperate one; but he did bring a mind agile, alert, vivid, impressible, humane, quick to see into things and to grasp the gist of them, and marvelous in its power of stating them—stating them with lucidity, with sparkling liveliness, with rough, incisive, and captivating force.

The moment of his arrival in America was one of supreme political excitement. The Congress of 1774 had but recently adjourned; and its measures for peaceful resistance to England through commercial non-intercourse had aroused the most violent discussions throughout the colonies. Like the majority of Americans down to the nineteenth of April, 1775, Paine had at first believed in the possibility of a peaceful solution of the trouble, and had earnestly desired reconciliation between England and her colonies. What his political opinions were at the beginning of his American career, he himself explained with perfect candor some years later: "I happened to come to America a few months before the breaking out of hostilities. I found the disposition of the people such that they might have been led by a thread, and governed by a reed. Their suspicion was quick and penetrating, but their attachment to Britain was obstinate; and it was at that time a kind of treason to speak against it. They disliked the ministry, but they esteemed the nation. Their idea of grievance operated without resentment; and their single object was reconciliation. Bad as I believed the ministry to be, I never conceived them capable of a measure so rash and wicked as the commencing of hostilities; much less did I imagine the nation would encourage it. I viewed the dispute as a kind of law suit, in which, I supposed, the parties would find a way either to decide or settle it. I had no thoughts of Independence or of arms. The world could not then have persuaded me that I should be either a soldier or an author. If I had any talents for either, they were buried in me, and might ever have continued so, had not the necessity of the times dragged and driven them into action. I had formed my plan of life, and con-

ceiving myself happy, wished everybody else so. But when the
country into which I had just set my foot, was set on fire about
my ears, it was time to stir. It was time for every man to stir.
Those who had been long settled had something to defend;
those who had just come had something to pursue; and the call
and the concern was equal and universal. For in a country
wherein all men were once adventurers, the difference of a few
years in their arrival could make none in their right."

Such, no doubt, is a true statement of Paine's opinions upon
American Independence early in 1775. But as the bitter events
of that year rapidly unfolded themselves, not a few Americans
became convinced that there was no true solution of the trouble
except in that very Independence which they had but a short
time before dreaded and denounced. Of such Americans,
Thomas Paine was one; and towards the end of the year,
through incessant study of passing events, and through incessant communication with the foremost minds in America, he
had filled his own mind with the great decisive elements of the
case, and was prepared to utter his thought thereon. Early in
January, 1776, he did utter it, in the form of a pamphlet, published at Philadelphia, and entitled *Common Sense*.

Before entering upon a study of this epoch-making pamphlet
—the first open and unqualified argument in championship of
the doctrine of American Independence—it is important for us
at least to glance at the previous history of American opinion
on the subject. No one who searches the writings which have
come down to us from that time, can have any doubt as to the
truth of this broad statement that, for the first ten or twelve
years of the Revolution, the entire Whig agitation was conducted on a perpetual disavowal of the purpose or the desire
for Independence. In every form in which a solemn affirmation
could be made and reiterated, it was affirmed by the Whigs during all those years that the only object of their agitation was to
obstruct and to defeat a bad ministerial policy, thereby to secure a redress of grievances; that, as for Independence, it was

the thing they abhorred, and it was mere calumny to accuse them of designing or of desiring it. Nearly all the greatest Whig pamphleteers prior to 1776—James Otis, Daniel Dulany, John Dickinson, and Alexander Hamilton—abjured Independence as a measure full of calamity and crime. The Stamp Act Congress, speaking in the name of the several colonies, declared that their connection with Great Britain was their "great happiness and security," and that they "most ardently" desired its "perpetual continuance." In January, 1768, the Massachusetts house of representatives sent to their agent a letter of instructions, written by James Otis, and thus defining their opposition to the renewal by parliament of its policy of taxing the colonies: "We cannot justly be suspected of the most distant thought of an Independency of Great Britain. Some, we know, have imagined this; . . . but it is so far from the truth that we apprehend the colonies would refuse it if offered to them, and would even deem it the greatest misfortune to be obliged to accept it." In June, 1774, the same legislative body elected delegates to the first Continental Congress; and in their letter of instructions, signed by Samuel Adams, they declared that "the restoration of union and harmony between Great Britain and the colonists" was "most ardently desired by all good men." The first Continental Congress, in its solemn petition to the king, adopted October 26, 1774, professed the most devoted loyalty: "We wish not a diminution of the prerogative. . . . Your royal authority over us and our connection with Great Britain we shall always carefully and zealously endeavor to support and maintain." In March, 1775, Benjamin Franklin, then in London, repeated the statement which he had made in the previous year to Lord Chatham, that he had never heard in America one word in favor of Independence "from any person, drunk or sober." In May, 1775, shortly after American blood had been shed at Lexington and Concord, George Washington, crossing the Potomac on his way to the second Continental Congress, was met midway in the river by a boat containing his friend, Jonathan Boucher; and while their boats touched, Boucher kindly warned Washington that the errand on which he was going would lead to civil war and to an effort for Independence. Such apprehensions were vigorously scouted by Washington, who then added, as Boucher says, "that if ever I heard of his joining in any such measures, I had his leave to set him down for everything wicked." Soon after Washington's arrival at Philadelphia, the Continental Congress resolved upon a dutiful petition to the king, assuring him that, although his ministry had forced hostilities upon them, yet they most ardently wished "for a restoration of the harmony formerly subsisting between" the mother country and the colonies. The Americans who had just fought at Lexington and Concord, and the Americans who, a few weeks later, were to fight at Bunker Hill, would have spurned as a calumny the accusation that their object in fighting was Independence. Washington's appointment as commander-in-chief, which was made two days before the battle of Bunker Hill, contained no intimation that he was to lead the armies in a struggle for Independence. As soon as the news of his appointment reached Virginia, his old military company there sent him their congratulations on the honor he had received, closing their letter with the wish that all his "counsels and operations" might be directed by Providence "to a happy and lasting union between us and Great Britain." On the 6th of July, 1775, the Congress which had thus appointed Washington to lead their armies against the troops of the king, adopted their celebrated declaration, "setting forth the causes and necessity of their taking up arms," wherein they say: "Lest this declaration should disquiet the minds of our friends and fellow-subjects in any part of the empire, we assure them that we mean not to dissolve that union which has so long and so happily subsisted between us, and which we sincerely wish to see restored. . . . We have not raised armies with ambitious designs of separating from Great Britain, and establishing Independent States." When, a few days later, that declaration was read to General Putnam's troops, parading on Prospect Hill, near Boston, they greeted, with three loud cries of

"Amen," the passage in which the Almighty was implored to dispose their adversaries "to reconciliation on reasonable terms." More than two months after the battle of Bunker Hill, Jefferson wrote to a kinsman of his that he was "looking with fondness towards a reconciliation with Great Britain." More than three months after that battle, the committee of Chester county, Pennsylvania, with Anthony Wayne as their chairman, issued a statement denying that in taking up arms, the people of that county intended "to overturn the constitution by declaring an Independency," and expressing their "abhorrence even of an idea so pernicious in its nature." As late as the 22d of October, 1775, when Jeremy Belknap went to the American camp to officiate as chaplain, he publicly prayed for the king. As late as December 25, 1775, the Revolutionary Congress of New Hampshire officially proclaimed their disavowal of any purpose "aiming at Independence,"—a disavowal which they incorporated into the new constitution for New Hampshire adopted on the 5th of January, 1776.

Such, then, upon the subject of Independence, was the attitude of all classes and parties in America during the first ten or twelve years of the Revolution. In just one sentiment all persons, Tories and Whigs, seemed perfectly to agree: namely, in abhorrence of the project of separation from the empire. Suddenly, however, and within a period of less than six months, the majority of the Whigs turned completely around, and openly declared for Independence, which, before that time, they had so vehemently repudiated. Among the facts necessary to enable us to account for this almost unrivalled political somersault, is that of the appearance in January, 1776, of the pamphlet entitled *Common Sense*.

This pamphlet was happily named: it undertook to apply common sense to a technical, complex, but most urgent and feverish, problem of constitutional law. In fact, on any other ground than that of common sense, the author of that pamphlet was incompetent to deal with the problem at all; since of law, of political science, and even of English and American history, he was ludicrously ignorant. But for the effective treatment of any question whatsoever that was capable of being dealt with under the light of the broad and rugged intellectual instincts of mankind—man's natural sense of truth, of congruity, of fair-play—perhaps no other man in America, excepting Franklin, was a match for this ill-taught, heady, and slashing English stranger.

From the tribunal of technical law, therefore, he carried the case to the tribunal of common sense; and in his plea before that tribunal, he never for a moment missed his point, or forgot his method. The one thing just then to be done was to convince the average American colonist of the period that it would be ridiculous for him any longer to remain an American colonist; that the time had come for him to be an American citizen; that nothing stood in the way of his being so, but the trash of a few pedants respecting the authority of certain bedizened animals called kings; and that whether he would or no, the alternative was at last thrust into his face upon the point of a bayonet—either to declare for national Independence, and a wide-spaced and resplendent national destiny, or to accept, along with subservience to England, the bitterness and the infamy of national annihilation.

The pamphlet begins with a rattling overture of pungent but crude affirmations concerning government in general, and concerning the English government in particular, all intended to rid the minds of its readers of any undue reverence for organized authority, especially for monarchical authority, and to convince a people with whom obedience to law had long been a second nature, that the hour had struck for them to legalize disobedience to law. Government has been often described as if it were identical with society; whereas government and society "are not only different, but have different origins. Society is produced by our wants, and government by our wickedness. . . . Society in every state is a blessing; but government, even in its best estate, is but a necessary evil; in its worst estate, an intolerable one. . . . Government, like dress, is the badge of lost innocence; the palaces of kings are built upon the ruins of the bowers of paradise." Government, in fact, is "a mode rendered necessary by the inability of moral virtue to govern the world." Such, according to Thomas Paine, is the origin of government; and as to its object, he declares it to be twofold—"freedom and security." And what is the true form of government? Whatever else it may be, surely it is not monarchy. That form of government which rests on "the distinction of men into kings and subjects," is one for which no "natural or religious reason can be assigned." "Male and female are the distinctions of nature; good and bad, the distinctions of heaven; but how a race of men came into the world so exalted above the rest, and distinguished like some new species, is worth enquiring into, and whether they are the means of happiness or of misery to mankind." "The nearer any government approaches to a republic, the less business there is for a king. . . . In England a king hath little more to do than to make war, and give away places; which, in plain terms, is to impoverish the nation, and set it together by the ears. A pretty business, indeed, for a man to be allowed eight hundred thousand sterling for, and worshiped into the bargain! Of more worth is one honest man to society, and in the sight of God, than all the crowned ruffians that ever lived."

Having thus dispatched, in a series of incisive and contemptuous propositions, the doctrine of king-craft as an intolerable method of governing mankind—supporting his opinions by elaborate and reverent quotations from the Bible—he soon reaches the specific business he has in hand, namely, the state of affairs in America. Here, at last, he is on the ground of tangible facts and of their natural interpretation; and here the vigor of his mind, his shrewdness of insight, his unhesitating confidence, the filmless lucidity of his style, his humor, his asperity, his epigrammatic gift, have victorious play, and give to his pages the most stimulating flavor. "The period of debate is closed. Arms, as the last resource, must decide the contest. . . . By referring the matter from argument to arms, a new era for politics is struck; a new method of thinking hath arisen. All plans, proposals, and so forth, prior to the nineteenth of April . . . are like the almanacs of last year."

Since the nineteenth of April, then, all talk of filial affection for England has become archaic, pointless, farcical; and for the American who, unaware of the change that has come upon the earth, still pleads that England is our mother, there is but one reply: "Then the more shame upon her conduct! Even brutes do not devour their young, nor savages make war upon their families."

To the objection that "as America has flourished under her former connection with Great Britain, the same connection is necessary towards her future happiness, and will always have the same effect," Paine is ready with a telling retort: "Nothing can be more fallacious than this kind of argument. We may as well assert that because a child has thrived upon milk, it is never to have meat; or that the first twenty years of our lives is to become a precedent for the next twenty. But even this is admitting more than is true; for I answer roundly that America would have flourished as much, and probably much more, had no European power had anything to do with her. The articles of commerce by which she has enriched herself, are the necessaries of life; and will always have a market while eating is the custom of Europe."

Moreover, the connection of America with England brings, according to Paine, not a solitary advantage to America; nay, it brings to her disadvantages and injuries without number. The greatest of all is this: our connection with England "tends directly to involve this continent in European wars and quarrels, and sets us at variance with nations who would otherwise seek our friendship, and against whom we have neither anger nor complaint. As Europe is our market for trade, we ought to form no partial connection with any part of it. It is the true interest of America to steer clear of European contentions, which she never can do while, by her dependence on Britain, she is made the make-weight in the scale of British politics."

Then, again, "it is repugnant to reason and the universal order of things, to all examples from former ages, to suppose that this continent can longer remain subject to any external power." There is something preposterous in the mere idea of a great nation on this side of the Atlantic remaining in a state of permanent pupilage to a great nation on the other side of the Atlantic: "A greater absurdity cannot be conceived of, than three millions of people running to their seacoast every time a ship arrives from London, to know what portion of liberty they should enjoy."

Furthermore, there is an obvious cosmographical argument for American Independence. A glance at the map will show that the subordination of America to England inverts the order of nature: "Small islands, not capable of protecting themselves, are the proper objects for kingdoms to take under their care; but there is something absurd in supposing a continent to be perpetually governed by an island. In no instance hath nature made the satellite larger than its primary planet; and as England and America, with respect to each other, reverse the common order of nature, it is evident that they belong to different systems: England to Europe, America to—itself!"

Aside from mere analogies, however, and looking directly at the welfare of America in the transaction of its own affairs, it is plain that Independence is a necessity: "As to government matters, it is not in the power of Britain to do this continent justice. The business of it will soon be too weighty and intricate to be managed with any tolerable degree of convenience, by a power so distant from us, and so very ignorant of us. . . . To be always running three or four thousand miles with a tale or a petition, waiting four or five months for an answer, which, when obtained, requires five or six more to explain it in, will in a few years be looked upon as folly and childishness. There was a time when it was proper, and there is a proper time for it to cease."

But if it be supposed for a moment that reconciliation were

actually brought about between England and America, what would be the result? The ruin of America. Why? First, because England would still be the governing power. And "is the power who is jealous of our prosperity, a proper power to govern us? . . . America is only a secondary object in the system of British politics. England consults the good of this country no further than it answers her own purpose. Wherefore, her own interest leads her to suppress the growth of ours, in every case which doth not promote her advantage, or in the least interferes with it." Secondly, because "even the best terms which we can expect to obtain can amount to no more than a temporary expedient, or a kind of government by guardianship, which can last no longer than till the colonies come of age." Thirdly, because "nothing but Independence . . . can keep the peace of the continent, and preserve it inviolate from civil wars."

But there are Americans who fear that if we separate ourselves from the control of the king of England, we shall lapse into anarchy. "Where, say some, is the king of America? I 'll tell you, friend, He reigns above, and doth not make havoc of mankind, like the royal brute of Britain. . . . A government of our own is our natural right; and when a man seriously reflects on the precariousness of human affairs, he will become convinced that it is infinitely wiser and safer to form a constitution of our own, in a cool, deliberate manner, while we have it in our power, than to trust such an interesting event to time and chance." "Ye who oppose Independence now, ye know not what ye do: ye are opening a door to eternal tryanny, by keeping vacant the seat of government. . . . To talk of friendship with those in whom our reason forbids us to have faith, and our affections, wounded through a thousand pores, instruct us to detest, is madness and folly. Every day wears out the little remains of kindred between us and them; and can there be any reason to hope that as the relationship expires, the affection will increase, or that we shall agree better, when we have ten times more and greater concerns to quarrel over than ever? Ye that tell us of harmony and reconciliation, can ye restore to us the time that is past? . . . The last cord now is broken. . . . There are injuries which nature cannot forgive; she would cease to be nature if she did. . . . O ye that love mankind! Ye that dare oppose, not only tyranny but the tyrant, stand forth! Every spot of the old world is overrun with oppression. Freedom hath been hunted round the globe. Asia and Africa have long expelled her. Europe regards her like a stranger; and England hath given her warning to depart. O! receive the fugitive; and prepare in time an asylum for mankind."

With all its crudities of thought, its superficiality, and its rashness of assertion, *Common Sense* is a masterly pamphlet; for in the elements of its strength it was precisely fitted to the hour, to the spot, and to the passions of men. Even its smattering of historical lore, and its cheap display of statistics, and its clumsy attempts at some sort of political philosophy, did not diminish the homage with which it was read by the mass of the community, who were even less learned and less philosophical than Paine, and who, at any rate, cared much more just then for their imperiled rights, than they did either for philosophy or for learning.

The power of the pamphlet lay in the fitness of its method, its tone, its scope. It brushes away the tangles and cobwebs of technical debate, and flashes common sense upon the situation. It was meant for plain men, in desperate danger, and desperately in earnest. Its thought is homely, always blunt, occasionally humorous, rugged, palpable, overpowering; with just enough of generous and contemptuous passion—love of freedom, hate of tyranny, and a consciousness of the latent, illimitable strength of its own cause. Its style never errs on the side of restraint; is never debilitated by any delicacy of feeling. Thomas Paine did not take up his pen in the service of the amenities. Here is no urbane concession to the foe. Here are the germs of that untempered invective which sometimes grew, at a later period of his life, into literary truculence and barbarism.

The immediate practical effects of this pamphlet in America, and the celebrity which it soon acquired in Europe as well as in America, are a significant part of its history as a potential literary document of the period. In every impassioned popular discussion there is likely to spring up a leader, who with pen or voice strikes in, at just the right moment, with the right word, so skillfully, so powerfully, that thenceforward the intellectual battle seems to be raging and surging around him and around the fiery word which he has sent shrilling through the air. So far as the popular discussion of American Independence is concerned, precisely this was the case, between January and July, 1776, with Thomas Paine and his pamphlet *Common Sense*.

It was originally published at Philadelphia on the ninth* of January, 1776, without the author's name. On the twentieth of that month, a second edition, with "large additions," was published by the same booksellers. On the twenty-fifth, another edition was announced by a firm of rival booksellers in Philadelphia, who state that "several hundred are already bespoke, one thousand for Virginia," and that the work was also about to be published in German. The edition thus announced made its appearance on the twentieth of February, being a pamphlet of fifty pages, and containing "large and interesting additions by the author." In the enormous tide of popular interest which soon bore the pamphlet into every port and inlet of American society, were speedily drowned the competitions of the two local booksellers who had begun by trying to monopolize the profits to be got from this brain-freighted and strong-winged commodity. In New York, Norwich, Providence, Newport, Salem, Newburyport, Charlestown, Boston, and elsewhere in America, it was soon reprinted, as well as in London, Newcastle-upon-Tyne, Edinburgh, Rotterdam, and Paris. Within

---

* The date of publication often given is 10 January, 1776, on the authority of an advertisement in *The Pennsylvania Journal*. Thus, Conway, *Life*, i. 61. But in *The Pennsylvania Evening Post*, for 9 January, 1776, there is an advertisement to the effect that the pamphlet was already out that day.

three months from the date of its first issue, at least one hundred and twenty thousand copies of it were sold in America alone. By that time, the pamphlet seemed to be in every one's hand and the theme of every one's talk.

In a very early edition, it was described on its title-page as "Written by an Englishman." In later issues this description was soon omitted; and in the enlarged edition of the twentieth of February, some reference was made to the public curiosity to know the authorship of the treatise: "Who the author of this production is, is wholly unnecessary to the public, as the object of attention is the doctrine, not the man. . . . He is unconnected with any party, and under no sort of influence, public or private, but the influence of reason and principle."

Of all writers then known to the American people, probably only three were much thought of at the time as likely to have produced this pamphlet. "Common Sense, when it first appeared," wrote John Adams long afterward, with characteristic aplomb, "was generally by the public ascribed to me or to Mr. Samuel Adams." Indeed, in some parts of Europe, particularly in France, the first rumor that it was written by a great American congressman vaguely named "Adams," seems to have remained in force for several years afterward; and in 1779, when John Adams himself arrived in France as a commissioner of Congress, he found himself welcomed as "le fameux Adams," the reputed author of *Common Sense,*—a pamphlet which, as he then wrote, "was received in France and in all Europe with rapture." In America, probably, the prevailing tendency was to ascribe it to Benjamin Franklin, who, indeed, on one occasion is said to have been expostulated with by a Loyalist lady of his acquaintance, for having in that pamphlet been so discourteous as to speak of their good king as "the royal brute of Britain." "Madam," replied Franklin, "let me assure you that I did not write 'Common Sense.' Moreover, if I had written it, I would not so have dishonored—the brute creation." In England, where Franklin was then better known than any other American, and where he had received personal affronts which would account, it was supposed, for any asperities of style, the pamphlet was for some time commonly spoken of as his—as in the case, for example, of an amusing story told in London in the summer of 1776, to the effect that the Prince of Wales had been discovered one day by his mother in the very act of reading, within the awful precincts of the palace, "Dr. Franklin's pamphlet 'Common Sense,' " and in response to the queen's searching questions, had refused to confess how he had come by the atrocious document.

Of all the contemporary testimonies to the immediate power of *Common Sense,* one of the earliest is that of General Charles Lee, who, on the twenty-fourth of January, 1776—fifteen days after the first issue of the pamphlet—thus wrote to Washington: "Have you seen the pamphlet 'Common Sense'? I never saw such a masterly, irresistible performance. It will, if I mistake not, in concurrence with the transcendent folly and wickedness of the ministry, give the 'coup-de-grace' to Great Britain. In short, I own myself convinced by the arguments, of the necessity of separation." On the thirty-first of January, one day after Washington had received Lee's letter, he thus wrote to Joseph Reed: "A few more of such flaming arguments as were exhibited at Falmouth and Norfolk, added to the sound doctrine and unanswerable reasoning contained in the pamphlet 'Common Sense,' will not leave numbers at a loss to decide upon the propriety of separation." A few days later, on the sixth of February, in an article which was published in *The Pennsylvania Evening Post,* a person in Maryland writes: "If you know the author of 'Common Sense,' tell him he has done wonders and worked miracles,—made Tories Whigs, and washed black-amores white." From South Carolina, on the fourteenth of February, rises this cry of delight: "Who is the author of 'Common Sense'? I can scarce refrain from adoring him. He deserves a statue of gold." On the twenty-fourth of February, a newspaper published in New York thus joins in the rising chorus of enthusiastic praise: "The pamphlet entitled 'Common Sense' is indeed a wonderful production. It is completely calculated for the meridian of North America. . . . This animated piece dispels, with irresistible energy, the prejudices of the mind against the doctrine of Independence, and pours in upon it such an inundation of light and truth, as will produce an instantaneous and marvelous change in the temper, in the views and feelings, of an American. The ineffable delight with which it is perused, and its doctrines imbibed, is a demonstration that the seeds of Independence, though imported with the troops from Britain, will grow surprisingly with proper cultivation in the fields of America." On the second of March, Mistress John Adams writes from Quincy to her husband in Philadelphia: "I am charmed with the sentiments of 'Common Sense,' and wonder how an honest heart . . . can hesitate one moment at adopting them." On the twelfth of March, a letter from Philadelphia says: " 'Common Sense' . . . is read to all ranks; and as many as read, so many become converted, though perhaps the hour before [they] were most violent against the least idea of Independence." A letter from Georgetown, South Carolina, on the seventeenth of March, says: " 'Common Sense' hath made Independents of the majority of the country." On the first of April, Washington, writing from Cambridge, thus speaks of the development of political thought among the people of Virginia: "My countrymen, I know, from their form of government and steady attachment heretofore to royalty, will come reluctantly into the idea of Independence, but time and persecution bring many wonderful things to pass; and by private letters which I have lately received from Virginia, I find 'Common Sense' is working a powerful change there in the minds of men." On the eighth of April, *The New York Gazette* says: "The subject of conversation throughout America for these few weeks past, hath been excited by a pamphlet called 'Common Sense.' " On the twelfth of April, a news-writer in New York says: "A pamphlet entitled 'Common Sense' has converted thousands to Independence, that could not endure the idea before." On the twenty-ninth of April, *The Boston Ga-*

zette says: "Had the spirit of prophecy directed the birth of a publication, it could not have fallen upon a more fortunate period than the time in which 'Common Sense' made its appearance. The minds of men are now swallowed up in attention to an object the most momentous and important that ever yet employed the deliberations of a people." Finally, on the seventh of June—the very day on which Richard Henry Lee introduced into Congress his resolutions for Independence—William Gordon, the historian of the Revolution, sets down these words respecting the influences that had prepared the public mind for the introduction of such resolutions: "The constant publications which have appeared and been read with attention, have greatly promoted the spirit of Independency; but but no one so much as the pamphlet under the signature of 'Common Sense,' written by Mr. Thomas Paine, an Englishman. . . . Nothing could have been better timed than this performance. In unison with the sentiments and feelings of the people, it has produced most astonishing effects, and been received with vast applause, read by almost every American, and recommended as a work replete with truth, and against which none but the partial and prejudiced can form any objections. It has satisfied multitudes that it is their true interest immediately to cut the Gordian knot by which the American colonies have been bound to great Britain, and to open their commerce, as an independent people, to all the nations of the world. It has been greatly instrumental in producing a similarity of sentiment through the continent, upon the subject under the consideration of Congress."

THOMAS PAINE'S *appeal to "common sense" bore fruit in July of 1776. Moses Coit Tyler, unlike many twentieth-century historians, was not satisfied with an explanation, no matter how complex and scholarly, of the intellectual and political sources of the Declaration of Independence. Instead he raised for his reader the basic questions: Was the document merely an incident in an obscure colonial revolt? Or, was it a statement of truth for all men, for all time?*

Thomas Jefferson and The Great Declaration

ON the twenty-first of June, 1775, Thomas Jefferson took his seat for the first time as a member of the Continental Congress, bringing with him into that famous assemblage, as we are told by an older member of it, "a reputation for literature, science, and a happy talent for composition. Writings of his were handed about, remarkable for the peculiar felicity of expression." He had then but recently passed his thirty-second birthday, and was known to be the author of two or three public papers of considerable note.

Of these, the first one, written in 1769, could hardly have been among those compositions of his which were handed about for the admiration of Congress: it consisted of the "Resolutions of the Virginia House of Burgesses" in response to the speech of their new governor, Lord Botetourt, and was remarkable for nothing so much as for its obsequious tone—especially for its meek assurance on behalf of the burgesses that, in all their deliberations, it should be their "ruling principle" to consider the interests of Virginia and those of Great Britain as "inseparably the same."

His second public paper, written in the early summer of 1774, indicates how perfectly, within that interval of five years, this adept at "felicity of expression" had passed from the

stage of deference, to something bordering on that of truculence, as regards the official custodians of authority. The extraordinary composition now referred to, was first published at
Williamsburg in the year in which it was written, and bears the
following title: "A Summary View of the Rights of British
America. Set Forth in Some Resolutions intended for the Inspection of the Present Delegates of the People of Virginia
now in Convention." Herein his majesty is informed, without
the waste of a single word in mere politeness, that "he is no
more than the chief officer of the people, appointed by the laws,
and circumscribed with definite powers, to assist in working
the great machine of government erected for their use, and
consequently subject to their superintendence." This, of course,
might be a somewhat novel and startling view of himself for
the "chief magistrate of the British empire" to take; but after
he shall have got accustomed to it, he would see, doubtless,
how eminently fitting it was that he should at last receive from
the people of America a "joint address, penned in the language of truth, and divested of those expressions of servility
which would persuade his majesty that we were asking favors,
and not rights." "Let those flatter who fear: it is not an American art. To give praise which is not due might be well from the
venal, but would ill become those who are asserting the rights
of human nature. They know, and will therefore say, that kings
are the servants, not the proprietors, of the people. Open your
breast, sire, to liberal and expanded thought. Let not the name
of George the Third be a blot in the page of history. . . . The
whole art of government consists in the art of being honest.
Only aim to do your duty, and mankind will give you credit
where you fail. No longer persevere in sacrificing the rights of
one part of the empire to the inordinate desires of another, but
deal out to all equal and impartial right. . . . This, sire, is the advice of your great American council, on the observance of which
may perhaps depend your felicity and future fame, and the
preservation of that harmony which alone can continue both in
Great Britain and America the reciprocal advantages of their

connection." Another notable state paper of Jefferson's, was one on which he had been engaged immediately prior to his departure from the legislature of Virginia, in order to take his seat in Congress—an "Address of the House of Burgesses," adopted June 12, 1775, and having reference to Lord North's plan for conciliating the American colonies. In this paper, the burgesses of Virginia are made to review the long record of political blunders and crimes perpetrated by the British government in its relation to America, and then to declare that, for the further management of the dispute, they looked to the General Congress.

Certainly, it is not strange that the more radical members of Congress welcomed among them this young man, who, being in opinion even more radical than themselves, also possessed so striking a talent for unabashed and sonorous talk to governors of royal provinces and even to kings. Moreover, he soon won the hearts of the speech makers in that body by being himself no speech maker; and while he thus avoided irritating collisions and rivalries with his associates, he commanded their further admiration by being always "prompt, frank, explicit, and decisive upon committees and in conversation"—not even Samuel Adams himself being more so. Accordingly, only three days after he had taken his seat, the great honor was paid him of being joined with the foremost political writer of the day— the author of the *Farmer's Letters*—as a special committee for preparing the declaration of the Americans on taking up arms. Furthermore, in less than a month after his arrival, this novice in congressional business was given the second place on a committee, consisting of such veterans as Franklin, John Adams, and Richard Henry Lee, appointed to draft the American reply to Lord North's conciliatory propositions.

Thus it came to pass, that when, early in June, 1776, Congress saw before it the probability of its soon adopting the tremendous resolution—"that these United Colonies are, and of right ought to be, free and independent States; that they are absolved from all allegiance to the British crown; and that all political connection between them and the state of Great Britain is, and ought to be, totally dissolved"—then Thomas Jefferson, receiving the largest number of votes, was placed at the head of the committee of illustrious men to whom was assigned the task of preparing a suitable Declaration of Independence, and thereby he became the draftsman of the one American state paper that has reached to supreme distinction in the world, and that seems likely to last as long as American civilization lasts.

It can hardly be doubted that some hindrance to a right estimate of the Declaration of Independence is occasioned by either of two opposite conditions of mind, both of which are often to be met with among us: on the one hand, a condition of hereditary, uncritical awe and worship of the American Revolution and of this state paper as its absolutely perfect and glorious expression; on the other hand, a later condition of cultivated distrust of the Declaration, as a piece of writing lifted up into inordinate renown by the passionate and heroic circumstances of its origin, and ever since then extolled beyond reason by the blind energy of patriotic enthusiasm. Turning from the former state of mind—which obviously calls for no further comment—we may note, as a partial illustration of the latter, that American confidence in the supreme intellectual merit of this all-famous document received a serious wound, some forty years ago, from the hand of Rufus Choate, when, with a courage greater than would now be required for such an act, he characterized it as made up of "glittering and sounding generalities of natural right." What the great advocate then so unhesitantly suggested, many a thoughtful American since then has at least suspected—that this famous proclamation, as a piece of political literature, cannot stand the test of modern analysis; that it belongs to the immense class of over-praised productions; that it is, in fact, a stately patchwork of sweeping propositions of somewhat doubtful validity; that it has long imposed upon mankind by the well-known effectiveness of verbal glitter and sound; that, at the best, it is an example of florid political declamation belonging to the sophomoric period of our national life—a period which, as we flatter ourselves, we have now outgrown.

Nevertheless, it is to be noted that, whatever authority the Declaration of Independence has acquired in the world, has been due to no lack of criticism, either at the time of its first appearance or since then—a fact which seems to tell in favor of its essential worth and strength. From the date of its original publication down to the present moment, it has been attacked again and again, either in anger or in contempt, by friends as well as by enemies of the American Revolution, by liberals in politics as well as by conservatives. It has been censured for its substance, it has been censured for its form: for its misstatements of fact, for its fallacies in reasoning; for its audacious novelties and paradoxes, for its total lack of all novelty, for its repetition of old and threadbare statements, even for its downright plagiarisms; finally, for its grandiose and vaporing style.

One of the earliest and ablest of its assailants was Thomas Hutchinson, the last civil governor of the colony of Massachusetts, who, being stranded in London by the political storm which had blown him thither, published there, in the autumn of 1776, his *Strictures upon the Declaration of the Congress at Philadelphia;* wherein, with an unsurpassed knowledge of the origin of the controversy, and with an unsurpassed acumen in the discussion of it, he traverses the entire document, paragraph by paragraph, for the purpose of showing that its allegations in support of American Independence are "false and frivolous."

A better written, and, upon the whole, a more effective arraignment of the great Declaration, was the celebrated pamphlet by an English barrister, John Lind, "An Answer to the Declaration of the American Congress"—a pamphlet evidently written at the instigation of the ministry, and sent abroad under its approval. Here, again, the manifesto of Congress is subjected to a searching criticism, in order to show that the theory of government put forward in its preamble is "absurd and visionary"; that its political maxims are not only "repugnant to the British constitution" but "subversive of every actual or imaginable kind of government"; and that its specific charges against the king and parliament are "calumnies"—since they allege as usurpations and as encroachments certain acts of government under George the Third identical in character with those which had been "constantly exercised by his predecessors and their parliaments," and which had been on many occasions recognized as constitutional by the American colonial assemblies. It is doubtful if any disinterested student of history, any competent judge of reasoning, will now deny to this pamphlet the praise of making out a strong case against the historical accuracy and the logical soundness of many parts of the Declaration of Independence.

Undoubtedly, the force of such censures is for us much broken by the fact, that those censures proceeded from men who were themselves partisans in the Revolutionary controversy and bitterly hostile to the whole movement which the Declaration was intended to justify. Such is not the case, however, with the leading modern English critics of the same document, who, while blaming in severe terms the policy of the British government toward the Thirteen Colonies, have also found much to abate from the confidence due to the official announcement of the reasons for our secession from the empire. For example, Earl Russell, after frankly saying that the great disruption proclaimed by the Declaration of Independence, was a result which Great Britain had "used every means most fitted to bring about," such as "vacillation in council, harshness in language, feebleness in execution, disregard of American sympathies and affections," also pointed out that "the truth of this memorable Declaration" was "warped" by "one singular defect," namely, its exclusive and excessive arraignment of George the Third "as a single and despotic tyrant," much like Philip the Second to the people of the Netherlands.

This temperate criticism from an able and a liberal English

statesman of the present century, may be said to touch the very core of the problem as to the historic justice of our great indictment of the last king of America; and there is deep significance in the fact, that this is the very criticism upon the document, which, as John Adams tells us, he himself had in mind when it was first submitted to him in committee, and even when, shortly afterwards, he advocated its adoption by Congress. After mentioning certain things in it with which he was delighted, he adds: "There were other expressions which I would not have inserted if I had drawn it up—particularly that which called the king tyrant. I thought this too personal; for I never believed George to be a tyrant in disposition and in nature. I always believed him to be deceived by his courtiers on both sides of the Atlantic, and, in his official capacity only, cruel. I thought the expression too passionate, and too much like scolding, for so grave and solemn a document; but, as Franklin and Sherman were to inspect it afterwards, I thought it would not become me to strike it out. I consented to report it."*

A more minute and a more poignant criticism of the Declaration of Independence has been made in recent years by still another English writer of liberal tendencies, who, however, in his capacity as critic, seems here to labor under the disadvantage of having transferred to the document which he undertakes to judge, much of the extreme dislike which he has for the man who wrote it—whom, indeed, he regards as a sophist, as a demagogue, as quite capable of inveracity in speech, and as bearing some resemblance to Robespierre "in his feline nature,

---

* The distinction here made by John Adams between the personal and the official character of George III, is quite pointless in its application to the Declaration of Independence; since it is of the King's official character only that the Declaration speaks. Moreover, John Adams's testimony in 1822 that he "never believed George to be a tyrant in disposition and in nature," is completely destroyed by John Adams's own testimony on that subject as recorded at an earlier period of his life. For example, in 1780, in a letter to M. Dumas, he thus speaks of George III—"Europe, in general, is much mistaken in that character; it is a pity that he should be believed to be so amiable; the truth is far otherwise. *Nerone neronior* is nearer the truth."

his malignant egotism, and his intense suspiciousness, as well as in his bloody-minded, yet possibly sincere, philanthropy." In the opinion of Professor Goldwin Smith, our great national manifesto is written "in a highly rhetorical strain"; "it opens with sweeping aphorisms about the natural rights of man, at which political science now smiles, and which . . . might seem strange when framed for slave-holding communities by a publicist who himself held slaves"; while, in its specifications of facts, it "is not more scrupulously truthful than are the general utterances" of the statesman who was its scribe. It charges that the several offensive acts of the king, besides "evincing a design to reduce the colonists under absolute despotism," "all had as their direct object the establishment of an absolute tyranny," are simply "propositions which history cannot accept." Moreover, the Declaration "blinks the fact that many of the acts, styled steps of usurpation, were measures of repression which, however unwise or excessive, had been provoked by popular outrage." "No government could allow its officers to be assaulted and their houses sacked, its loyal lieges to be tarred and feathered, or the property of merchants sailing under its flag to be thrown by lawless hands into the sea." Even "the preposterous violence and the manifest insincerity of the suppressed clause" against slavery and the slave-trade, "are enough to create suspicion as to the spirit in which the whole document was framed."

Finally, as has been already intimated, not even among Americans themselves has the Declaration of Independence been permitted to pass on into the enjoyment of its superb renown, without much critical disparagement at the hands of statesmen and historians. No doubt Calhoun had its preamble in mind, when he declared that "nothing can be more unfounded and false" than "the prevalent opinion that all men are born free and equal"; for "it rests upon the assumption of a fact which is contrary to universal observation." Of course, all Americans who have shared to any extent in Calhoun's doctrines respecting human society, could hardly fail to agree with him in regarding as fallacious and worthless those general propositions in the Declaration which seem to constitute its logical starting point, as well as its ultimate defense.

Perhaps, however, the most frequent form of disparagement to which Jefferson's great state paper has been subjected among us, is that which would minimize his merit in composing it, by denying to it the merit of originality. For example, Richard Henry Lee sneered at it as a thing "copied from Locke's treatise on government." The author of a life of Jefferson, published in the year of Jefferson's retirement from the presidency, suggests that the credit of having composed the Declaration of Independence "has been perhaps more generally, than truly, given by the public" to that great man. Charles Campbell, the historian of Virginia, intimates that some expressions in the document were taken without acknowledgment from Aphra Behn's tragi-comedy, *The Widow Ranter, or, The History of Bacon in Virginia.* John Stockton Littell describes the Declaration of Independence as "that enduring monument at once of patriotism, and of genius and skill in the art of appropriation"—asserting that "for the sentiments and much of the language" of it, Jefferson was indebted to Chief Justice Drayton's charge to the grand jury of Charleston delivered in April, 1776, as well as to the declaration of independence said to have been adopted by some citizens of Mecklenburg County, North Carolina, in May, 1775. Even the latest and most critical editor of the writings of Jefferson calls attention to the fact, that a glance at the declaration of rights, as adopted by Virginia on the 12th of June, 1776, "would seem to indicate the source from which Jefferson derived a most important and popular part" of his famous production.* By no one, however, has the charge of a lack of originality been pressed with so much decisiveness as by John Adams, who took evident pleasure in speaking of it as a document in which were merely "recapitulated" previous and

* Paul Leicester Ford, *The Writings of Thomas Jefferson*, i. Introd. xxvi.

well-known statements of American rights and wrongs, and who, as late as in the year 1822, deliberately wrote that "there is not an idea in it but what had been hackneyed in Congress for two years before. The substance of it is contained in the declaration of rights and the violation of those rights, in the journals of Congress, in 1774. Indeed, the essence of it is contained in a pamphlet, voted and printed by the town of Boston, before the first Congress met, composed by James Otis, as I suppose, in one of his lucid intervals, and pruned and polished by Samuel Adams."*

Perhaps nowhere in our literature would it be possible to find a criticism brought forward by a really able man against any piece of writing, less applicable to the case, and of less force or value, than is this particular criticism by John Adams and others, as to the lack of originality in the Declaration of Independence. Indeed, for such a paper as Jefferson was commissioned to write, the one quality which it could not properly have had—the one quality which would have been fatal to its acceptance either by the American Congress or by the American people—is originality. They were then at the culmination of a tremendous controversy over alleged grievances of the most serious kind—a controversy that had been fiercely raging for at least twelve years. In the course of that long dispute, every phase of it, whether as to abstract right or constitutional privilege or personal procedure, had been presented in almost every conceivable form of speech. At last, they had resolved, in view of all this experience, no longer to prosecute the controversy as members of the empire: they had resolved to revolt, and casting off forever their ancient fealty to the British crown, to separate from the empire, and to establish themselves as a new nation among the nations of the earth. In this emer-

* Thus, the ingenuous reader has the happiness of seeing the eternal fitness of things complied with, and the chief intellectual merit of the Declaration of Independence brought back to the place where it belongs, and there divided between the town of Boston, James Otis, and the Adams family.

gency, as it happened, Jefferson was called upon to put into form a suitable statement of the chief considerations which prompted them to this great act of revolution, and which, as they believed, justified it. What, then, was Jefferson to do? Was he to regard himself as a mere literary essayist, set to produce before the world a sort of prize dissertation—a calm, analytic, judicial treatise on history and politics with a particular application to Anglo-American affairs—one essential merit of which would be its originality as a contribution to historical and political literature? Was he not, rather, to regard himself as, for the time being, the very mouthpiece and prophet of the people whom he represented, and as such required to bring together and to set in order, in their name, not what was new, but what was old; to gather up into his own soul, as much as possible, whatever was then also in their souls—their very thoughts and passions, their ideas of constitutional law, their interpretations of fact, their opinions as to men and as to events in all that ugly quarrel; their notions of justice, of civic dignity, of human rights; finally, their memories of wrongs which seemed to them intolerable, especially of wrongs inflicted upon them during those twelve years by the hands of insolent and brutal men, in the name of the king, and by his apparent command?

Moreover, as the nature of the task laid upon him made it necessary that he should thus state, as the reasons for their intended act, those very considerations both as to fact and as to opinion which had actually operated upon their minds, so did it require him to do so, to some extent, in the very language which the people themselves, in their more formal and deliberate utterances, had all along been using. In the development of political life in England and America, there had already been created a vast literature of constitutional progress— a literature common to both portions of the English race, pervaded by its own stately traditions, and reverberating certain great phrases which formed, as one may say, almost the vernacular of English justice, and of English aspiration for a free, manly, and orderly political life. In this vernacular the Declaration of Independence was written. The phraseology thus characteristic of it, is the very phraseology of the champions of constitutional expansion, of civic dignity and of progress, within the English race ever since Magna Charta; of the great state papers of English freedom in the seventeenth century, particularly the Petition of Right in 1629, and the Bill of Rights in 1689; of the great English charters for colonization in America; of the great English exponents of legal and political progress—Sir Edward Coke, John Milton, Algernon Sidney, John Locke; finally, of the great American exponents of political liberty and of the chief representative bodies, whether local or general, which had convened in America from the time of the Stamp Act Congress until that of the Congress which resolved upon our Independence. To say, therefore, that the official Declaration of that resolve is a paper made up of the very opinions, beliefs, unbeliefs, the very sentiments, prejudices, passions, even the errors in judgment and the personal misconstructions—if they were such—which then actually impelled the American people to that mighty act, and that all these are expressed in the very phrases which they had been accustomed to use, is to pay to that state paper the highest tribute as to its fitness for the purpose for which it was framed.

Of much of this, also, Jefferson himself seems to have been conscious; and perhaps never does he rise before us with more dignity, with more truth, than when, late in his lifetime, hurt by the captious and jangling words of disparagement then recently put into writing by his old comrade, to the effect that the Declaration of Independence "contained no new ideas, that it is a commonplace compilation, its sentiments hackneyed in Congress for two years before, and its essence contained in Otis's pamphlet," Jefferson quietly replied that perhaps these statements might "all be true: of that I am not to be the judge. . . . Whether I had gathered my ideas from reading or reflection, I do not know. I know only that I turned to neither book nor pamphlet while writing it. I did not consider it as any part of

my charge to invent new ideas altogether, and to offer no sentiment which had ever been expressed before."

Before passing from this phase of the subject, however, it
should be added that, while the Declaration of Independence
lacks originality in the sense just indicated, in another and
perhaps in a higher sense, it possesses originality—it is indi-
vidualized by the character and the genius of its author. Jefferson gathered up the thoughts and emotions and even the
characteristic phrases of the people for whom he wrote, and
these he perfectly incorporated with what was already in his
own mind, and then to the music of his own keen, rich, passionate, and enkindling style, he mustered them into that
stately and triumphant procession wherein, as some of us still
think, they will go marching on to the world's end.

There were then in Congress several other men who could
have written the Declaration of Independence, and written it
well—notably, Franklin, either of the two Adamses, Richard
Henry Lee, William Livingston, and, best of all—but for his
own opposition to the measure—John Dickinson; but had any
one of these other men written the Declaration of Independence, while it would have contained, doubtless, nearly the
same topics and nearly the same great formulas of political
statement, it would yet have been a wholly different composition from this of Jefferson's. No one at all familiar with his
other writings as well as with the writings of his chief contemporaries, could ever have a moment's doubt, even if the
fact were not already notorious, that this document was by
Jefferson. He put into it something that was his own, and that
no one else could have put there. He put himself into it—his
own genius, his own moral force, his faith in God, his faith in
ideas, his love of innovation, his passion for progress, his invincible enthusiasm, his intolerance of prescription, of injustice, of cruelty, his sympathy, his clarity of vision, his affluence
of diction, his power to fling out great phrases which will long
fire and cheer the souls of men struggling against political un-
righteousness. And herein lies its essential originality, perhaps

the most precious, and indeed almost the only, originality ever attaching to any great literary product that is representative of its time. He made for himself no improper claim, therefore, when he directed that upon the granite obelisk at his grave should be carved the words—"Here was buried Thomas Jefferson, author of the Declaration of Independence."

If the Declaration of Independence is now to be fairly judged by us, it must be judged with reference to what it was intended to be—namely, an impassioned manifesto of one party, and that the weaker party, in a violent race quarrel; of a party resolved, at last, upon the extremity of revolution, and already menaced by the inconceivable disaster of being defeated in the very act of armed rebellion against the mightiest military power on earth. This manifesto, then, is not to be censured because, being avowedly a statement of its own side of the quarrel, it does not also contain a moderate and judicial statement of the opposite side; or because, being necessarily partisan in method, it is likewise both partisan and vehement in tone; or because it bristles with accusations against the enemy so fierce and so unqualified as now to seem in some respects overdrawn; or because it resounds with certain great aphorisms about the natural rights of man, at which, indeed, political science cannot now smile except to its own discomfiture and shame—aphorisms which are likely to abide in this world as the chief source and inspiration of heroic enterprises among men for self-deliverance from oppression.

Taking into account, therefore, as we are bound to do, the circumstances of its origin, and especially its purpose as a solemn and piercing appeal to mankind, on behalf of a small and weak nation against the alleged injustice and cruelty of a great and powerful one, it still remains our duty to enquire whether, as has been asserted in our time, history must set aside either of the two central charges embodied in the Declaration of Independence.

The first of these charges affirms that the several acts complained of by the colonists, evinced "a design to reduce them under absolute despotism," and had as their "direct object the establishment of an absolute tyranny" over the American people. Was this, indeed, a groundless charge, in the sense intended by the words "despotism" and "tyranny"—that is, in the sense commonly given to those words in the usage of the English-speaking race? According to that usage, it was not an oriental despotism that was meant, nor a Greek tyranny, nor a Roman, nor a Spanish. The sort of despot, the sort of tyrant, whom the English people, ever since the time of King John and especially during the period of the Stuarts, had been accustomed to look for and to guard against, was the sort of tyrant or despot that could be evolved out of the conditions of English political life. Furthermore, he was not by them expected to appear among them at the outset in the fully developed shape of a Philip or an Alva in the Netherlands. They were able to recognize him, they were prepared to resist him, in the earliest and most incipient stage of his being—at the moment, in fact, when he should make his first attempt to gain all power over his people by assuming the single power to take their property without their consent. Hence it was, as Edmund Burke pointed out in the house of commons only a few weeks before the American Revolution entered upon its military phase, that in England "the great contests for freedom . . . were from the earliest times chiefly upon the question of taxing. Most of the contests in the ancient commonwealths turned primarily on the right of election of magistrates, or on the balance among the several orders of the state. The question of money was not with them so immediate. But in England it was otherwise. On this point of taxes the ablest pens and most eloquent tongues have been exercised, the greatest spirits have acted and suffered. . . . They took infinite pains to inculcate, as a fundamental principle, that in all monarchies the people must in effect themselves, mediately or immediately, possess the power of granting their own money, or no shadow of liberty could subsist. The colonies draw from you, as with their life-blood, these ideas and principles. Their love of liberty, as with you, fixed and attached on their specific point of taxing. Liberty might be safe or might be endangered in twenty other particulars without their being much pleased or alarmed. Here they felt its pulse; and as they found that beat, they thought themselves sick or sound."

Accordingly, the meaning which the English race on both sides of the Atlantic were accustomed to attach to the words "tyranny" and "despotism," was a meaning to some degree ideal: it was a meaning drawn from the extraordinary political sagacity with which that race is endowed, from their extraordinary sensitiveness as to the use of the taxing-power in government, from their instinctive perception of the commanding place of the taxing-power among all the other forms of power in the state, from their perfect assurance that he who holds the purse with the power to fill it and to empty it, holds the key of the situation,—can maintain an army of his own, can rule without consulting parliament, can silence criticism, can crush opposition, can strip his subjects of every vestige of political life; in other words, he can make slaves of them, he can make a despot and a tyrant of himself. Therefore, the system which in the end might develop into results so palpably tyrannic and despotic, they bluntly called a tyranny and a despotism in the beginning. To say, therefore, that the Declaration of Independence did the same, is to say that it spoke good English. Of course, history will be ready to set aside the charge thus made in language not at all liable to be misunderstood, just so soon as history is ready to set aside the common opinion that the several acts of the British government, from 1763 to 1776, for laying and enforcing taxation in America, did evince a somewhat particular and systematic design to take away some portion of the property of the American people without their consent.

The second of the two great charges contained in the Declaration of Independence, while intimating that some share in the blame is due to the British parliament and to the British people, yet fastens upon the king himself as the one person chiefly responsible for the scheme of American tyranny therein set forth, and culminates in the frank description of him as "a prince whose character is thus marked by every act which may define a tyrant." Is this accusation of George the Third now to be set aside as unhistoric? Was that king, or was he not, chiefly responsible for the American policy of the British government between the years 1763 and 1776? If he was so, then the historic soundness of the most important portion of the Declaration of Independence is vindicated.

Fortunately, this question can be answered without hesitation, and in few words; and for these few words, an American writer of to-day, conscious of his own bias of nationality, will rightly prefer to cite such as have been uttered by the ablest English historians of our time, who have dealt with the subject. Upon their statements alone it must be concluded, that George the Third ascended his throne with the fixed purpose of resuming to the crown many of those powers which by the constitution of England did not then belong to it, and that in this purpose, at least during the first twenty-five years of his reign, he substantially succeeded—himself determining what should be the policy of each administration, what opinions his ministers should advocate in parliament, and what measures parliament itself should adopt. "The king desired," says Sir Erskine May, "to undertake personally the chief administration of public affairs, to direct the policy of his ministers, and himself to distribute the patronage of the crown. He was ambitious not only to reign, but to govern." "Strong as were the ministers, the king was resolved to wrest all power from their hands, and to exercise it himself." "But what was this, in effect, but to assert that the king should be his own minister? . . . The king's tactics were fraught with danger, as well to the crown itself, as to the constitutional liberties of the people."

Already, prior to the year 1778, according to Lecky, the king had "laboriously built up" in England a "system of personal government"; and it was because he was unwilling to have this system disturbed, that he then refused, "in defiance of the most

earnest representations of his own minister and of the most
eminent politicians of every party . . . to send for the greatest
of living statesmen at the moment when the empire appeared
to be in the very agonies of dissolution. . . . Either Chatham or
Rockingham would have insisted that the policy of the country
should be directed by its responsible ministers, and not dictated by an irresponsible sovereign." This refusal of the king
to adopt the course which was called for by the constitution,
and which would have taken the control of the policy of the
government out of his hands, was, according to the same great
historian, an act "the most criminal in the whole reign of
George the Third, . . . as criminal as any of those acts which led
Charles the First to the scaffold."

Even so early as the year 1768, according to John Richard
Green, "George the Third had at last reached his aim." In the
early days of the ministry which began in that year, "his influence was felt to be predominant. In its later and more disastrous
days it was supreme; for Lord North, who became the head of
the ministry on Grafton's retirement in 1770, was the mere
mouthpiece of the king. 'Not only did he direct the minister,'
a careful observer tells us, 'in all important matters of foreign
and domestic policy, but he instructed him as to the management of debates in parliament, suggested what motions should
be made or opposed, and how measures should be carried. He
reserved for himself all the patronage, he arranged the whole
cast of the administration, settled the relative place and pretensions of ministers of state, law officers, and members of the
household, nominated and promoted the English and Scotch
judges, appointed and translated bishops and deans, and dispensed other preferments in the church. He disposed of military
governments, regiments, and commissions, and himself ordered
the marching of troops. He gave and refused titles, honors, and
pensions.' All this immense patronage was steadily used for the
creation and maintenance of a party in both houses of parliament attached to the king himself. . . . George was, in fact,
sole minister during the fifteen years which followed; and the

shame of the darkest hour of English history lies wholly at his door."

Surely, until these tremendous verdicts of English history shall be set aside, there need be no anxiety in any quarter as to the historic soundness of the two great accusations which together make up the principal portion of the Declaration of Independence. In the presence of these verdicts, also, even the passion, the intensity of language, in which these accusations are uttered, seem to find a perfect justification. Indeed, in the light of the most recent and most unprejudiced expert testimony, the whole document, both in its substance and in its form, seems to have been the logical response of a nation of brave men to the great words of the greatest of English statesmen, as spoken in the house of commons precisely ten years before: "This kingdom has no right to lay a tax on the colonies. . . . Sir, I rejoice that America has resisted. Three millions of people so dead to all the feelings of liberty as voluntarily to submit to be slaves, would have been fit instruments to have made slaves of the rest."

It is proper for us to remember that what we call criticism, is not the only valid test of the genuineness and worth of any piece of writing of great practical interest to mankind: there is, also, the test of actual use and service in the world, in direct contact with the common sense and the moral sense of large masses of men, under various conditions, and for a long period. Probably no writing which is not essentially sound and true has ever survived this test.

Neither from this test has the great Declaration any need to shrink. Probably no public paper ever more perfectly satisfied the immediate purposes for which it was sent forth. From one end of the country to the other, and as fast as it could be spread among the people, it was greeted in public and in private with every demonstration of approval and delight. To a marvelous degree, it quickened the friends of the Revolution for their great task. "This Declaration," wrote one of its signers but a few days after it had been proclaimed, "has had a glorious effect—has made these colonies all alive." "With the Independency of the American States," said another political leader a few weeks later, "a new era in politics has commenced. Every consideration respecting the propriety or impropriety of a separation from Britain is now entirely out of the question. . . . Our future happiness or misery, therefore, as a people, will depend entirely upon ourselves." Six years afterward, in a review of the whole struggle, a great American scholar expressed his sense of the relation of this document to it, by saying, that "into the monumental act of Independence," Jefferson had "poured the soul of the continent."

Moreover, during the century and a quarter since the close of the Revolution, the influence of this state paper on the political character and the political conduct of the American people has been great beyond all calculation. For example, after we had achieved our own national deliverance, and had advanced into that enormous and somewhat corrupting material prosperity which followed the adoption of the constitution, the development of the cotton interest, and the expansion of the republic into a trans-continental power, we fell, as is now most apparent, under an appalling national temptation—the temptation to forget, or to repudiate, or to refuse to apply to the case of our human brethren in bondage, the very principles which we ourselves had once proclaimed as the basis of every rightful government, and as the ultimate source of our own claim to an untrammeled national life. The prodigious service rendered to us in this awful moral emergency by the Declaration of Independence was, that its public repetition, at least once every year, in the hearing of vast throngs of the American people, in every portion of the republic, kept constantly before our minds, in a form of almost religious sanctity, those few great ideas as to the dignity of human nature, and the sacredness of personality, and the indestructible rights of man as mere man, with which we had so gloriously identified the beginnings of our national existence, and upon which we had proceeded to erect all our political institutions both for the nation and for the States. It did, indeed, at last become very hard for us to listen each year to the preamble of the Declaration of Independence, and still to remain the owners and users and catchers of slaves; still harder, to accept the doctrine that the righteousness and prosperity of slavery was to be taken as the dominant policy of the nation. The logic of Calhoun was as flawless as usual, when he concluded that the chief obstruction in the way of his system, was the preamble of the Declaration of Independence. Had it not been for the inviolable sacredness given by it to those sweeping aphorisms about the natural rights of man, it may be doubted whether, under the vast practical inducements involved, Calhoun might not have succeeded in winning over an immense majority of the American people to the support of his compact and plausible scheme for making slavery the basis of the republic. It was the preamble of the Declaration of Independence which elected Lincoln, which sent forth the Emancipation Proclamation, which gave victory to Grant, which ratified the Thirteenth Amendment.

Moreover, we cannot doubt that the permanent effects of the great Declaration on the political and even the ethical ideals of the American people are wider and deeper than can be measured by our experience in grappling with any single political problem; for they touch all the spiritual springs of American national character, and they create, for us and for all human beings, a new standard of political justice and a new principle in the science of government. "Much ridicule, a little of it not altogether undeserved," says a brilliant English scholar of our time, who is also nobly distinguished in the sphere of English statesmanship, "has been thrown upon the opening clause of the Declaration of Independence, which asserts the inherent natural right of man to enjoy life and liberty, with the means of acquiring and possessing property, and pursuing and obtaining happiness and safety. Yet there is an implied corollary in this which enjoins the highest morality that in our present state we are able to think of as possible. If happiness is the right of our neighbor, then not to hinder him but to help him in its pursuit, must plainly be our duty. If all men have a claim, then each man is under an obligation. The corollary thus involved is the corner-stone of morality. It was an act of good augury thus to inscribe happiness as entering at once into the right of all, and into the duty of all, in the very head and front of the new charter, as the base of a national existence, and the first principle of a national government. The omen has not been falsified. The Americans have been true to their first doctrine. They have never swerved aside to set up caste and privilege, to lay down the doctrine that one man's happiness ought to be an object of greater solicitude to society than any other man's, or that one order should be encouraged to seek its prosperity through the depression of any other order. Their example proved infectious. The assertion in the New World, that men have a right to happiness and an obligation to promote the happiness of one another, struck a spark in the Old World. Political construction in America immediately preceded the last violent stage of demolition in Europe."*

We shall not here attempt to delineate the influence of this state paper upon mankind in general. Of course, the emergence of the American Republic as an imposing world-power is a phenomenon which has now for many years attracted the attention of the human race. Surely, no slight effect must have resulted from the fact that, among all civilized peoples, the one American document best known, is the Declaration of Independence, and that thus the spectacle of so vast and beneficent a political success has been everywhere associated with the assertion of the natural rights of man. "The doctrines it contained," says Buckle, "were not merely welcomed by a majority of the French nation, but even the government itself was unable to withstand the general feeling." "Its effect in hastening the approach of the French Revolution . . . was indeed most remarkable." Elsewhere, also, in many lands, among many peoples, it has been appealed to again and again as an inspiration for political courage, as a model for political conduct; and if, as the brilliant English historian just cited has affirmed, "that

* John Morley, *Edmund Burke: A Historical Study*, 161–162.

noble Declaration . . . ought to be hung up in the nursery of every king, and blazoned on the porch of every royal palace," it is because it has become the classic statement of political truths which must at last abolish kings altogether, or else teach them to identify their existence with the dignity and happiness of human nature.

It would be unfitting, in a work like the present, to treat of the Declaration of Independence without making more than an incidental reference to its purely literary character.

Very likely, most writings—even most writings of genuine and high quality—have had the misfortune of being read too little. There is, however, a misfortune—perhaps, a greater misfortune—which has overtaken some literary compositions, and these not necessarily the noblest and the best—the misfortune of being read too much. At any rate, the writer of a piece of literature which has been neglected, need not be refused the consolation he may get from reflecting that he is, at least, not the writer of a piece of literature which has become hackneyed. Just this is the sort of calamity which seems to have befallen the Declaration of Independence. Is it, indeed, possible for us Americans, near the close of the nineteenth century, to be entirely just to the literary quality of this most monumental document—this much belauded, much bespouted, much beflouted document?—since, in order to be so, we need to rid ourselves, if we can, of the obstreperous memories of a lifetime of Independence Days, and to unlink and disperse the associations which have somehow confounded Jefferson's masterpiece with the rattle of fire-crackers, with the flash and the splutter of burning tar-barrels, and with that unreserved, that gyratory and perspiratory, eloquence now for more than a hundred years consecrated to the return of our fateful Fourth of July.

Had the Declaration of Independence been, what many a revolutionary state paper is, a clumsy, verbose, and vaporing production, not even the robust literary taste and the all-forgiving patriotism of the American people could have endured the weariness, the nausea, of hearing its repetition, in ten thousand different places, at least once every year, for so long a period. Nothing which has not supreme literary merit has ever triumphantly endured such an ordeal, or ever been subjected to it. No man can adequately explain the persistent fascination which this state-paper has had, and which it still has, for the American people, or for its undiminished power over them, without taking into account its extraordinary literary merits— its possession of the witchery of true substance wedded to perfect form—its massiveness and incisiveness of thought, its art in the marshaling of the topics with which it deals, with symmetry, its energy, the definiteness and limpidity of its statements,* its exquisite diction—at once terse, musical, and electrical; and, as an essential part of this literary outfit, many of those spiritual notes which can attract and enthrall our hearts —veneration for God, veneration for man, veneration for principle, respect for public opinion, moral earnestness, moral courage, optimism, a stately and noble pathos, finally, self-sacrificing devotion to a cause so great as to be herein identified with the happiness, not of one people only, or of one race only, but of human nature itself.

Upon the whole, this is the most commanding and the most pathetic utterance, in any age, in any language, of national grievances and of national purposes; having a Demosthenic momentum of thought, and a fervor of emotional appeal such as Tyrtaeus might have put into his war-songs. Indeed, the Declaration of Independence is a kind of war-song; it is a stately and a passionate chant of human freedom; it is a prose lyric of civil and military heroism. We may be altogether sure that no genuine development of literary taste among the American people in any period of our future history can result in serious misfortune to this particular specimen of American literature.

---

* Much has been said of the generalities, whether glittering or otherwise, of the Declaration; yet they who have most objected to its teachings seem to have found them sufficiently specific and distinct. Its famous assertion that "all men are created equal," has been complained of as liable to be misconstrued; "but," as a recent biographer of Jefferson cleverly says, "no intelligent man has ever misconstrued it, except intentionally."

THE *Declaration of Independence was a Rubicon not all men could cross. For some who had argued faithfully and well for the colonial cause, the Declaration of Independence was both a national and a personal tragedy.*

John Dickinson of Pennsylvania was one of those men.

John Dickinson

THE year 1765, which is marked by the first contributions of John Dickinson to the literature of the American Revolution, presents him to us as an accomplished young barrister of Philadelphia, already noted for his large reading in history and politics, already noted for the purity and brilliance of his English style. He was born in 1732, on the eastern shore of Maryland, at Crosia-Doré—an estate which even then for nearly a century had been the seat of the Dickinson family, as it still is after the lapse of a second century and more than the half of a third. Having been carefully educated by private tutors at home, he read law for three years in the office of John Moland of Philadelphia. In 1753, he was entered of the Middle Temple, London, where he resided for three years, having for fellow-students Edward Thurlowe, Lloyd Kenyon, and William Cowper. In 1760, he began his political career by taking a seat as member of the assembly of Delaware. In 1762, according to a usage then not uncommon, he was transferred to the assembly of Pennsylvania; and in that body he served with great distinction until 1765, and again from 1770 until the expiration of the colonial government in 1776. Moreover, in 1765 he represented Pennsylvania in the Stamp Act Congress, as he did also in the several sessions of the Continental Congress from 1774 until some time in July, 1776. Having, by his opposition to the proposal for American Independence, incurred the deep dislike and distrust of the more radical members of the party to which he belonged, he left his seat in Congress in order to take command of a brigade of Pennsylvania troops called out to aid in resisting the threatened attack of the British upon New York; and on the tenth of August, from his camp at Elizabethtown, New Jersey, he thus wrote to his friend, Charles Thomson, secretary of Congress: "The enemy are moving, and an attack on New York is quickly expected. As for myself, I can form no idea of a more noble fate than, after being the constant advocate for and promoter of every measure that could possibly lead to peace or prevent her return from being barred up; after cheerfully and deliberately sacrificing my popularity and all the emoluments I might certainly have derived from it, to principle; after suffering all the indignities that my countrymen now bearing rule are inclined, if they could, so plentifully to shower down upon my innocent head,—than willingly to resign my life, if Divine Providence shall please so to dispose of me, for the defense and happiness of those unkind countrymen whom I cannot forbear to esteem as fellow-citizens, amidst their fury against me."

Notwithstanding the lofty principle upon which he thus acted, and the nobility of his devotion to the safety of his imperiled countrymen, he was pursued, even into the field of battle, by the enmity of his late associates, unable, as is apt to be the case with all revolutionary associates, to pardon the man who, having gone with them a part of the way, hesitated to go with them the whole of it. "I had not been ten days in camp at Elizabethtown," he wrote, "when I was by my persecutors turned out of Congress. While I was exposing my person to every hazard, and lodging every night within half a mile of the enemy, the members of the convention at Philadelphia, resting in quiet and safety, ignominiously voted me, as unworthy of my seat, out of the national senate." By a studied insult, likewise, he was driven soon afterward to resign his commission in the army. Upon his return to Pennsylvania, he served for a short time in its legislature, and then withdrew to an estate of his in Delaware, resolved to retire for awhile from all participation in politics, but to volunteer as a private soldier at the next call for troops. In this capacity he carried a musket in the battle of Brandywine. In May, 1779, he appeared once more in Congress, but as a member from Delaware, serving, however, only until the autumn of that year. In 1781, he was made governor of Delaware. In 1782, he was made governor of Pennsylvania, and as such was serving the commonwealth at the close of the Revolution.

This is the man who, being thus occupied during all those years by great practical employments in peace and war, yet had such productiveness in literary labor and so exquisite a genius as to win for himself the title of "Penman of the American Revolution." By the author of a recent sketch of his life, he has been described as "the great colonial essayist." By the editor of the latest edition of his writings, it has been claimed for him that, in the literature of the Revolution, he is "as preëminent as Washington in war, Franklin in diplomacy, and Morris in finance."

No other man in those days had a finer gift for putting into form—into luminous, urbane, and stately form—the constitutional and political principles on which, in his opinion, the American opposition to the British ministry was to be conducted; and, prior to the middle of 1776, no other man was so much employed by the several public bodies with which he was connected, in giving expression to those principles in the great state papers of the time. It was he who, in 1765, drafted the "Resolutions in relation to the Stamp Act," adopted by the assembly of Pennsylvania, as well as the "Declaration of Rights," and the "Petition to the King," adopted by the Stamp Act Congress. It was he who, in July, 1774, wrote the "Resolves" promulgated by the convention of Pennsylvania; also, their "Instructions to the Representatives in Assembly," and their elaborate "Essay on the Constitutional Power of Great Britain over the Colonies in America." It was he who, in October, 1774, wrote the "Address of Congress to the Inhabitants of the Province of Quebec" and the first "Petition of Congress to the

King's Most Excellent Majesty." It was he who, in the early summer of 1775, wrote the second "Petition of Congress to the King's Most Excellent Majesty," as well as "The Declaration by the Representatives of the United Colonies of North America, now met in Congress at Philadelphia, setting forth the Causes and Necessity of their taking up Arms."* It was he who, in November, 1775, and again in June, 1776, wrote the "Instructions" of Pennsylvania to its representatives in Congress; who, in July, 1776, wrote the "Revision of the Bill of Rights" for the State of Pennsylvania; who, at about the same time, wrote the first draft of the "Articles of Confederation," as then submitted to Congress; who, finally, in May, 1779, wrote the "Address of Congress to the Several States on the Present Situation of Affairs."

But besides these imposing official expressions of the argument and sentiment of the American Revolution, John Dickinson likewise gave a more personal utterance to them, in almost innumerable ways, through the public press. During a period reaching back to at least three years prior to the Stamp Act, and reaching forward to at least one year subsequent to the Declaration of Independence, he was an almost constant writer of political essays for the newspapers, of broadsides, and of other fugitive productions, the most of which, as he probably intended they should be, are now quite beyond the possibility of recognition. A mere glance at the list of his miscellaneous writings upon Revolutionary topics—so far as those writings are known to us—can hardly fail to give the reader a lively impression of the literary energy and versatility of the man, and of the vastness of the work he did during those tremendous years, in molding the opinions of his countrymen, and in conveying impulse and direction to events which have since acquired a world-wide celebrity and influence. Thus, in November, 1765, he issued, as a broadside, a stirring "Address to

* Tyler attributed this entire document to Dickinson. Modern scholars argue that Jefferson wrote the last four and one-half paragraphs. S. E. Morison, *Sources and Documents Illustrating the American Revolution 1764–1788* (London: Oxford University Press, 1951), pp. xxxvi, 144. [Ed.]

Friends and Countrymen on the Stamp Act"; and this he re-
enforced by publishing in the following month a plausible and
strong pamphlet, entitled "The Late Regulations respecting
the British Colonies Considered." In 1766, under the signature
of "A North American," he published "An Address to the Committee of Correspondence in Barbadoes"—a paper bearing
upon its title-page a sarcastic motto adapted, rather than precisely quoted, from Shakespeare:

> This word rebellion hath froze them up,
> Like fish in a pond.

On the second of December, 1767, in "The Pennsylvania
Chronicle," he began the publication of a series of essays, which
soon attained to a greater reputation, on both sides of the Atlantic, than had been reached by any previous production in
American literature—the "Letters from a Farmer in Pennsylvania," twelve in number, the last one appearing on the fifteenth of February, 1768. In April of that year, he published
at Philadelphia "An Address read at a Meeting of Merchants
to consider Non-Importation"—an appeal which three months
later he supplemented by a "Letter" to the same merchants on
the same subject. In July, 1768, he published "A Song for
American Freedom"—a rather clumsy hymn of patriotic duty
and enthusiasm, which, however, so perfectly fitted the needs
and the moods of the friends of the Revolution that, in spite of
its lack of poetic merit, it became, in all parts of the land, and
down to the outbreak of hostilities, the most popular lyric produced among us during that period. In November, 1773, he published "Two Letters on the Tea-Tax." In May, 1774, he published "Letters to the Inhabitants of the British Colonies"—
these letters being four in number. In December, 1775, he published a "Speech to the Assembly of New Jersey." In July,
1776, he published "An Essay for a Frame of Government in
Pennsylvania."

To him who now reads that John Dickinson, having opposed
in Congress the resolution for American Independence, im-

mediately thereafter left that body in order to lead a brigade of American troops against the British, it will probably seem either that he had somewhat too suddenly repented of his opposition to Independence, or else that he was guilty of conduct inconsistent with his principles. Neither inference would be correct. In truth, his conduct throughout that particular emergency was in perfect accord with all his political teachings, which involved, especially, these two principles: first, that it was the ancient and manly method of loyal Englishmen, in cases of extreme danger, to make demand for political rights with arms in their hands, and even embodied in military array against the king's troops; and, secondly, that every citizen, having said and done his best to secure the prevalence of his own view, was bound to submit himself to the decision of the community to which he belonged, and help to carry it out. Indeed, no other American who finally supported the American Revolution in its ultimate issue—that of secession from the empire—exhibited, from first to last, a more perfect familiarity, or a more perfect sympathy, with the great historic precedents set by the English people in the management of fundamental controversies between subjects and their sovereign.

Both by nature and by culture, John Dickinson was a conservative, having an uncommon horror of all changes that violated the sequences of established law. His philosophy of politics was practical, rather than merely speculative: it was the product of an orderly and peace-loving mind, revering the dignity of human nature, familiar with political history, trained to the solution of legal problems by the maxims and methods of English law, and convinced that every dispute between man and man could better be settled by reason and by good humor, than by brute fury and brute force. In the alarming differences which had arisen between the American portion of the British empire and the sovereign power, he saw no difficulties which could not under such treatment be happily adjusted, if, indeed, both parties to the controversy sincerely desired them to be so adjusted. Accordingly, in all his writings, whether official or personal, his endeavor was to place the American claim on historic constitutional grounds—such as Englishmen at home must respect; to persuade all Americans, in the assertion of their rights, to be fearless and firm, as their English ancestors had always been under similar circumstances; to persuade both Americans and Englishmen that they were alike interested in a wise, just, and lasting settlement of this great dispute, and that, in its discussion, the exercise of amenity and of good humor would be of the greatest use. Always he prefers to fight English oppression by English principles against oppression; to shew to the people of England, that it was their own rulers, and not the Americans, who were violating the constitution; and that the demands of the Americans, so far from being the spawn of a factious or revolutionary temper, were derived immediately from "the records, statutes, lawbooks, and most approved writers of our mother-country—those 'dead but most faithful counselors' (as Sir Edward Coke calls them) 'who cannot be daunted by fear, nor muzzled by affection, reward, or hope of preferment, and therefore may safely be believed.' "

"We well know," he wrote in 1774, "that the colonists are charged by many persons in Great Britain, with attempting to obtain . . . a total Independence on her. As well we know the accusation to be utterly false. . . . NOLUMBUS LEGES ANGLIAE MUTARI. This is the rebellion with which we are stigmatized. We have committed the like offense, that was objected by the polite and humane Fimbria against a rude senator of his time: we have 'disrespectfully refused to receive the whole weapon into our body.' We could not do it, and—live; but that must be acknowledged to be a poor excuse, equally inconsistent with good breeding and the supreme legislature of Great Britain. For these ten years past, we have been incessantly attacked. Hard is our fate, when, to escape the character of rebels, we must be degraded into that of slaves; as if there was no medium between the two extremes of anarchy and despotism, where innocence and freedom could find repose and safety. Why should we be exhibited to mankind as a people adjudged by parliament unworthy of freedom? The thought alone is insupportable.

Even those unhappy persons, who have had the misfortune of being born under the yoke of bondage . . . no sooner breathe the air of England, though they touch her shore only by accident, than they instantly become freemen. Strange contradiction! The same kingdom, at the same time, the asylum and the bane of liberty!

"To return to the charge against us, we can safely appeal to that Being, from whom no thought can be concealed, that our warmest wish and utmost ambition is, that we and our posterity may ever remain subordinate to, and dependent upon, our parent state. This submission our reason approves, our affection dictates, our duty commands, and our interest enforces. If this submission, indeed, implies a dissolution of our constitution, and a renunciation of our liberty, we should be unworthy of our relation to her, if we should not frankly declare, that we regard it with horror; and every true Englishman will applaud this just distinction, and candid declaration. Our defense necessarily touches chords in unison with the fibres of his honest heart. They must vibrate in sympathetic tones. If we, his kindred, should be base enough to promise the humiliating subjection, he could not believe us. We should suffer all the infamy of the engagement, without finding the benefit expected from being thought as contemptible as we should undertake to be.

"But this submission implies not such insupportable evils; and our amazement is inexpressible, when we consider the gradual increase of these colonies from their small beginnings in the last century to their late flourishing condition, and how prodigiously, since their settlement, our parent state has advanced in wealth, force, and influence, till she has become the first power on the sea, and the envy of the world,—that these our better days should not strike conviction into every mind, that the freedom and happiness of the colonists are not inconsistent with her authority and prosperity. . . . What unknown offenses have we committed against her within these ten years, to provoke such an unexampled change in her conduct towards us? In the last war, she acknowledged us repeatedly to be faithful, dutiful, zealous, and useful in her cause. Is it criminal in us that our numbers, by the favor of Divine Providence, have greatly increased? That the poor choose to fly from their native countries in Europe to this continent? Or, that we have so much improved these woods, that if we can be forced into an unsuccessful resistance, avarice itself might be satiated with our forfeitures?

"It cannot with truth be urged that projects of innovation have commenced with us. Facts and their dates prove the contrary. Not a disturbance has happened on any part of this continent, but in consequence of some immediately preceding provocation. . . . Our highest pride and glory has been, with humble and unsuspecting duty to labor in contributing to elevate her to that exalted station she holds among the nations of the earth, and which, we still ardently desire and pray, she may hold, with fresh accessions of fame and prosperity, till time shall be no more.

"These being our sentiments, and, we are fully convinced, the sentiments of our brethren throughout the colonies, with unspeakable affliction we find ourselves obliged to oppose that system of dominion over us, arising from counsels pernicious both to our parent and to her children; to strive, if it be possible, to close the breaches made in our former concord, and stop the sources of future animosities. And may God Almighty, who delights in the titles of just and merciful, incline the hearts of all parties to that equitable and benevolent temper, which is necessary solidly to establish peace and harmony, in the place of confusion and dissension."

If we attempt to estimate the practical effects of John Dickinson's work as a political writer during the American Revolution, we shall find it not easy to disentangle and to separate them from the practical effects of his work as a politician. The two lines of power were closely interwoven: each, in the main, helped the other, as each was liable, in its turn, to be hindered by the other. At any rate, just as the politico-literary influence of James Otis was, upon the whole, predominant in America from 1764 until 1767, so, from the latter date until some months after the outbreak of hostilities in 1775, was the politico-literary influence of John Dickinson predominant here. Moreover, as he succeeded to James Otis in the development of Revolutionary thought, so was he, at last, succeeded by Thomas Paine, who held sway among us, as the chief writer of political essays, from the early part of 1776 until the close of the Revolution itself.

The prodigious decline in the influence of John Dickinson, at the approach of the issue of Independence, is a thing not hard to explain: it was due in part to his personal characteristics, in part to the nature of his opinions. From the beginning of the troubles until some months after the first shedding of blood, in 1775, public opinion in America had set strongly in favor of making demand—even armed demand—for our political rights, but without any rupture of the colonial tie. It was, therefore, a period calling for clear and resolute statements of our claims, but with loyalty, urbanity, and tact. To be the chief literary exponent of such a period, John Dickinson was in every way fitted by talent, by temperament, by training. A man of wealth, cultivation, and elegant surroundings, practically versed in the law and in politics, considerate, cautious, disinclined to violent measures and to stormy scenes, actuated by a passion for the unity and greatness of the English race and for peace among all men, it was his sincere desire that the dispute with the mother country should be so conducted as to end, at last, in the perfect establishment of American constitutional rights within the empire, but without any hurt or dishonor to England, and without any permanent failure in respect and kindness between her and ourselves.

Nevertheless, in 1775, events occurred which gave a different aspect to the whole dispute, and swept an apparent majority of the American people quite beyond the sphere of such ideas and methods. John Dickinson's concession to parliament of a legislative authority over us, even to a limited extent, was roughly discarded; instead of which was enthroned among us the unhistoric and makeshift doctrine that American allegiance was due not at all to parliament, but to the crown only. Moreover, the moderation of tone, the urbane speech, the civility in conduct, exemplified by Dickinson in all his dispute with England, then became an anachronism and an offense. We were plunged at last into civil war—we had actually reached the stage of revolution; and the robust men who then ruled the scene, being of opinion that revolutions are apt to take place in some disregard of urbanity, and that civil wars have a peculiar tendency to give prominence to whatever is uncivil, were disposed, with no little contempt, to brush aside the moderate, conservative, and courteous Dickinson, who, either for advice or for conduct, seemed to them to have no further function to perform in the American world. His "Farmer's Letters" were declared by Jefferson to have been "really an 'ignis fatuus,' misleading us from true principles." Even Edward Rutledge, who, in June, 1776, agreed with Dickinson in his opposition to the plan for Independence, nevertheless expressed some impatience with his intellectual fastidiousness and nicety—declaring that the "vice of all his productions, to a considerable degree," was "the vice of refining too much." Of course, to an impetuous and blustering man of affairs like John Adams, such a political theorist as John Dickinson, with his qualms and his scruples and his splitting of hairs, could have seemed but a "piddling genius," who, for a whole year before the proclamation of American Independence, had been giving "a silly cast to our whole doings." This celebrated sneer of John Adams's, which occurs in a letter of his written from Philadelphia in July, 1775, was followed, in April, 1777, by an allusion to the same person, by the same letter-writer, implying that, as he thought, the public had in the meantime come over to his contemptuous opinion of Dickinson: "The Farmer turns out to be the man that I have seen him to be these two years. He is in total neglect and disgrace here. I am sorry for it, because of the forward part he took in the beginning of the controversy. But there is certainly such a thing as falling away in politics, if there is none in grace."

In the close quarters and heated air of the actual conflict, John Dickinson, it may be, could hardly have expected to receive appreciation, forbearance, or even simple justice, from his angry political associates, then playing a desperate game which, for many of them, meant either success or the scaffold. It will be the privilege of Time through her mouthpiece, History, to temper somewhat the harsh estimates which prevailed during the later portion of his life, respecting this able, brilliant, and noble-minded man.

*PERVASIVE as the struggle with England undoubtedly
was, the lives of some men were relatively untouched
by it. The Quaker, John Woolman, could live a religious life and write beautifully of it. The Frenchman, Crevecoeur, could write that "here individuals
of all nations are melted into a new race of men . . ."*

*Yet both men, the provincial mystic and the culti-
vated European, were in a real way a part of the
process that created a new nation. In their own lives
and writing they provided the beginnings of an answer to the question that Crevecoeur himself asked:
"What, then, is the American, this new man?"*

Two Apostles of Quietness and Good Will

IT is no slight distinction attaching to American literature for
the period of the Revolution, that in a time so often characterized as barren of important literary achievement, were produced two of the most perfect examples of autobiography to be
met with in any literature. One of these, of course, is Franklin's
Autobiography, the first, the largest, and the best part of which
was written in 1771—a work that has long since taken its place
among the most celebrated and most widely read of modern
books. Almost at the very time at which that fascinating story
was begun, the other great example of autobiography in our
Revolutionary literature was finished—*The Journal of John
Woolman*, a book which William Ellery Channing long afterward described as "beyond comparison the sweetest and purest
autobiography in the language." It is a notable fact, however,
that while these two masterpieces in the same form of literature
are products of the same period, they are, in respect of personal
quality, very nearly antipodal to each other; for, as Franklin's
account of himself delineates a career of shrewd and somewhat
selfish geniality, of unperturbed carnal content, of kindly
systematic and most successful worldliness, so the autobi-

ography of Woolman sets forth a career which turns out to be one of utter unworldliness, of entire self-effacement, all in obedience to an Unseen Leadership, and in meek and most tender devotion to the happiness of others—especially slaves, poor toiling white people, and speechless creatures unable to defend themselves against the inhumanity of man.

John Woolman, who was of a spirit so unpresuming that he would have wondered and have been troubled to be told that any writing of his was ever to be dealt with as literature, was born in 1720 in Northampton, New Jersey, his father being a farmer, and of the Society of Friends. Until his twenty-first year, he lived at home with his parents, and, as he expresses it, "wrought on the plantation." Having reached his majority, he took employment in the neighboring village of Mount Holly, in a shop for general merchandise. In this occupation he passed several years; after which, as he writes, "I was thoughtful of some other way of business; perceiving merchandize to be attended with much cumber in the way of trading in these parts. My mind, through the power of truth, was in a good degree weaned from the desire of outward greatness, and I was learning to be content with real conveniences that were not costly; so that a way of life free from much entanglements, appeared best for me, though the income might be small. . . . I saw that an humble man, with the blessing of the Lord, might live on a little; and that where the heart was set on greatness, success in business did not satisfy the craving, but that commonly, with an increase of wealth, the desire of wealth increased. There was a care on my mind so to pass my time, that nothing might hinder me from the most steady attention to the voice of the true Shepherd. My employer, though now a retailer of goods, was by trade a tailor, and kept a servant man at that business; and I began to think about learning the trade, expecting that if I should settle, I might by this trade and a little retailing of goods, get a living in a plain way without the load of great business. I mentioned it to my employer, and we soon agreed on terms; and then, when I had leisure from the affairs of merchandize, I worked with his man. I believed the hand of Providence pointed out this business for me, and was taught to be content with it, though I felt at times a disposition that would have sought for something greater. But, through the revelation of Jesus Christ, I had seen the happiness of humility, and there was an earnest desire in me to enter deep into it; and at times this desire arose to a degree of fervent supplication, wherein my soul was so environed with heavenly light and consolation, that things were made easy to me which had been otherwise. . . . I then wrought at my trade as a tailor; carefully attending meetings for worship and discipline; and found an enlargement of gospel love in my mind, and therein a concern to visit Friends in some of the back settlements of Pennsylvania and Virginia; and being thoughtful about a companion, I expressed it to my beloved friend, Isaac Andrews, who then told me that he had drawings to the same places, and also to go through Maryland, Virginia, and Carolina. . . . I opened the case in our monthly-meeting; and Friends expressing their unity therewith, we obtained certificates to travel as companions,—his from Haddonfield, and mine from Burlington."

The story of John Woolman, as thus far told, brings us to the point where he began to give himself almost wholly to the true work of his life—that of an apostle, with a need to go from land to land in fulfillment of his apostleship, and able, like one of the greatest of all apostles, to minister to his own necessities by the labors of a lowly trade. For, long before he set out upon these travels, even from his early childhood, he had entered, as he thought, into the possession of certain treasures of the spirit which he could not hoard up for himself alone—which, if he could but share them with others, would make others rich and happy beyond desire or even imagination. As we study John Woolman along the pages upon which he has made record of his inmost nature, we shall be inclined to infer that the traits which made him the man he was, were these: first, a singularly vivid perception of the reality and worth of things spiritual; secondly, such a passion of desire for all that is like God, that whatsoever he met with in himself or in others which was otherwise, grieved him with an ineffable sorrow; thirdly, love, taking every form of adoration for the Highest Love, and of sympathy and effort on behalf of all God's creatures, great and small; next, humility; next, directness, simplicity, sincerity; next, refinement. Certainly, the power of this book cannot be conveyed by detached passages, and in all cases must be without effect, save upon natures that are prepared for it; yet of what has just now been said, some verification may be had in sentences like these, taken here and there from it. "I was taught to read near as soon as I was capable of it; and as I went from school one seventh day, I remember, while my companions went to play by the way, I went forward out of sight, and sitting down I read the twenty-second chapter of the Revelation: 'He shewed me a pure river of water of life, clear as crystal, proceeding out of the throne of God and of the Lamb, &c.' And in reading it, my mind was drawn to seek after that pure habitation." "I . . . was early convinced in my mind, that true religion consisted in an inward life, wherein the heart doth love and reverence God the Creator, and learns to exercise true justice and goodness, not only toward all men, but also toward the brute creatures; that as the mind was moved, by an inward principle, to love God as an invisible incomprehensible Being, by the same principle it was moved to love Him in all His manifestations in the visible world; that, as by His breath the flame of life was kindled in all animal sensible creatures, to say we love God as unseen, and at the same time exercise cruelty toward the least creature moving by His life, or by life derived from Him, was a contradiction in itself." "I looked upon the works of God in this visible creation, and an awfulness covered me; my heart was tender and often contrite and universal love to my fellow creatures increased in me." "Some glances of real beauty may be seen in their faces, who dwell in true meekness." "When I eat, drank, and lodged free-cost with people who lived in ease on the hard labor of slaves, I felt uneasy; and as my mind was inward to the Lord, I found from place to place this uneasiness return upon me at times through the whole visit." "This trade of importing slaves from their native country . . . was frequently the subject of my serious thoughts. And I saw in these southern provinces so many vices and corruptions, increased by this trade and this way of life, that it appeared to me as a dark gloominess hanging over the land. And though now many willingly run into it, yet in future the consequences will be grievous to posterity: I express it as it hath appeared to me, not once nor twice, but as a matter fixed on my mind." "I was then carried in spirit to the mines, where poor oppressed people were digging rich treasures for those called Christians; and heard them blaspheme the name of Christ, at which I was grieved—for His name to me was precious." "About this time, a person at some distance lying sick, his brother came to me to write his will. I knew he had slaves, and asking his brother, was told he intended to leave them as slaves to his children. As writing is a profitable employ, and as offending sober people was disagreeable to my inclination, I was straitened in my mind; but as I looked to the Lord, He inclined my heart to His testimony. And I told the man, that I believed the practice of continuing slavery to this people was not right, and had a scruple in my mind against doing writings of that kind; that though many in our society kept them as slaves, still I was not easy to be concerned in it, and desired to be excused from going to write the will. I spake to him in the fear of the Lord, and he made no reply to what I said, but went away. He also had some concerns in the practice, and I thought he was displeased with me. In this case, I had a fresh confirmation, that acting contrary to present outward interest, from a motive of divine love and inward regard to truth and righteousness, and thereby incurring the resentments of people, opens the way to a treasure better than silver, and to a friendship exceeding the friendship of men." "A neighbor received a bad bruise in his body, and sent for me to bleed him; which being done, he desired me to write his will. I took notes; and amongst other things, he told me to which of his children he gave his young negro. I considered the pain and distress he was in, and knew not how it would end; so I wrote his will, save only that part concerning his slave, and carrying it to his bed-side, read it to him, and then told him, in a friendly way, that I could not write any instruments by which my fellow creatures were made slaves, without bringing trouble to my own mind. I let him know that I charged nothing for what I had done, and desired to be excused from doing the other part in the way he proposed. We then had a serious conference on the subject. At length, he agreeing to set her free, I finished his will." "We were taught by renewed experience to labor for an inward stillness; at no time to seek for words, but live in the spirit of truth, and utter that to the people which truth opened in us." "The natural man loveth eloquence, and many love to hear eloquent orations; and if there is not a careful attention to the gift, men who have once labored in the pure Gospel ministry, growing weary of suffering and ashamed of appearing weak, may kindle a fire, compass themselves about with sparks, and walk in the light—not of Christ who is under suffering, but of that fire which they, going from the gift, have kindled; and that, in hearers, which is gone from the meek suffering state into the worldly wisdom, may be warmed with this fire, and speak highly of these labors. That which is of God gathers to God, and that which is of the world, is owned by the world."

Thus, the autobiography of John Woolman was the gradual and secret growth of many years, beginning when he was of the age of thirty-six, and added to from time to time until, at the age of fifty-two, being in the city of York, in England, about the business of his Master, he was stricken down of the small pox, whereof he died. Besides this story of his life, he left several ethical and religious essays: "Some Considerations on the Keeping of Negroes"; "Considerations on Pure Wisdom, and Human Policy, on Labor, on Schools, and on the Right

Use of the Lord's Outward Gifts"; "Considerations on the True Harmony of Mankind, and How it is to be Maintained"; finally, "A Word of Remembrance and Caution to the Rich"—the last being in some respects the most impressive of all his essays, with a striking applicability to problems now vexing the civilized world.

While these essays set forth, without reserve and without censoriousness, the very altruism of Jesus Christ, which, as Woolman thought, must first live in the hearts of men, both rich and poor, before the distinctions of outward condition will cease to occasion bitterness and violence upon earth, it is fitting here to add, that, like the autobiography, all these writings are, as Whittier has said, in the style "of a man unlettered, but with natural refinement and delicate sense of fitness, the purity of whose heart enters into his language." "The secret of Woolman's purity of style," said Channing, "is that his eye was single, and that conscience dictated the words." There is about John Woolman's writings that unconventionality of thought, that charity without pretense, that saintliness without sanctimony or sourness, that delicacy, that untaught beauty of phrase, by which we are helped to understand the ardor of Charles Lamb's love for him, as uttered in his impulsive exhortation to the readers of the Essays of Elia: "Get the writings of John Woolman by heart." "A perfect gem!" wrote Henry Crabb Robinson, in 1824, of Woolman's *Journal,* which Lamb had shortly before made known to him. "His is a 'schöne Seele.' An illiterate tailor, he writes in a style of the most exquisite purity and grace. His moral qualities are transferred to his writings." Perhaps, after all, the aroma that lingers about Woolman's words is best described by Woolman's true spiritual successor in American literature, in the saying that he who reads these writings becomes sensible "of a sweetness as of violets."*

In 1782, just as the people of England were beginning to adjust themselves to the fact that their obstreperous American

* Whittier, Introd. to *The Journal of John Woolman,* 34.

children had finally come of age, and were giving rather too many proofs of their capacity to set up political housekeeping on their own account, there was published in London an American book about these same American children and their big country, but written with a sweetness of tone and, likewise, with a literary grace and a power of fascination, then quite unexpected from the western side of the Atlantic. It presented itself to the public behind this ample title-page: *Letters from an American Farmer, describing certain provincial situations, manners, and customs, not generally known, and conveying some idea of the late and present interior circumstances of the British Colonies in North America: written for the information of a friend in England, by J. Hector St. John, a farmer in Pennsylvania.*

The name of the author as thus given upon his title-page, was not his name in full, but only the baptismal portion of it. By omitting from the book his surname, which was Crevecoeur, he had chosen to disguise to the English public the fact—which could hardly have added to his welcome among them—that though he was an American, he was not an English American, but a French one—having been born in Normandy, and of a noble family there, in 1731. Moreover, this is not his only device for self-concealment; for, throughout the book, he writes under the character of a simple-hearted American farmer who, born in America, and with but slight education, and with no opportunity for travel beyond the bounds of his native land, has inherited his farm from his American father, and has learned, almost within the horizon of that farm, his best lessons concerning this world and other worlds and the meaning of life everywhere.

In reality, however, while really an American farmer, Crevecoeur was a man of education, of refinement, of varied experience in the world. When but a lad of sixteen, he had removed from France to England; when but twenty-three, he had emigrated to America. Here, in due time, he had taken unto himself an American farm, and an American wife, and with true

French graciousness and tact had quickly assimilated the ways of life, especially of rural life, in his adopted country. It is probable that he was of the Society of Friends—which may partly account for his coming to America and especially to Pennsylvania, as well as for many peculiarities of his book— some of its local and personal allusions, its gentle tone, its spirituality, its mysticism, its tender but firm championship of the poor Indian and the poor slave, and, above all, its prevailing reticence concerning the ferocious political and military controversies of the Revolution. At any rate, being a man of quite uncommon literary cultivation, and having the vivacity and the imaginative flexibility of his race, having also a fondness both for human fellowship and for solitude, and the power to look upon life, even in a wilderness, through the eyes of a scholar, a philosopher, and an idealist, he threw himself with full delight into the primitive free spirit of the new world—its consciousness of ample room and of escape from tradition, its helpfulness, its frank customs, crude labors, artless pleasures— and all these he was able, at last, to interpret to the old world in a series of idyllic descriptions which, surely, could not be fallacious or misleading—except, of course, to people who were not scholars, philosophers, and idealists, or who, at least, had not his faculty of seeing in this world those beautiful realities that are invisible always to the mere bodily sight.

As an account of the American colonies, this book makes no pretension either to system or to completeness; and yet it does attain to a sort of breadth of treatment by seizing upon certain representative traits of the three great groups of colonies. For the northern group, he has five letters, devoted to Nantucket, Martha's Vineyard, and Cape Cod. For the middle group, he has two letters, evidently founded upon his own experience as the possessor of a farm in Pennsylvania, on "the edge of the great wilderness, three hundred miles from the sea": one of these letters being descriptive of "the situation, feelings, and pleasures of an American farmer," and the other of the "distresses of a frontier-man." For the southern group, he has but one letter, dealing with Charleston, South Carolina, and with the more harrowing and tragic form of the slave-labor system as prevalent in that region. The remaining letters—four in number—are taken up with a variety of topics, all having their interpretative value; such as the genius and the achievements of John Bartram the American botanist, his own observations upon natural history in America, and especially some aspects of the race-problem there, which he deals with in answer to the question—"What is an American?"

If we would come at once into contact with Crevecoeur's habit and tone of thought—a delicate and joyous perception of phenomena, and a divination of their meaning as seen by him through a haze of noble idealizing sentiment—we can perhaps do no better than to turn to his discussion of this very question —a question still often asked and perhaps never yet fully answered. Premising that the people of the colonies "are a mixture of English, Scotch, Irish, French, Dutch, Germans, and Swedes," and that "from this promiscuous breed that race now called Americans have arisen," he repeats the enquiry—"What, then, is the American, this new man? He is neither an European, nor the descendant of an European: hence that strange mixture of blood, which you will find in no other country. I could point out to you a family, whose grandfather was an Englishman, whose wife was Dutch, whose son married a French woman, and whose present four sons have now four wives of different nations. He is an American, who, leaving behind him all his ancient prejudices and manners, receives new ones from the new mode of life he has embraced, the new government he obeys, and the new rank he holds. He becomes an American by being received in the broad lap of our great 'alma mater.' Here individuals of all nations are melted into a new race of men, whose labors and posterity will one day cause great changes in the world. Americans are the western pilgrims, who are carrying along with them that great mass of arts, sciences, vigor, and industry, which began long since in the east. They will finish the great circle. The Americans were once scattered all over Europe. Here they are incorporated into one of the finest systems of population which has ever appeared, and which will hereafter become distinct by the power of the different climates they inhabit. The American ought therefore to love this country much better than that wherein either he or his forefathers were born. Here the rewards of his industry follow, with equal steps, the progress of his labor. His labor is founded on the basis of nature—self-interest: can it want a stronger allurement? Wives and children, who before in vain demanded of him a morsel of bread, now, fat and frolicsome, gladly help their father to clear those fields whence exuberant crops are to arise, to feed and to clothe them all, without any part being claimed either by a despotic prince, a rich abbot, or a mighty lord. Here religion demands but little of him,—a small voluntary salary to the minister, and gratitude to God: can he refuse these? The American is a new man, who acts upon new principles; he must therefore entertain new ideas, and form new opinions. From involuntary idleness, servile dependence, penury, and useless labor, he has passed to toils of a very different nature, rewarded by ample subsistence.— This is an American."

It is probable that not many passages in these letters were more enjoyed at the time, or are more likely to last in our literature as delightful examples of description at first hand, than those in which the author gives the results of his keen and sympathetic watchfulness of nature in the New World— such as his account of the intrusive swallow and the submissive wren, or of the bee-hunt, or of the battle between the water-snake and the black-snake—all of which, indeed, are contributions to natural history as well as to literature.

There are in this book two distinct notes—one of great peace, another of great pain. The earlier and larger portion of the book gives forth this note of peace: it is a prose pastoral of life in the New World, as that life must have revealed itself to a well-appointed American farmer of poetic and optimistic temper, in the final stage of our colonial era, and just before the influx of the riot and bitterness of the great disruption. What he thus writes breathes such deep tranquillity as might have its pulse in some leafy dale of Arcadia. Evidently this American farmer has found some happy valley—some peace-encircled spot—where, in modest competence, and with a "holiday-rejoicing spirit," he can plough his fields, and angle in his brooks, and take note of the splendors of sun-rise, and become acquainted with his birds and bees and squirrels and other furtive creatures— including even his own wife and children. Those political busy-bodies who, in the enjoyment of the utmost freedom, have yet thrown themselves into the anguish of imaginary slavery through their gratuitous speculations over the taxing-power of parliament, have no message for him. At present he hears them not. He celebrates the comfort of American life—its opportunity—its thoughtfulness—its dignity—its beneficence. From his far-away plantation he stretches out his hands and shares in the "secret communion among good men throughout the world." Happy with enough, he has no hatred for those who have more. "I envy no man's prosperity, and wish no other portion of happiness than that I may live to teach the same philosophy to my children." He exults in the largeness, equality, facility, of life in this land: "Here we have in some measure, regained the ancient dignity of our species: our laws are simple and just; we are a race of cultivators; our cultivation is unrestrained, and therefore everything is prosperous and flourishing. For my part, I had rather admire the ample barn of one of our opulent farmers, who himself felled the first tree in his plantation, and was first founder of his settlement, than study the dimensions of the temple of Ceres. I had rather record the progressive steps of this industrious farmer, throughout all the stages of his labors and other operations, than examine how modern Italian convents can be supported without doing anything but singing and praying." He is glad to think that American society "is not composed, as in Europe, of great lords who possess everything, and of a herd of people who have nothing. Here are no aristocratical families, no courts, no kings, no bishops, no ecclesiastical dominion, no invisible power giving to a few a very visible one." "We are a people of cultivators, scattered over an immense territory, communicating with each other by means of good roads and navigable rivers, united by the silken bands of mild government, all respecting the laws, without dreading their power, because they are equitable." He loves to think of America "as the asylum of freedom, as the cradle of future nations, and the refuge of distressed Europeans." "We know, properly speaking, no strangers: this is every person's country." He is fond of giving us glimpses of his own serene and manly relations to life, as he sits "smoking a contemplative pipe" on his piazza, or as he plows his low ground holding his "little boy on a chair which screws to the beam of the plow." No struggle for existence, no carking care, keeps him from enjoying the sights and sounds of nature about him: "The pleasure I receive from the warblings of the birds in the spring is superior to my poor description, as the continual succession of their tuneful notes is for ever new to me. I generally rise from bed about that indistinct interval which, properly speaking, is neither night nor day; for this is the moment of the most universal vocal choir. Who can listen unmoved to the sweet love-tales of our robins, told from tree to tree, or to the shrill cat-birds? The sublime accents of the thrush, from on high, always retard my steps, that I may listen to the delicious music. The variegated appearances of the dew-drops, as they hang to the different objects, must present, even to a clownish imagination, the most voluptuous ideas. The astonishing art which all birds display in the construction of their nests, ill-provided as we may suppose them with proper tools, their neatness, their convenience, always make me ashamed of the slovenliness of our houses. Their love to their dame, their incessant careful attention, and the peculiar songs they address to her while she tediously incubates their eggs, remind me of my duty, could I ever forget it. Their affection to their helpless little ones is a lovely precept; and, in short, the whole economy of what we proudly call the brute creation, is admirable in every circumstance; and vain man, though adorned with the additional gift of reason, might learn from the perfection of instinct, how to regulate the follies, and how to temper the errors, which this second gift often makes him commit. This is a subject on which I have often bestowed the most serious thoughts. I have often blushed within myself, and been greatly astonished, when I have compared the unerring path they all follow,—all just, all proper, all wise, up to the necessary degree of perfection—with the coarse, the imperfect, systems of men."

This note of peace holds undisturbed through the first half of the book, and more. Not until, in the latter half of it, the author comes to describe slavery in the far-south, likewise the harsh relations between the colonists and the Indians, finally the outbreak of the tempest of civil war, does his book give out its second note—the note of pain. His observations upon slavery are penetrating, and while never censorious, are yet pitiless in their justice and their moral purity. Moreover, the barbarism —perhaps, the necessary barbarism—of its penal methods, is set forth by him in a single picture, that of the caged negro; a picture, which has genuine literary power—quietness of stroke, absolute sureness, vividness, and pathos, and a self-enforcing logic which no dialectics can refute or escape. "I was not long since invited to dine with a planter who lived three miles from ——, . . . In order to avoid the heat of the sun, I resolved to go on foot, sheltered in a small path leading through a pleasant wood. I was leisurely travelling along, attentively examining some peculiar plants which I had collected, when all at once I felt the air strongly agitated, though the day was perfectly calm and sultry. I immediately cast my eyes toward the cleared ground, from which I was but a small distance, in order to see whether it was not occasioned by a sudden shower; when at that instant a sound, resembling a deep rough voice, uttered, as I thought, a few inarticulate monosyllables. Alarmed and surprised, I precipitately looked all around, when I perceived, at about six rods distance, something resembling a cage, suspended to the limbs of a tree, all the branches of which appeared covered with large birds of prey, fluttering about and anxiously endeavoring to perch on the cage. Actuated by an involuntary motion of my hands, more than by any design of my mind, I fired at them: they all flew to a short distance, with a most hideous noise, when, horrid to think and painful to repeat, I perceived a negro suspended in the cage, and left there to expire! I shudder when I recollect that the birds had already picked out his eyes; his cheek bones were bare; his arms had been attacked in several places; and his body seemed covered with a multitude of wounds. From the edges of the hollow sockets, and from the lacerations with which he was disfigured, the blood slowly dropped and tinged the ground beneath. No sooner were the birds flown, than swarms of insects covered the whole body of this unfortunate wretch, eager to feed on his mangled flesh and to drink his blood. I found myself suddenly arrested by the power of affright and terror; my nerves were convulsed; I trembled, I stood motionless, involuntarily contemplating the fate of this negro in all its dismal latitude. The living spectre, though deprived of his eyes, could still distinctly hear, and in his uncouth dialect begged me to give him some water to allay his thirst. Humanity herself would have recoiled back with horror; she would have balanced whether to lessen such reliefless distress, or mercifully with one blow to end this dreadful scene of agonizing torture. Had I had a ball in my gun, I certainly should have despatched him; but, finding myself unable to perform so kind an office, I sought, though trembling, to relieve him as well as I could. A shell ready fixed to a pole, which had been used by some negroes, presented itself to me; I filled it with water, and with trembling hands I guided it to the quivering lips of the wretched sufferer. Urged by the irresistible power of thirst, he endeavored to meet it, as he instinctively guessed its approach by the noise it made in passing through the bars of the cage. 'Tankè you, whitè man;

tankè you; putè somè poison and givè me.' 'How long have you been hanging there?'—I asked him. 'Two days, and me no die; the birds, the birds, aaah me!' Oppressed with the reflections which this shocking spectacle afforded me, I mustered strength enough to walk away, and soon reached the house where I intended to dine. There I heard that the reason for this slave's being thus punished, was on account of his having killed the overseer of the plantation. They told me that the laws of self-preservation rendered such executions necessary, and supported the doctrine with the arguments generally made use of to justify the practice, with the repetition of which I will not trouble you at present."

In the final chapter of the book, entitled "Distresses of a Frontier Man," the note of pain, which has begun to be heard still earlier, rises into something like a wail; for, the twofold horrors, first of impending attacks by Indians, and, secondly, of civil war between white men, have at last reached the once happy home of this bucolic philosopher and quietist. "The hour is come at last, that I must fly from my house and abandon my farm. But what course shall I steer, enclosed as I am? . . . Whichever way I look, nothing but the most frightful precipices present themselves to my view, in which hundreds of my friends and acquaintances have already perished. Of all animals that live on the surface of this planet, what is man when no longer connected with society, or when he finds himself surrounded by a convulsed and a half-dissolved one!" "I am a lover of peace, —what must I do? . . . I am conscious that I was happy before this unfortunate Revolution. I feel that I am no longer so; therefore I regret the change. . . . If I attach myself to the mother-country, which is three thousand miles from me, I become what is called an enemy to my own region; if I follow the rest of my countrymen, I become opposed to our ancient masters. Both extremes appear equally dangerous to a person of so little weight and consequence as I am, whose energy and example are of no avail. As to the argument, on which the dispute is founded, I know but little about it. Much has been said and written on both sides, but who has a judgment capacious and clear enough to decide? . . . Books tell me so much, that they inform me of nothing. . . . Alas, how should I unravel an argument in which reason herself has given way to brutality and bloodshed? What then must I do? I ask the wisest lawyers, the ablest casuists, the warmest patriots, for I mean honestly. Great Source of Wisdom! inspire me with light sufficient to guide my benighted steps out of this intricate maze! Shall I discard all my ancient principles, shall I renounce that name, that nation, which I held once so respectable? . . . On the other hand, shall I arm myself against that country where I first drew breath, against the play-mates of my youth, my bosom-friends, my acquaintances? . . . Must I be called a parricide, a traitor, a villain; lose the esteem of all those whom I love, to preserve my own; be shunned like a rattle-snake, or be pointed at like a bear?"

By its inclusion of these sombre and agonizing aspects of life in America, the book gains, as is most obvious, both in authenticity and in literary strength. Nevertheless, with even these tremendous abatements from the general scene of human felicity presented by the New World, the reader is tempted to infer that, after all, felicity is the permanent fact there, and that suffering is but a temporary accident. It is not hard to understand why, at such a time, a book like this should soon have made its way into the languages of Europe, particularly those of France, Germany, and Holland; nor why it should have fascinated multitudes of readers in all parts of the continent, even beguiling many of them—too many of them, perhaps—to try their fortunes in the blithe and hospitable portion of the planet where the struggle for existence seemed almost a thing unknown. In England, likewise, the book won for itself, as was natural, a wide and gracious consideration; its praises lasted among English men of letters as long, at least, as until the time of Hazlitt and Charles Lamb; while its idealized treatment of rural life in America wrought quite traceable effects upon the imaginations of Campbell, Byron, Southey, Coleridge, and furnished not a few materials for such captivating and airy schemes of literary colonization in America as that of "Pantisocracy."*

* These men planned a community based on "the principles of an abolition of individual property"; they chose a site on the Susquehanna River in Pennsylvania but never came to America. Arthur E. Bestor, Jr., *Backwoods Utopias* (Philadelphia: University of Pennsylvania Press, 1950), p. 37. [Ed.]

SECURE *in the historian's wisdom of hindsight, we can say that the United States of America began when John Smith and company founded Jamestown in May of 1607 and that the American Revolution was an inevitable result of the chain of events that began on that bit of swampland. Be that as it may, by 1783 a new nation, and perhaps a new breed of man, had come into being. One man seems to embody the characteristics of this new nation: moralist, inventor, scientist, printer, publisher, author, politician, diplomat, he had a European reputation not because he was a European but just because he was an American. That man was Benjamin Franklin.*

Franklin in the Literature of the Revolution

ONE peculiarity attaching to Franklin's part in the American Revolution arises from the fact that nearly the whole of that Revolution took place in his absence. In November, 1764, he went to England as the agent of Pennsylvania, charged with the duty of protesting against the passage of the Stamp Act; and in England he remained for nearly eleven years. Returning to America in May, 1775, he remained here only until October, 1776, when, "at the age of seventy-two or seventy-four, and at the risk of his head," as Horace Walpole wrote, he "bravely embarked on board an American frigate" as commissioner to the court of France. In France he then remained until September, 1785. Coming back to America in that year, he died in 1790. Thus, during the twenty years which may be set apart as the period of the American Revolution, Franklin himself was in America only two years and a half.

Nevertheless, it is doubtful if any other brain than his had more to do with the shaping of the thought of the American Revolution, or any other hand a more potent pressure in the ordering of its event. Though separated from his country by the breadth of the Atlantic, never was there a moment during all those years when his country was not conscious of his inseparable and indispensable connection with the development of its destiny. Indeed, in that very spectacle of his personal absence from the scene of great transactions over which he was believed to wield a tremendous control, was something to give an added stimulus to the imaginations of men, and to enhance both in America and in Europe the vast influence which he had in both. From his modest lodgings in London during the first eleven years of the Revolution, from his quiet hotel in a suburb of Paris during the last eight years of it, he seemed to be the arch-magician, who, by his mastery of the secrets of nature, knew how to send abroad over land and sea invisible forces to sway mankind to his will. Under such circumstances, it is easy to perceive how his renown as an electrician threw a weird and an exaggerating light upon his prestige as a statesman and a revolutionist. "Our colonies might be well enough," was a saying among Englishmen in 1774, "were it not for Dr. Franklin, who has, with a brand lighted from the clouds, set fire to all America." In 1775, Samuel Johnson depicted Franklin as a "master of mischief" who had taught his countrymen "how to put in motion the engine of political electricity, . . . and to give the great stroke by the name of Boston." Among the innumerable prints of Franklin scattered through France, were many that represented him as an old philosopher serenely seated in his chair, with flashes of lightning playing in the sky above his head, while beneath the portrait was some inscription attributing to him the power to use that lightning as his ally in the liberation of America and of mankind: as, under the drawing by Carmontelle—

On l'a vu désarmer les Tirans et les Dieux:

or, under the portrait by Cochin—

C'est l'honneur et l'appui du nouvel hémisphère;
Les flots de l'Océan s'abaissent à sa voix;
Il réprime ou dirige à son gré le tonnerre:
Qui désarme les dieux, peut-il craindre les rois?

It was for a similar use that Turgot produced his incomparable line

Eripuit coelo fulmen, septrumque tyrannis.

With the grotesque humor even then characteristic of much popular writing in America, one of our own newspapers sent forth, in 1777, the droll announcement, that Dr. Franklin was about "to produce an electrical machine of such wonderful force that, instead of giving a slight stroke to the elbows of fifty or a hundred thousand men who are joined hand in hand, it will give a violent shock even to nature herself, so as to disunite kingdoms, join islands to continents, and render men of the same nation strangers and enemies to each other; and that, by a certain chemical preparation from oil, he will be able to smooth the waves of the sea in one part of the globe, and raise tempests and whirlwinds in another, so as to be universally acknowledged for the greatest physician, politician, mathematician, and philosopher, this day living."

At the time of his voyage to England in 1764—that being his third voyage thither—he was already the most celebrated person that his country had then produced—a fact sufficiently attested by Hume's salutation of him as "the first philosopher and indeed the first great man of letters" for whom Europe was beholden to America. He was then fifty-eight years of age, and independent in his private circumstances. He had known a long and varied experience in commercial life, in politics, in legislative and administrative work. He had been a successful journalist, under the somewhat petty and clumsy conditions of journalism in those days. He was the projector of many mechanical and institutional devices for adding to the welfare and happiness of the human race. He was distinguished beyond all other men of his time in the one branch of science to which the men of his time were looking with the greatest interest. Finally, he was the author of a multitude of writings, covering a wide range of subjects, some of which had already made their way wherever the English language was known, and were read and relished for their shrewdness, their wit, their practical helpfulness, their alliance of prudence with generosity and good humor, their pure, pithy, and sparkling style.

It is a trait of Franklin as a man of letters, that while in his early life he took infinite pains to become a good writer, he did so, apparently, not from mere literary ambition, but chiefly as a means to some immediate practical end—particularly that of getting on in the world. Accordingly, nearly everything he wrote was sent forth alone, and without his name, and was then allowed to shift for itself without any further pains or care on his part. This seeming freedom from solicitude as to the whereabouts or the well-being of his literary children, may be noted in the reply he made, during his second residence in England, to a request from Lord Kames for copies of all his published writings: "I had daily expectations of procuring some of them from a friend to whom I formerly sent them when I was in America, and postponed writing to you, till I should obtain them; but at length he tells me he cannot find them. Very mortifying this to an author—that his works should so soon be lost! So I can only send you my 'Observations on the Peopling of Countries,' which happens to have been reprinted here; 'The Description of the Pennsylvania Fireplace,' a machine of my contriving; and some little sketches that have been printed in the 'Grand Magazine,' which I should hardly own, did I not know that your friendly partiality would make them seem at least tolerable."

The disposition, as shewn in these sentences, humorously to underrate his own performances and by all means to avoid every sort of self-glorification, does not leave him at any time; and whoever, in 1764, desired to know what Franklin had then done in letters, had still to get other testimony than Franklin's. Already, so early as in 1751, and without his knowledge, had been published in London a collection of his scientific writings, entitled *Experiments in Electricity made at Philadelphia*—a little book which was made larger in 1752, and again larger in

1754, and was also many times republished on the continent in Latin, French, German, and Italian. His greatest prolificacy, however, had been in writings of a more general kind, dealing shrewdly and often playfully with traits of human nature, with the vices and foibles of society, with ethical and religious subjects, with all aspects of current politics in America as touching finance, the treatment of Indians, the treatment of negroes, military preparations, forms of government both colonial and intercolonial, and the relations of the colonies to England. Besides innumerable juvenile experiments in prose and verse—ballads, lampoons, burlesques, paragraphs, disquisitions, epigrams, emblems, proverbs—the most of which, happily, are lost beyond recovery—he had published the essays of "The Busy-Body"; several dialogues in the manner of Xenophon, such as "Public Men," and "Concerning Virtue and Pleasure"; the satirical letters of "Celia Single," "Anthony Afterwit," and "Alice Adder-tongue"; "Articles of Belief and Acts of Religion"; "Self-Denial not the Essence of Virtue"; "On True Happiness"; "The Waste of Life"; "A Modest Inquiry into the Nature of a Paper Currency"; "On Government"; "The Importance of Gaining and Preserving the Friendship of the Indians"; "Observations concerning the Increase of Mankind and the Peopling of Countries"; "Plain Truth, or, Serious Considerations on the Present State of the City of Philadelphia and the Province of Pennsylvania"; "Plan of Union for the Colonies"; and "The Interest of Great Britain Considered with regard to her Colonies and the Acquisition of Canada and Guadaloupe." Finally, no other class of his writings down to that time had appealed to so numerous and so eager a multitude of readers, as those in which he undertook to teach men the art of worldly prosperity, as "Necessary Hints to those that would be Rich," and "The Way to Wealth as Clearly Shown in the Preface of an Old Almanac entitled 'Poor Richard Improved,'" the latter containing the humorous and needle-witted speech of Father Abraham, which, as a recent biographer of Franklin has truly said, "is the most famous piece of literature the colonies produced."

Undoubtedly, his best work in letters was done after the year
1764, and thenceforward down to the very year of his death;
for, to a degree not only unusual but almost without parallel in
literary history, his mind grew more and more vivacious with
his advancing years, his heart more genial, his inventiveness
more sprightly, his humor more gay, his style brighter, keener,
more deft, more delightful. Yet even in these earlier writings
of his, Franklin is always Franklin; and their vast popularity
and effectiveness were due to qualities essentially the same as
those which marked his later and still better work: the pure
English of the best writers and the best talkers, simplicity, brevity, lightness of touch, strength without effort, the absence of
declamation and of rhetorical parade, melody, point, extraordinary insight into human nature together with a frank identifi-
cation of himself with its frailties, a singular desire and gift for
helping other people to solve their most troublesome problems,
and, finally, pervading all, and giving irresistible charm to all,
his humor—a humor which perfectly answers to Thackeray's
fine definition of it as something made up of "wit and love,"
the best humor being "that which contains most humanity, that
which is flavored throughout with tenderness and kindness."
Writing in 1758 to his sister Jane, whom he dearly loved, and
who was very devout according to the severe Calvinistic manner of the period, Franklin quotes an acrostic wherein religion
is likened to a building, of which faith, hope, and charity are
the three stories. "Faith," says he, in commenting upon this
bit of imagery, "is then the ground floor, hope is up one pair of
stairs. My dear beloved Jenny, don't delight so much to dwell
in those lower rooms, but get as fast as you can into the garret,
for in truth the best room in the house is charity. For my part,
I wish the house was turned upside down—it is so difficult,
when one is fat, to go upstairs; and not only so, but I imagine
hope and faith may be more firmly built upon charity, than
charity upon faith and hope."

Yet no one could read far in Franklin and conclude that his
charity was of the soft and eyeless sort. To a writer who en-
quired by what means he could find out the faults of the girl

whom he was courting, and especially whether she had the virtues she seemed to have, Franklin replied, "Commend her among her female acquaintance." As a maker of epigrams, the man who wrote, "The noblest question in the world is, what good may I do in it," and "Keep your eyes wide open before marriage, half shut afterwards," and "Deny thyself for self's sake," and "He is no clown that drives the plow, but he that does clownish things," and "He that can have patience, can have what he will," also wrote, "Three may keep a secret, if two of them are dead," and "Sal laughs at everything you say; why? because she has fine teeth," and "God heals—the Doctor takes the fee," and "Who has deceived thee so oft, as thyself?" and "Search others for their virtues, thyself for thy vices," and "The proof of gold is fire; the proof of a woman, gold; the proof of a man, woman."

For the period of the Revolution, the writings of Franklin fall naturally into two principal divisions—first, those connected with the Revolutionary controversy, and, secondly, those almost entirely apart from it.

Among the latter, of course, are to be reckoned his numerous papers on scientific discoveries and mechanical inventions; a considerable number of his personal letters—these being, perhaps, the wisest and wittiest of all his writings; many short sketches, usually playful in tone, often in the form of apologues or parables; finally, the first, and the best, part of his *Autobiography,* which, during the hundred years succeeding its first publication in 1791, has probably been the most widely read book of its class in any language, and which, "treated as a piece of writing, and judged as literature . . . must be pronounced," according to a recent critic, "the equal of Robinson Crusoe, one of the few everlasting books in the English language." Here, then, as a product of Franklin's general literary activity during the Revolutionary period, is a considerable body of literature not concerned in the strifes of that bitter time, almost faultless in form, and so pervaded by sense, gayety, and kindness, as to

be among the most precious and most delightful of the intellectual treasures of mankind.

Among so many pieces of writing, there must be an inequality of merit; and perhaps some of those which have been most
frequently quoted and most loudly praised, are not altogether
the most deserving of it, such as "The Whistle," and "An Economical Project," both of which bear traces of a conscious effort
at pleasantry, and of pleasantry, also, which, as Lord Jeffrey
said, has in it "something childish." On the other hand, the delicious trifle entitled "The Ephemera: An Emblem of Human
Life," and the "Dialogue between Franklin and the Gout," are
executed, as Lord Jeffry also declared, "with the lightness and
spirit of genuine French compositions"; while "A Parable of
Persecution," and we may add, "A Parable of Brotherly Love,"
"A Tale of Poor Jacques Montrésor," and the latter part of the
essay on "The Handsome and Deformed Leg," have "all the
point and facility of the fine pleasantries of Swift and Arbuth-
not, with something more of directness and apparent sincerity."
It may be doubted, also, whether for spontaneity, grace, and
pure frolic, all inspired and illuminated by that sort of gallantry which can best be described as Parisian, any of his so-
called "Bagatelles" is now more charming than the love-chal-
lenge of this septuagenarian widower addressed to the brilliant
and not immature Madame Helvetius, widow of the famous
philosopher whose name she was so proud to bear: "Mortified
at the barbarous resolution pronounced by you so positively
yesterday evening, that you would remain single the rest of
your life as a compliment to the memory of your husband, I
retired to my chamber. Throwing myself upon my bed, I
dreamt that I was dead, and was transported to the Elysian
Fields. I was asked whether I wished to see any persons in particular; to which I replied that I wished to see the philosophers.
'There are two who live here at hand in this garden; they are
good neighbors, and very friendly towards one another.'—'Who
are they?'—'Socrates and Helvetius.'—'I esteem them both
highly; let me see Helvetius first, because I understand a little

French, but not a word of Greek.' I was conducted to him; he received me with much courtesy, having known me, he said, by character, some time past. He asked me a thousand questions relative to the war, the present state of religion, of liberty, of the government in France. 'You do not inquire, then,' I said, 'after your dear friend Madame Helvetius; yet she loves you extremely. I was in her company not more than an hour ago.' 'Ah,' said he, 'you make me recur to my past happiness, which ought to be forgotten in order to be happy here. For many years I could think of nothing but her, though at length I am consoled. I have taken another wife, the most like her that I could find; she is not indeed altogether so handsome, but she has a great fund of wit and good sense, and her whole study is to please me. She is at this moment gone to fetch the best nectar and ambrosia to regale me; stay awhile, and you will see her.' 'I perceive,' said I, 'that your former friend is more faithful to you than you are to her; she has had several good offers, but has refused them all. I will confess to you that I loved her extremely; but she was cruel to me, and rejected me peremptorily for your sake.' 'I pity you, sincerely,' said he, 'for she is an excellent woman, handsome and amiable. But do not the Abbé de la R. . . . and the Abbé M. . . . visit her?' 'Certainly they do; not one of your friends has dropped her acquaintance.' 'If you had gained the Abbé M. . . . with a bribe of good coffee and cream, perhaps you would have succeeded; for he is as deep a reasoner as Duns Scotus or St. Thomas; he arranges and methodizes his arguments in such a manner that they are almost irresistible. Or if by a fine edition of some old classic you had gained the Abbé de la R. . . . to speak against you, that would have been still better, as I always observed that when he recommended anything to her, she had a great inclination to do directly the contrary.' As he finished these words the new Madame Helvetius entered with the nectar, and I recognized her immediately as my former American friend, Mrs. Franklin! I reclaimed her, but she answered me coldly: 'I was a good wife to you for forty-nine years and four months, nearly half a century; let that content you. I have formed a new connection here, which will last to eternity.'—Indignant at this refusal of my Eurydice, I immediately resolved to quit those ungrateful shades, and return to this good world again, to behold the sun, and you! Here I am; let us avenge ourselves!"

Of course, of chief importance for the purpose of our present studies, are those writings of Franklin which deal with the controversies of the American Revolution, and which, while they may be called controversial writings, illustrate in a delightful way Franklin's habit of eliminating from all controversy its churlish and merely rasping traits. He has himself told us how he came to acquire his method. As a somewhat forward lad, he had fallen into a disputatious habit—"a very bad habit," as he afterwards came to see. "Persons of good sense, I have since observed, seldom fall into it, except lawyers, university men, and men of all sorts that have been bred at Edinburgh." From this disagreeable habit his escape seems to have been due, in the first instance, to his good luck in meeting with a copy of Xenophon's "Memorable Things of Socrates," wherein he found many examples of the Socratic method of conducting a dispute: "I was charmed with it, adopted it, dropt my abrupt contradiction and positive agumentation, and put on the humble inquirer and doubter." "I continued this method some years, but gradually left it, retaining only the habit of expressing myself in terms of modest diffidence, never using, when I advanced anything that may possibly be disputed, the words 'certainly,' 'undoubtedly,' or any others that give the air of positiveness to an opinion, but rather say, . . . 'I imagine it to be so,' or, 'it is so, if I am not mistaken.' " Accordingly, in the long and angry disputes of the American Revolution, the part taken in them by Franklin was very much like that which Socrates might have taken had he been born in Boston in the early part of the eighteenth century, had he been for many years a printer and a politician in Philadelphia, and had he filled at London and Paris the diplomatic stations that were filled by Franklin. Indeed, the likeness between Franklin and Socrates was more than superficial; for besides the plebeian origin of both and some trace of plebeian manners which clung to both, and the strain of animal coarseness from which neither was ever entirely purified, they both had an amazing insight into human nature in all its grades and phases, they were both indifferent to literary fame, they were both humorists, they both applied their great intellectual gifts in a disciplinary but genial way to the improvement of their fellow-men, and in dealing controversially with the opinions of others they both understood and practised the strategy of coolness, playfulness, an unassuming manner, moderation of statement, the logical parallel, and irony.

Being officially employed in Europe during nearly the entire period of the American Revolution, he was everywhere recognized as something far more than the official representative of America. Through his fame in science and letters, through his intimacy with great men, through the picturesqueness and the fascination of his personality, finally, through his journalistic sense in detecting from day to day the set of the winds and tides of public opinion and how to avail himself of both in the interests of his country, he became, in fact, the one conspicuous interpreter to Europe of the grievances and the purposes of America, and the one conspicuous interpreter to America of the attitude of Europe.

In studying the mass of Franklin's literary contributions to the Revolutionary controversy between 1763 and 1783, we shall find much help in noting that his relation to that controversy had two strongly contrasted phases: first, his sincere and most strenuous desire that the dispute should not pass from the stage of words to that of blows, and thence to a struggle for American secession from the empire; and, secondly, after the stage of blows had been reached, his championship of American secession through war as the only safe or honorable course then left to his countrymen. The line of division between these two phases of opinion and action, falls across the spring and early

summer of 1775. Prior to that time, all his writings, serious or
jocose, are pervaded by the one purpose of convincing the
English people that the American policy of their government
was an injustice and a blunder, and of convincing the American
people that their demand for political rights would certainly
be satisfied, if persisted in steadily and without fear, but also
without disloyalty and without unseemly violence. Subsequent
to that time, having accepted with real sorrow the alternative
of war and of war for American secession, all his writings, serious or jocose, are pervaded by the one purpose of making that
war a successful one—a result to which, as a writer, he could
best contribute by such appeals to public opinion in America
as should nourish and quicken American confidence in their
own cause, and by such appeals to public opinion in Europe as
should win for that cause its moral and even its physical support. For reasons that must be obvious, his general literary
activity was far greater during the first phase of this controversy, than during the second.

Rising above the throng of his writings upon the American
question in all its varying issues and aspects, from the beginning to the end, are some eight or ten productions which stand
out as most worthy of mention in this place.

The first of these is the celebrated pamphlet entitled "The
Examination of Doctor Benjamin Franklin, in the British
House of Commons, relative to the Repeal of the American
Stamp Act, in 1766." Though a mere report of a certain memorable transaction in parliament, this pamphlet is, in reality,
the result of a most consummate piece of political and editorial
craftsmanship on the part of Franklin himself—a master without a master in the art of touching the springs of popular conviction and sympathy. First published in London in 1767, it
had in England "a great run," as even Franklin permitted himself to acknowledge. Being promptly translated into French, it
was also widely circulated upon the continent, and for its pithy,
dramatic, and amusing way of putting the American case, it

was read by multitudes of people in many countries who thus got their first distinct impression as to the nature of the trouble then brewing in America, and as to the American people themselves—their number, character, resources, dispositions, opinions, purposes. Moreover, if the pamphlet thus gave a great impulse to the American cause in Europe—an impulse which was at once transmitted with tremendous effect to America, also—not less did it contribute to the reputation and standing of Franklin himself on both sides of the Atlantic; for, by its incidental and modest exhibition of his marvelous presence of mind, under the shower of questions that were rained upon him in the House of Commons, of his unfailing resources both in knowledge and in argument, of his frankness, reasonableness, shrewdness, wit, temper, tact, good humor, it simply extended to the public outside the house the impression he had produced inside it, namely, that thenceforward, upon the American question, this elderly and quiet philosopher was to be reckoned with as a statesman and a diplomat of the first order. "From this examination of Doctor Franklin," said the *Gentleman's Magazine* for July, 1767, "the reader may form a clearer and more comprehensive idea of the state and disposition of America, and of the expediency or inexpediency of the measure in question, and of the character and conduct of the minister who proposed it, than from all that has been written upon the subject in newspapers and pamphlets, under the titles of essays, letters, speeches, and considerations, from the first moment of its becoming the object of public attention till now."

Early in the year 1768, under the guise of an Englishman having unusual acquaintance with the colonies, he published in the *London Chronicle* a long and sprightly article on the "Causes of American Discontents before 1768." Though greatly mutilated and weakened by the editor of the journal in which it first appeared—so that, as Franklin complained, with its teeth drawn and its nails pared, it could "neither scratch nor bite," and could only "paw and mumble"—there was enough left of it to shew Franklin's great skill in winning favor for his side of the question by a novel and a half-grumbling presentation of its claims, and even by an ironical disparagement of them.

So, too, in 1774, over the signature of "A Londoner," he contributed to the *Public Advertiser* a series of short articles "On the Rise and Progress of the Differences between Great Britain and her American Colonies," in which, with the frankness of a discontented Englishman, he caustically exposes the dunce-like methods of the ministry in dealing with the American problem, and the stupid pertinacity of those writers for the English press who seemed to think that they were solving that problem by calling the Americans hard names and by propagating all sorts of calumnies against them. "Surely," exclaims the "Londoner" at the close of his last article, "the great commerce of this nation with the Americans is of too much importance to be risked in a quarrel which has no foundation but ministerial pique and obstinacy! . . . Will our reviling them as cheats, hypocrites, scoundrels, traitors, cowards, tyrants, etc., etc., according to the present mode in all our papers, make them more our friends, more fond of our merchandize? Did ever any tradesman succeed, who attempted to drub customers into his shop? And will honest John Bull, the farmer, be long satisfied with servants that before his face attempt to kill his plough-horses?"

Probably no writer ever understood better than he how to make dull subjects lively, and how, by consequence, to attract readers to the consideration of matters in themselves unattractive. As he well knew, the European public, whether upon the continent or in Great Britain, were not likely to give their days and nights to the perusal of long and solemn dissertations on the rights and wrongs of his countrymen in the other hemisphere. Accordingly, such dissertations he never gave them, but, upon occasion, brief and pithy and apparently casual statements of the American case; exposing, also, the weak points of the case against his own, by means of anecdotes, epigrams, jeux-d'esprit; especially contriving to throw the whole argument into some sort of dramatic form—as in "A Dialogue between Britain, France, Spain, Holland, Saxony, and America," or as in "A Catechism relative to the English Debt"; or, again, setting forth in pictorial form some stirring aspect of the dispute, as, in 1774, his famous emblematic drawing to illustrate "the result of England's persistence in her policy towards the colonies," wherein Britannia is represented as a huge desolate female-figure occupying a conspicuous place on the globe, but with all her limbs—that is, her colonies—cut off and lying scattered about—these dismembered limbs being severally labelled Virginia, New England, Pennsylvania, and New York. In this sorry plight, as Franklin says in the "Explanation" accompanying the picture, Britannia lifts "her eyes and mangled stumps to Heaven; her shield, which she is unable to wield, lies useless by her side; her lance has pierced New England; the laurel branch has fallen from the hand of Pennsylvania; the English oak has lost its head, and stands a bare trunk, with a few withered branches; briers and thorns are on the ground beneath it; the British ships have brooms at their topmast heads, denoting their being on sale; and Britannia herself is seen sliding off the world,—no longer able to hold its balance,—her fragments overspread with the label, 'Date obolum Belisario.' "

It remains to be mentioned that Franklin's favorite weapon in political controversy—a weapon, which, perhaps, no other writer in English since Dean Swift, has handled with so much cleverness and effect—was that of satire in the form of ludicrous analogue, thereby burlesquing the acts and pretensions of his adversary, and simply overwhelming him with ridicule. His very first dash into the Revolutionary controversy after his arrival in England in 1764, furnishes a case in point; when, in a letter to a newspaper, over the signature of "A Traveler," he chaffs the English public about their habit of swallowing preposterous stories concerning the colonies, as then commonly told them in their journals—himself, however, ironically maintaining the truth of these very stories, and even capping them by others just as true: as the one about the tails of the American sheep being "so laden with wool, that each has a little car or wagon on four little wheels to support and keep it from trailing on the ground"; or, as the one about the inhabitants of Canada "making preparations for a cod and whale fishery this summer in the upper lakes. Ignorant people may object that the upper lakes are fresh, and that cod and whales are salt-water fish; but let them know, sir, that cod, like other fish, when attacked by their enemies, fly into any water where they can be safest; that whales, when they have a mind to eat cod, pursue them wherever they fly, and that the grand leap of the whale in the chase up the Falls of Niagara is esteemed, by all who have seen it, as one of the finest spectacles in nature."

Moreover, with Franklin, as had been the case with Dean Swift before him, this species of satire took a form at once so realistic and so comically apt, as to result in several examples of brilliant literary hoaxing—a result which, in the controversy then going on, was likely to be beneficial to the solemn and self-satisfied British Philistine of the period, since it compelled him for once to do a little thinking, and also to stand off and view his own portrait as it then appeared to other people, and even in spite of himself to laugh at his own portentous and costly stupidity in the management of an empire that seemed already grown too big for him to take proper care of. Of Franklin's work in the vein of literary burlesque, three pieces claim mention for their pre-eminent wit and point: first, "Rules for Reducing a Great Empire to a Small One," secondly, "An Edict by the King of Prussia," both printed in the English newspapers in the early autumn of 1773; and, thirdly, a pretended letter of instructions "From the Count de Schaumbergh to the Baron Hohendorf commanding the Hessian Troops in America," this being dated at Rome, 18 February, 1777.

Referring to the first two of these pieces, soon after their publication, Franklin told his son that his object in writing them was to expose the conduct of England toward the colonies, "in a short, comprehensive, and striking view, and stated, therefore, in out-of-the-way forms, as most likely to take the general attention." "In my own mind," he adds, "I preferred the first, as a composition, for the quantity and variety of the matter contained, and a kind of spirited ending of each paragraph. But I find that others here generally prefer the second." Probably, the chief reason for the greater attention paid in England to the second piece is to be found in the more direct and palpable character of its satire, dealing as it did with ideas and even phrases then uncommonly familiar to the English public. It made its appearance in the midst of the busy preparations then in progress for sending out the guileful tea-ships; when, of course, the very air was vibrant with allusions to the almost limitless claims of the mother country upon her American children, to the propriety and beauty of the English laws for controlling the commerce and manufactures of the colonies, and, above all, to the base ingratitude of England's American children in objecting to being taxed at will by their affectionate national parent. Under these circumstances it occurred to Franklin to set forth in some lively way the absurdity of all this; especially, that it was an argument which proved much more than its inventors would care to be responsible for. If, indeed, England had such limitless claims upon the American colonies because she was their mother country, why had not Germany, the mother country of England, the same claims upon her? This idea, accordingly, Franklin worked out in a manner thoroughly Franklinian—causing to be published, first, in the *Public Advertiser*, what purported to be a solemn edict of Frederick the Great—"Given at Potsdam, this twenty-fifth day of the month of August, one thousand seven hundred and seventy-three, and in the thirty-third year of our reign"— wherein that monarch, in a tone of command very natural to him, uses the characteristic words of the English acts of parliament regulating the commerce and manufactures of the American colonies, and then proclaims on behalf of Prussia the same regulations over "the island of Great Britain": "And all per-

sons in the said island are hereby cautioned not to oppose in
any wise the execution of this our edict, or any part thereof,
such opposition being high treason; of which all who are suspected shall be transported in fetters from Britain to Prussia,
there to be tried and executed according to the Prussian law."

In England this travesty made a great hit; all the more so
for the reason, as Franklin explained to his son, "that people
in reading it were, as the phrase is, 'taken in,' till they had got
half through it, and imagined it a real edict, to which mistake,
I suppose, the king of Prussia's character contributed." Some
of its effects, the author himself had the good luck to witness,
and in a way of which he has left an amusing account. Having
sent his satire to the newspaper, he immediately went down
to the country-seat of his friend, Lord le Despencer, where
among other guests happened to be Paul Whitehead, the poet.
One morning while most of the company were chatting in the
breakfast-parlor, Whitehead "came running in to us out of
breath, with the paper in his hand. 'Here!' says he, 'here 's news
for ye! Here 's the king of Prussia claiming a right to this kingdom!' All stared, and I as much as anybody; and he went on
to read it. When he had read two or three paragraphs, a gentleman present said: 'Damn his impudence; I dare say we shall
hear by next post, that he is upon his march with one hundred
thousand men to back this.' Whitehead, who is very shrewd,
soon after began to smoke it, and looking in my face said, 'I 'll
be hanged if this is not some of your American jokes upon us.'
The reading went on, and ended with abundance of laughing,
and a general verdict that it was a fair hit." Indeed, Lord Mansfield, who, of course, was not in that company, called the satire
"very able and very artful," and expressed the belief that it
"would do mischief by giving here a bad impression of the
measures of government, and in the colonies by encouraging
them in their contumacy," all of which, certainly, was precisely
the effect which it was intended to have.

The last of the three specimens of the satire above mentioned,
the Count de Schaumbergh's letter of instructions, seems to

have been written by Franklin not long after his arrival in France in the latter part of 1776, and was intended to hold up to the execration of the civilized world both parties in the transaction by which the king of England bought of certain petty princes in Germany the troops with which to butcher his late American subjects. In some respects, this is the most powerful of all the satirical writings of Franklin. More, perhaps, than is the case with any other work of his, it displays, with marvelous subtlety and wit, that sort of genius which can reproduce with minute and perfect verisimilitude the psychological processes of some monstrous crime against human nature—a crime which it thus portrays both to the horror and the derision of mankind. "Since the death of Swift," says John Bigelow in referring to this pretended letter of the Hessian trafficker in the bodies and souls of his subjects, "who, besides Franklin, was sufficiently a master of this kind of satire to have written it?"

As Franklin was by far the greatest man of letters on the American side of the Revolutionary controversy, so a most luminous and delightful history of the development of thought and emotion during the Revolution might be composed, by merely bringing together detached sayings of Franklin, humorous and serious, just as these fell from his tongue or pen in the successive stages of that long conflict: it would be a trail of light across a sea of storm and gloom.

Nevertheless, not by illustrative fragments of what he wrote or said, any more than by modern descriptions however vivid, can an adequate idea be conveyed of the mass, the force, the variety, the ease, the charm, of his total work as a writer during those twenty tremendous years. Undoubtedly, his vast experience in affairs and the sobriety produced by mere official responsibility, had the effect of clarifying and solidifying his thought, and of giving to the lightest products of his genius a sanity and a sureness of movement which, had he been a man of letters only, they could hardly have had in so high a degree. It is only by a continuous reading of the entire body of Franklin's Revolutionary writings, from grave to gay, from lively to severe, that any one can know how brilliant was his wisdom, or how wise was his brilliance, or how humane and gentle and helpful were both. No one who, by such a reading, procures for himself such a pleasure and such a benefit, will be likely to miss the point of Sydney Smith's playful menace to his daughter—"I will disinherit you, if you do not admire everything written by Franklin."

Bibliographical Note

Moses Coit Tyler's *A History of American Literature* was first published by G. P. Putnam's Sons (New York) in 1878. The original book was in two volumes; the first volume covered the years 1607 through 1676 and the second the period between 1676 and 1765. A second printing of this edition was issued in 1879. Eighteen years later, in 1897, G. P. Putnam's Sons published Tyler's *The Literary History of the American Revolution 1763–1783*. Again, there were two volumes—the first for the years 1763–1776. The second brought the story to a conclusion with the year 1783. In 1897 the Putnam company also published in two forms a new and revised edition of *A History of American Literature*. One version retained the original two volume format; the second version was a one-volume "student's edition."

The books were not printed again until 1941 when Barnes and Noble (New York) issued the two volumes of *The Literary History of the American Revolution 1763–1783* as a part of the Facsimile Library Publications. Randolph Greenfield Adams wrote an introduction for this printing. *A History of American Literature 1607–1765* (the original two volumes in one) with a foreword by Howard Mumford Jones was published in 1949 by Cornell University Press (Ithaca, New York). Then, in 1957, using Howard Mumford Jones's foreword, the Frederick Ungar Publishing Company (New York) reissued the two-volume version of *The Literary History of the American Revolution 1763–1783*. This edition was given a second printing in 1963 by the same publisher as a part of their American Classics series.

Tyler's literary histories have appeared in paperback only once: in 1962 Collier Books (New York) published a two volume in one edition of *A History of American Literature 1607–1765* with a new foreword by Perry Miller. The next year, 1963, Peter Smith (Gloucester, Massachusetts) printed a clothbound edition of the paperback. The four volumes have not been published again, although at least the Ungar edition of the Revolution volumes and the Collier paperback version of *A History of American Literature 1607–1765* are still readily available.

Index